Equity and Well-Being

Equity is an abstract concept covering philosophical issues such as fairness and social justice, making its definition and measurement complex. This volume tackles these complexities head-on. The book is enriched with many empirical analyses and provides a comprehensive analysis of equity ranging from concepts and measurements to empirical illustrations and policy implications.

After an extensive discussion on equity in the introduction, this volume begins with a chapter on well-being, where the concepts of functioning and capability are discussed. This is followed by a few chapters on what an equitable distribution is and how equity can be measured. The volume then provides a definition and a methodology to measure equitable growth, examining the relationship between growth, inequality, and poverty. It also presents various empirical illustrations and country-specific experiences with three country case studies, which assess whether health and education services are equitable in developing Asia, examining the extent to which these social services favor the poor as well as the policy challenges to a more equitable delivery of these services. Finally, these country studies provide evidence-based policy recommendations to improve equity in social service delivery in developing countries.

Achieving social equity has long been an important policy goal. There are relatively few studies on equity. This book aims to help fill this gap with an in-depth analysis of the issues associated with equity, covering its concept, measurement, and policy practices and implications.

Dr Hyun Hwa Son is currently a senior economist in the Economics and Research Department of the Asian Development Bank (ADB). Before joining ADB in March 2007, she was a poverty specialist/economist at the United Nations Development Programme. She also worked for the World Bank in Washington D.C., and held an academic position at Macquarie University in Sydney, Australia. She has worked and published extensively on poverty, inequality, pro-poor growth, inclusive growth, health and education, and public policies.

Equity and Well-Being

Measurement and policy practice

Hyun Hwa Son

Routledge
Taylor & Francis Group

LONDON AND NEW YORK

First published 2011
by Routledge
2 Park Square, Milton Park, Abingdon, Oxfordshire OX14 4RN

Simultaneously published in the USA and Canada by Routledge
711 Third Avenue, New York, NY 10017

First issued in paperback 2014

*Routledge is an imprint of the Taylor & Francis Group, an informa
business*

6 ADB Avenue, Mandaluyong City
1550 Metro Manila, Philippines
Tel: +63 2 632 4444
Fax: +63 2 636 2444
www.adb.org

British Library Cataloguing in Publication Data
A catalogue record for this book is available from the British Library

Library of Congress Cataloging in Publication Data
A catalog record for this book has been requested

ISBN 13: 978-0-415-69269-4 (hbk)
ISBN 13: 978-1-138-01886-0 (pbk)

Typeset in Times New Roman
by Cenveo Publisher Services

Contents

Figures

Tables

Preface

Even though equity has long been an important policy goal, inequity persists globally. In the 1980s, governments were typically more interested in addressing cost constraints and improving efficiency than in promoting equity. The situation had improved by the end of the 1990s, when many governments and international organizations prioritized equity in their development agenda. And this emphasis has continued into the new millennium, as governments increasingly focus on policies and programs to reduce inequity.

But despite the renewed attention, there are still few studies on the subject. This book aims to help fill this gap with an in-depth analysis of the issues associated with equity, including its concept and measurement, policy practices, and implications. As is widely acknowledged, equity is an abstract concept covering philosophical issues such as fairness and social justice, making its definition and measurement complex. This book tackles the complexity. Aside from discussing the conceptual issues surrounding equity, the text is enriched with many empirical analyses that reveal clear policy implications. As such, its comprehensive analysis ranges from concepts and measurements to empirical illustrations and policy implications.

This book was born out of work done for the Asian Development Bank's regional technical assistance (RETA) project on Equity in the Delivery of Public Services in Selected Developing Member Countries, its chapters presenting several of the background papers produced under the RETA project. It is hoped the book can benefit those working in the development field, including academics, practitioners, and policymakers.

There are a number of people I would like to acknowledge. I owe Dr Ifzal Ali, former Chief Economist of the Asian Development Bank, considerable thanks for encouraging me to become the leader of the RETA project and thus steering me onto the path to writing this book. I am grateful for his insights and inspirations on development issues, and I benefitted enormously from numerous discussions with him during his tenure as the Chief Economist in the Economics and Research Department. To the same extent, I am grateful to Dr Juzhong Zhuang, Deputy Chief Economist of the Asian Development Bank, for encouraging me to write the book, and I am thankful for his overall guidance.

I have also benefitted greatly from the many discussions I had about the issues surrounding equity and public service delivery with many government officials in Nepal, the Philippines, Sri Lanka, Lao People's Democratic Republic, and Indonesia before the launch of the project. These discussions deepened my understanding of economic development in Asia. I would like to express my particular gratitude to Dr Lava Deo Awasthi of Nepal, who was Joint Secretary at the Ministry of Education, for his support. My passion for this project was ignited by his enthusiasm about development issues in Nepal.

Many scholars in this field have helped me in various stages of manuscript preparation: some read a few chapters and provided me with insightful comments and suggestions, while others helped me clarify the many conceptual and practical issues related to equity. Among those, I would like to acknowledge Professors Nanak Kakwani, Jacques Silber, and Ernesto Pernia for sharing their in-depth knowledge on the subject and also for their tolerance of my ignorance.

In addition, I am grateful to the authors who prepared the country chapters— Chapters 9, 10, and 11—for their patience and hard work in going through many rounds of revisions. Finally, I would like to thank Emmanuel San Andres and Eric Van Zant for providing excellent research assistance and editing of the manuscripts.

Abbreviations

APIS	annual poverty indicators survey
BESRA	Basic Education Sector Reform Agenda
BHS	*Barangay* health station
CBMS	community-based monitoring system
CBS	Central Bureau of Statistics
CCT	conditional cash transfer
CFS	Consumer Finance and Socioeconomic Survey
DCS	Department of Census and Statistics
DHS	Demographic and Health Survey
DOE	Department of Education
DOH	Department of Health
EIO	equity index of opportunity
FGT	Foster–Greer–Thorbecke
GDP	gross domestic product
GNP	gross national product
HDI	human development index
HIES	Household Income and Expenditure Survey
HPI	human poverty indicator
MDG	Millenium Development Goal
MOE	Ministry of Education
MOHP	Ministry of Health and Population
NCR	National Capital Region
NDHS	National Demographic and Health Survey
OI	opportunity index
PEGR	poverty equivalent growth rate
PME	Provincial Ministry of Education
PMOH	Provincial Ministry of Health
PPP	*Pantawid Pamilyang Pilpino*
PPP	purchasing power parity/pro-poor policy
RHU	rural health unit
SBA	skilled birth attendant

SEF   School Education Fund
SES   socioeconomic survey
UNDP   United Nations Development Programme
VAT   value added tax
WDR   World Development Report

Introduction

What is equity?

Equity and economics often make for awkward company. It seems that economists talk quite often about equity, but there is little agreement about what exactly is being talked about or whether it should concern economists at all. The dictionary defines "equity" as "justice" or "fairness"—concepts one is more likely to come across in political or legal literature than in the calculus-filled tomes of economics. After all, in the world of profit-maximizing firms and utility-maximizing consumers, equity has no place: whether economic output is owned by one or equally shared, Pareto efficient allocations and equilibrium prices will be determined. Nothing in general equilibrium theory requires that all actors in the economy should have some minimum level of consumption or that the distribution of goods should be equitable. However, despite the mechanical neatness and analytical rigor of this "equity-less" economy, economists have grappled with the question of equity, from Bentham's (1781) "greatest possible quantity of happiness" to Marxian (1867) socialism, and Sen's (1993) capabilities approach. So, what exactly do we mean by "equity?"

Equity in the vernacular sense is synonymous with justice and fairness; thus, equity is about putting things right,[1] to give to one what one is due. Putting this squarely in economic terms, equity is about finding the "right" distribution of some good among individuals in a society. Economists often find it conceptually difficult to deal with the question of fairness and distribution. While economic theory regularly considers atomistic persons, firms, or countries, distribution necessitates thinking of societies—many different individuals living and interacting together. Rather than thinking of faceless representative persons (or households or firms), arriving at a definition of a fair distribution requires thinking of all the individuals' heterogeneous characteristics and circumstances. Equity requires a definition of what individuals in particular circumstances are entitled to, be it some minimum level of happiness or some share of society's production.

Adam Smith, whose notion of the "invisible hand" was the inspiration for competitive equilibrium theory, actually considered the question of equity. In *Wealth of Nations* (1776), Smith writes, "No society can surely be flourishing and happy, of which the far greater part of the members are poor and miserable."

(Book I, Section 8, paragraph 35). More than two centuries onward, economists are still defining equity in terms of some concept of societal happiness: Kaplow and Shavell (2002) define equity as a distribution of resources that maximizes social welfare. This, however, does not tell us much about what is "right" distribution as there is no clear definition of how to aggregate individual welfare into social welfare. Bentham's (1781) strict utilitarianism implies a simple addition of individual welfare to calculate social welfare, implying perfect social substitutability of one individual's welfare for another's. Assuming that interpersonal comparisons of welfare are even possible (i.e., welfare is measured in cardinal rather than ordinal terms), Bentham's definition of equity would allow for the tyranny of the majority. If a policy benefits, say, 90% of the population at the expense of the other 10%, then it would be an equitable policy. To protect the interests of the minority, Rawls (1971) proposes a "maximin" approach to deriving social welfare—society's welfare is only as high as the welfare of the worst-off individual, and a fair distribution is achieved by maximizing the lot of the worst-off. This approach is blind to the welfare of all other individuals who are not the worst-off; thus, extreme inequality is acceptable so long as the minimum welfare is maximized. However, improving the lot of the worst-off can come at the expense of justice itself. As Nozick (1974) would argue, there is not much justice in taking away a person's hard-earned possessions to benefit someone else; in fact, the confiscation of legitimately obtained property is itself the definition of injustice. Other ways of aggregating individual welfare into social welfare—what we call social welfare functions—fall somewhere between the extremes of Bentham's strict utilitarianism and Rawls' maximin. That said, there is no economic theory that informs us which is the "right" welfare function for a given society. Any formulation of a social welfare function will have implicit assumptions on weights and desirable distributions, which reflect the economist's value judgments of what is "right" distribution.

Note that equity is not the same as equality, although the two are related and, quite often, used interchangeably. Equality, in its usual connotation, means that each individual has the same amount of some measurable good, be it income, welfare, or utility. Equality is easy enough to measure and it does not need to know individual identities—either the good is distributed equally or it isn't. On the other hand, equity necessitates looking into individual circumstances and relative positions. Are all individuals equal? How do we determine whether or not two unique individuals are equal? Once circumstances and relative positions are determined, equity then necessitates thinking about what individuals are due. Do equal individuals deserve equal treatment and equal welfare? Is it just to treat unequals equally? In principle, therefore, equity could be achieved even if the distribution of some measured good is unequal (Le Grand 1991). That said, it is quite understandable why equity and equality are confused with each other (apart from the obvious reason that they are near homonyms). While equal distribution of a good is not a necessary condition to achieve equity, equal treatment of equal individuals is. This concept has been the hallmark of discussions on social justice since Aristotle's *Nicomachean Ethics* postulated that society must "treat like cases as like" (Ross 1998). Thus, a belief that all persons are equal necessitates a definition of equity as a state of equality in all respects.

Equity and economic thought

Equity, unlike efficiency, is essentially a moral issue. Economics prides itself as the queen of the social sciences in its ability to analyze social problems with the objectivity and precision one usually sees in the natural sciences. It is able to formulate falsifiable hypotheses, test them empirically, and develop scientific conclusions. It is happy to relegate justice and fairness issues to parliament and the courts in its pursuit of efficiency (cf. Coase 1960; Cooter and Ulen 2000). Equity, however, requires economists to think about the very issues economics would like to relegate to the other social sciences. Somehow, economists have to reconcile their faceless and atomistic *homo economicus* with human circumstances and suffering. Economists have indeed tried to reconcile these two opposing thoughts—models incorporating various definitions of equity have been proposed to suit different fields of enquiry. Equity in growth theory often revolves around the treatment of different generations (Svensson 1980; Arrow et al. 1995): is it fair for current consumption to constrain future consumption? Equity in public economics, on the other hand, revolves around vertical and horizontal equity in taxation (Atkinson and Stiglitz 1980): who should be taxed (or subsidized) and by how much? Meanwhile, equity in regulation considers fairness vis-à-vis incentive compatibility (Zajac 2001): when is it "right" to constrain or regulate successful firms, if at all? Among the fields of economics, however, it is development economics that needs to consider equity the most. Discussions of poverty, inequality, and inclusive growth—how to expand and distribute the economic pie—all revolve around equity.

In thinking of equity, economists are immediately confronted with a difficult question: What is it that we want to equitably distribute? One answer that comes to mind is happiness—otherwise termed as welfare or utility (Bentham 1781; Mill 1848; Harsanyi 1976)—until one realizes that it is almost impossible to measure, much less distribute. Thus, an index of happiness or welfare that is measurable and distributable needs to be found. Income is a commonly used index for this purpose as it represents everything a person can purchase, which will presumably maximize one's utility. However, income as an index of happiness falters when one considers that the level of utility from income is only as good as one's choice set (Le Grand 1984)—a millionaire cannot benefit much from his wealth if there is nothing he considers worth buying or if he has no access to the one item he needs (e.g., a life-saving drug). From here economists turn to other goods that are more closely related to "well-being", such as access to basic needs (International Labour Organisation 1977), total consumption (Slesnick 1994), rights and freedoms (Steiner 1994; Van Parijs 1995), capabilities and functionings (Sen 1993), opportunities (Dworkin 1981), and basic liberties (Rawls 1993). Note, however, that one's selection of the good to be distributed could determine the implied social welfare function to be used. For example, selecting basic needs would require a function closer to Rawls' maximin approach as persons are expected to require some minimum level of needs; on the other hand, selecting total consumption would require a function that allows some interpersonal substitutability.

A prevailing view is that equity is achieved if there is equality in opportunities and resources while allowing for inequalities in outcomes (Dworkin 1981; Roemer 1998). Also known as resource egalitarianism, this point of view assumes that all people are equal. It then argues that if opportunities are distributed equally, then any inequality in outcomes—say, in terms of income or consumption—observed henceforth is due to the subsequent decisions made by individuals. Society, represented by the state, needs to ensure that opportunities are distributed equally, but people themselves should decide how to use their opportunities and reap the results of their efforts. This view satisfies moral concepts of personal responsibility and provides socially beneficial incentives for productive effort. However, resource egalitarianism fails to account for variables and events that are external to the individual but nevertheless have an impact on outcomes. For example, random events like the weather can determine the outcome of decisions. Likewise, externalities of other peoples' actions can have a negative impact on personal outcomes. In these cases, resource egalitarianism may not necessarily result in equitable outcomes.

About this book

So should economists even concern themselves with questions of equity? Posner (2003) argues that economics has nothing to say in matters of distribution because justice and fairness cannot be reduced to the quantifiable terms favored by economics. Farber (2003), who sees economics as having something to contribute to discussions on equity, concedes that, ultimately, one has to look outside economics to find a meaningful discussion of equity. Given the normative nature of equity and the difficulties of modeling and measuring it, why can't economists just relegate it to parliament and the courts, or at least the other social sciences?

To this we can actually give a positive answer: economists' concern for equity is an expression of what Adam Smith (1759) terms "sympathy": we see how inequity affects others, mirror it in ourselves, and abhor it. Sympathy in this sense is not just a sentimental notion coined by romantic 18th century moral philosophers; it is an objective human trait observed across cultures that challenges the economists' constructed concept of *homo economicus*. Fehr and Schmidt (1999) in various experiments show that humans exhibit inequality aversion and would like to minimize inequality in outcomes. For example, Fehr and Schmidt (1999), Heinrich et al. (2004) and Oosterbeek, Sloof, and van der Keulen (2004) show that there is a consistent tendency toward equal distributions in ultimatum games, which is remarkable considering that the Nash equilibrium of ultimatum games is to have highly unequal distributions. In experiment after experiment, test subjects exhibit qualities of fair play and inequality aversion, even if these qualities work against their personal interests. In other words, humans—economists included—have an ingrained sense of what is fair and just. As Adam Smith would say, it is in our nature to consider equity in our research, and economists have a lot to contribute to society's discussion of how to equitably distribute the gains of production. And that is why we wrote this book, which discusses conceptual, technical, and empirical issues of equity. It begins with issues surrounding the concept and measurement of equity and goes on to operationalize these concepts of equity through empirical studies on various sectors of the economy, such as education and health.

The volume starts with a chapter on "What is well-being?", which provides a critical evaluation of the alternative approaches to defining well-being, including the concepts of functioning and capability, where deprivation encompasses non-income dimensions. Chapters 2 and 3 are devoted to what an equitable distribution is and how equity can be measured. Chapter 2 argues that equity should not only measure dispersions in the distribution of income, but should also have a close link with social welfare. It discusses two measures of distribution—the Lorenz curve and the Bonferroni curve—and their related numerical indices, the Gini index and the Bonferroni index. Since both indices are used to measure relative inequality, these are not adequate measures from a social justice point of view. In this context, this chapter introduces absolute measures of inequality that would be sensitive to an increase in the absolute gap between the rich and poor. These absolute measures are modified from the Gini and Bonferroni indices, and it is argued that they are more relevant from social justice perspectives. The chapter extends its discussion to social welfare functions, which is particularly instrumental in evaluating the social welfare impacts of government policies. It provides policy insights into understanding different forms of the social welfare function and shows that the Bonferroni social welfare index can be a better measure than the Gini social welfare index if the main objective of policymakers is to maximize the welfare of the poor.

The discussion of conceptual issues of equity is deepened and becomes technically rigorous in Chapter 3. This chapter "On the concept of equity in opportunity" argues that measuring the equity of opportunity in society is an essential ingredient in the formulation of policies and programs that promote inclusive growth. In this chapter, equity of opportunity is defined and measured through the theoretical framework of the social opportunity function, a concept similar to the social welfare function. The functional and graphical distribution of opportunity is discussed through the generalized Lorenz curve and the Bonferroni curve, while complete ranking of distributions is achieved through their related numerical indices: the concentration index and the Bonferroni index of opportunity, respectively. The concepts of relative and absolute measures of equity of opportunity are then introduced and a social opportunity index that considers both the amount and distribution of opportunity is developed. These measures are used to analyze changes in the opportunities for healthcare and education in the Philippines from 1998 to 2007.

Chapter 4 tackles patterns of growth, discussing the relationship between growth, inequality, and poverty. There has been intense debate over the relationship among the three. It has been argued that growth in average incomes automatically trickles down to benefit the poor. The opposing view to this trickle-down argument puts the distribution of income and wealth at center stage, arguing that reductions in inequality are required to combat poverty. This side includes adherents of the notion of "immiserizing growth"—that is, the idea that growth in average incomes may well occur at the same time as large groups of people are being increasingly impoverished. During the 1990s, the proliferation of quality data on income distribution from a number of countries has allowed rigorous empirical testing of standing debates. This chapter assesses the pattern of growth through its linkages to changes in poverty and inequality using data from 25 developing Asian countries during 1981–2005. It provides an *ex post* analysis that evaluates whether the growth process in a country has been equitable or inequitable. For this purpose, the chapter applies a measure called the "poverty equivalent growth rate" (Kakwani and Son 2008), which shows how the benefits of growth have been shared between the poor and the non-poor over time.

Chapter 5 examines the issue of redistribution through taxation and introduces a tool to assess a government's fiscal policy from an equity point of view. Different taxes have different impacts on distribution. Generally, personal income taxes and property taxes are progressive, increasing equality by taxing the rich more and the poor less. On the other hand, indirect taxes on consumption are usually regressive because the poor consume a larger share of their income than the rich. By and large, the overall tax system in developing countries is regressive (Gemmell and Morrissey 2005), mainly because developing countries tend to rely more heavily on indirect taxes that include taxes on goods and services and international trade. For instance, indirect taxes in Thailand constituted about half of total tax revenue (45%) in 2009. Indirect taxes generally offset the equity gains that could be achieved through progressive direct taxation. One way to increase progressivity of indirect taxes is to target these taxes on goods and services consumed at different rates by the rich and the poor. For example, government can lower or eliminate the value added tax on products that make up a large proportion of the poor household's consumption (e.g., basic food items) while increasing taxes on luxury products that are generally consumed by the rich. Thus, in the selection of taxable items one should give careful consideration to the consumption patterns of the population. The chapter provides a tool to assess government tax and expenditure policies from an equity perspective based on people's consumption patterns.

Social protection is a means for direct government intervention to address equity. Social protection systems not only protect people during times of economic crisis, but also represent an investment in future growth. Chapter 6 looks into key issues relating to social protection programs and largely focuses on targeting. This chapter introduces a new targeting indicator that is a function of four factors: the percentage of the poor targeted by the program, the percentage of the population that can be covered by the program, Type I error (i.e., probability of excluding the poor from a given program), and Type II error (i.e., probability of including the non-poor in the program). This indicator measures the association between the poverty status of households or individuals and the selection of beneficiary households or individuals—a higher value for this indicator suggests the program has better targeting ability. The chapter goes on to discuss the issue of coverage, which is relevant to a program's efficiency as well as its impacts on poverty reduction. This issue arises because, in many cases, the number of beneficiaries is not equal to the number of poor people in the population. While too many beneficiaries can mean resources are being wasted, too few beneficiaries means poverty impacts are minimal. Most targeted programs suffer from a severe mismatch that reduces the targeting power of the programs—even if we have perfect information about the poor, the program can still suffer from a mismatch if, by design, not all the poor can be reached. This issue is addressed through an indicator that measures the extent to which the mismatch reduces targeting efficiency.

Chapter 7 provides an *ex ante* assessment of the implementation of the conditional cash transfer (CCT) program. *Ex ante* impact evaluation of social protection programs similar to that carried out in this chapter would be useful in answering a number of policy-relevant counterfactual questions that *ex post* evaluations would be unable to answer. This evaluation has been done with the Philippines' CCT program called the *Pantawid Pamilyang Pilipino*. The study investigates the impact of CCT on current poverty, and the impact of this extra money on school attendance under different transfer amounts and different targeting criteria, such as universal targeting, geographical targeting, targeting of the poor, and progressive targeting.

To what extent can aggregate income measures such as per-capita gross domestic product (GDP) explain people's standards of living? Can growth in per-capita GDP alone bring about significant improvements in people's standards of living in a reasonable period of time? Chapter 8 seeks to answer these questions by comparing achievements and inequities in the standards of living of different countries at different stages of economic development. In particular, this chapter assesses the performance of countries in different regions of Asia over the period 2000–07, testing for the statistical relationship between indicators of the countries' standards of living and per-capita GDP. It finds that to achieve social progress, patterns of investment in human development matter more than economic growth *per se*. Results also show that convergence in standards of living would take longer than the convergence in per capita incomes, implying that economic growth should be complemented by an improvement in living standards in order for human and social development to be achieved. It proposes not only the enlargement of the economic pie and the allocation of resources toward basic services, but also the development of policies and institutions that will enable the continuous and efficient delivery of quality basic social services. An important message emerging from the analysis of Chapter 8 is that the quality of public social services in health and education is important to growth.

The next three chapters deal with the issue of equity in education and health services in three developing countries: the Philippines, Nepal, and Sri Lanka. Deprivation of education and health services not only indicates poverty, but is also part of the very definition of poverty itself. The poor need access to at least a minimum level of education and health services to escape poverty and contribute to society. However, a lack of income means they have few or no resources to procure the very services that can bring them out of poverty. Chapters 9, 10, and 11 show that the poor have the least opportunity to avail themselves of education and health services, with many having little or no access even to basic healthcare or education. However, it is not enough that the poor are able to avail themselves of basic social services; these services need to be delivered with at least acceptable quality. A poor boy may attend school, but the quality may be so poor that he ends up learning nothing; likewise, a woman may have antenatal care, but its quality may be so poor that she cannot justify the cost of travel to get it. Finally, even when governments spend on social sectors, the rich may benefit rather than the poor. These three issues—accessibility, equitability, and distribution of public resources—are critical in achieving equity in the delivery of education and health services. Chapters 9, 10, and 11 present case studies on the Philippines, Nepal, and Sri Lanka, respectively. The Philippines' presents a case in which people have access to education and health services, but the quality is often of concern. By contrast, Nepal suffers from both poor accessibility and poor quality of these services. Sri Lanka, meanwhile, stands out from neighbouring Asian economies for its better development indicators and also can yield policy lessons in improving the delivery of education and health services.

Note

1 Note that the root of the word "justice" is the Latin *jus*, which means rightness, and the Latin *justitia* literally means "to put things right".

1 What is well-being?

Introduction

Poverty is defined as the "pronounced deprivation in well-being" in the 2000/01 *World Development Report* (WDR). But what does well-being mean? How do we define it? And what are the elements necessary to ensure a decent level of well-being? These are not easy questions to answer. Several approaches have been used to describe well-being in the socioeconomic literature, important among them are basic needs, economic growth, quality of life, and welfare. How do these approaches differ? And which approach is the most appropriate to describe well-being? This chapter, briefly, deals with these broad questions.

In any society some people enjoy higher levels of well-being than others. In this context, poverty may be viewed as the low level of well-being of some sections of society. Poverty becomes a concern if some sections of society are so deprived that they are unable to function with dignity. As the 2000/01 WDR writes, to be poor "is to be hungry, to lack shelter and clothing, to be sick and not cared for, to be illiterate and not schooled."

This chapter evaluates the alternative approaches that have been applied in the literature to define well-being. It then discusses the concepts of functioning and capability pioneered by Sen (1985, 1999), which in recent years had led to poverty being largely defined as capability deprivation. Although this approach makes the concept of poverty broader and more closely related to the actual lives people lead, a distinction must be made between capability deprivation in general and poverty in particular. Poverty is concerned with the inadequacy of command over resources needed to generate socially determined basic capabilities, whereas capability deprivation is more general and may be caused by a host of factors, of which command over resources may not be the most important. Thus, poverty is not necessary for a person to suffer capability deprivation.

Does economic growth mean more well-being?

Gross domestic product (GDP) per capita and related aggregate income measures are widely used to assess the economic performance of countries. The rate of change in real GDP per capita has become a standard economic indicator used by economists, politicians, and business analysts in economic debates. Despite the popularity of economic growth as a measure of success, it is being increasingly realized that it is an inadequate measure of change in the well-being of the society concerned. Higher economic growth does not necessarily mean a higher level of well-being for the people.

GDP as conventionally measured excludes many factors that contribute to well-being, while incorporating other factors that have an adverse effect on it. For instance, GDP does not include non-market production in the economy: the contribution made by housewives to output can be quite substantial but it is not included in GDP. On the other hand, as growth in economic production leads to increased pollution, people spend more money protecting themselves from the resulting ill-effects. These expenditures are included in GDP, but they do not necessarily add to well-being. Moreover, the pollution itself contributes to the people's ill-being, but this is not netted out of the output that caused them in GDP measures.

This is not to suggest that economic growth is unimportant for well-being. Economic growth provides people with greater command over goods and services and thus gives them greater utility. Per-capita income is an important explanatory variable for determining key education and health indicators—such as life expectancy at birth, literacy rate, enrollment rate, child mortality rate, and birth attended by skilled health worker—all of which reflect people's well-being. In other words, people's choice sets can be expanded through economic growth, but we need to remember that this is not exactly the same concept as well-being.

The benefits of economic growth are seldom shared equally. Some people may enjoy a large share of economic benefits, while a large proportion of people may be completely bypassed by economic growth. Thus, economic growth does not necessarily imply a higher level of well-being for every individual belonging to a society. If our objective is to enhance the well-being of every single individual in society, then economic growth is not an appropriate indicator to judge the changes in aggregate well-being. Instead, it should be supplemented with other indicators that are more closely associated with individual living standard. According to the 2010 Human Development Report, "economic growth is a means and not an end of development." This is indeed a forceful statement, suggesting that there is no automatic translation from high growth in gross national income to progress in human development.

Functionings and capabilities

People want income because it allows them to possess commodities, which they then consume. The higher their income, the greater the command people will have over these commodities. The possession of commodities, including services, provides people with the means to lead a better life; thus, the possession of commodities or opulence is closely related to the quality of life people enjoy. However, it is merely a means to an end. As Sen (1985) points out, "ultimately, the focus has to be on what we can or cannot do, can or cannot be." Therefore, well-being must be seen as individual achievements and not as means that individuals possess. Well-being or standard of living is not about the possession of commodities; rather, it is about living. Along these lines of reasoning, Amartya Sen developed the ideas of "functionings and capabilities." While functioning is an achievement, capability is the ability to achieve. Thus, functionings are directly related to what kind of life people actually lead, whereas capabilities are concerned with the freedom people have in the choice of life they lead.

Income allows an individual to purchase commodities with which he or she generates various functionings. But not all individuals can convert commodities into functionings to the same degree. For instance, a disabled person may not be able to do many things that an able-bodied individual can do with the same commodity. As such, in measuring well-being or standard of living, our focus ought to be on the achievements of people and not merely on the commodities they possess.

It may seem obvious that the higher the income people have, the greater will be their capabilities. After all, it is an observed fact that developed countries do have a higher standard of living than developing countries. But the relationship between the two is not as simple as it appears. Consider, for example, a country which has succeeded in reducing its mortality rate so much that its per-capita GDP falls because of the resulting increase in population; in this case, can we say conclusively whether the country's living standard has improved or deteriorated? The answer is not clear: the fall in per-capita income suggests that the country has become poorer, but, at the same time, the country has increased the capability of its citizens to live a longer life. This example demonstrates the complex nature of the relationship between income and the capabilities that people possess.

Utility functions and happiness

Real income measures based on the utility maximization hypothesis are widely used to capture changes in people's welfare. In the literature, an individual's utility is defined in terms of his or her consumption of goods and services. It is assumed that a typical individual allocates his or her fixed income to various goods and services in such a way that his or her utility is maximized. The prices of goods and services play a crucial role in the construction of real income measures. This literature in welfare economics has resulted in the development of "price" and "real income" indices that are widely used in practice.

The main drawback of the real income approach is that the utility function implicit in the approach is narrowly defined as a function of a commodity bundle. As such, this approach does not take account of the characteristics of the people—that is, what people can or cannot do. It merely provides an index of "opulence" or an index of the command people have over commodities. Sen (1989, p. 64) is highly critical of this approach because it reflects only "what one has rather than what one gets from what one has." As argued earlier, well-being is about living.

Quality of life may be enhanced by opulence, but opulence alone is not well-being.

On the other hand, it is not uncommon to reason that, ultimately, it is the subjective happiness of people that really counts, rather than faceless commodity bundles or per-capita GDP. Is it thus more appropriate to measure well-being in terms of the degree of happiness? The answer is no. On this subject, Sen (1989) argues that living standards cannot be the same as happiness. More specifically, he writes that:

> If an immensely rich able-bodied, healthy, well-educated person were to tell us that he is unhappy, we would have no prime foci reason to disbelieve him (he could be really unhappy), but we would scarcely think that his unhappiness indicates that his standard of living is low. He is unhappy despite his high standard of living. The fact that we see nothing unbelievable or absurd in such a possibility indicates quite clearly that the notion of living standard and that of utility or happiness are not identical. The former may be typically very important to the latter, but they are not the same things.
>
> (Sen 1989, p. 65)

People can be happy or unhappy irrespective of how they live. In India, many people live in severe poverty with no access to the basic amenities of life, and yet, they may still be happy because of the belief that they will be better-off in their next life. Indeed, they believe that the more they suffer in this life, the better-off they will be in their next. Such religious beliefs may help alleviate people's sufferings, but these beliefs are not necessarily correlated with people's standards of living. Well-being is about people's capabilities to do things. The more capabilities people have, the higher is their well-being. Yet, higher well-being may or may not make people happier.

It is not suggested that happiness or unhappiness is entirely based on a person's state of mind. People may be unhappy because they are unable to do things they want or have limited capabilities to function. If large numbers of people express unhappiness, it is a good indicator that they have lost some basic capabilities and it is worthwhile to pay attention to its causes. In this regard, the degree of happiness (or unhappiness) can, in some circumstances, be a good indicator of people's well-being (or ill-being). But then again, happiness is not the same as well-being. Moreover, happiness can only be measured through people's perceptions, which may change drastically over a short period. Therefore, the level of happiness alone would not be a stable indicator of well-being because it could change without any change in the people's actual living standards.

Basic needs

In the 1950s and 1960s, growth in per-capita GDP (or related income measures) was the principal yardstick for measuring economic development. The dominant ideology at that time was that economic growth would create widespread prosperity by creating more jobs and more goods and services. The benefits of economic growth would eventually "trickle down" to the poor.

By the early 1970s, it became clear that economic growth did not help the poor. The level of poverty remained persistently high despite the rapid economic growth in many countries. Consequently, dissatisfaction with growth-oriented policies became widespread. International organizations, particularly the World Bank, shifted the focus of their development strategies from growth to meeting people's basic needs. Greater emphasis was thus placed on the eradication of poverty and meeting people's basic needs in education, health, and housing.

The basic needs approach involves providing people with a minimum basket of goods. This approach, clearly, is more closely related to people's living standards than growth in an aggregated income measure. The higher the satisfaction of people's basic needs, the greater will be their well-being. However, this approach again places its entire emphasis on the possession of commodities and not on people. Well-being must reflect what lives people are able to lead rather than the bundle of commodities they possess. As individuals differ from one to another, their needs are also different. A basic bundle of commodities given to an individual may not necessarily result in the same achievements for another individual.

Well-being defined on the basis of functionings and capabilities is focused on people—specifically on the lives they lead and on their achievements. This is a more general approach in the sense that it takes into account many aspects of life other than the fulfillment of basic needs. Well-being is a more complex concept, while the basic needs approach is rather narrow. For instance, it says nothing about the political and civil liberties people may or may not be enjoying. As Dasgupta (1993) points out, to ignore political and civil liberties when we evaluate the quality of life is simply grotesque.

Human development index

The United Nations Development Programme (UNDP) defines human development as both the process of widening people's choices and the level of their achieved well-being. This definition is closely related to Sen's conceptualization of standard of living in terms of "capabilities" and "functionings": while the former concept refers to the choices people have, the latter refers to the actual levels of well-being. The two approaches, which seem to have the same motivation, put people ahead of commodities.

As its name suggests, human development may narrowly be interpreted as the development of people's potential. It is important to develop people's potential so that they have wider choices, but the development of potential is not enough if no environment exists for them to utilize it. What's important is what people can do with their potential, not just what they possess. For instance, we may succeed in improving the educational levels of people living in a certain region, but if the region does not provide enough job opportunities, then their well-being may not necessarily improve, even with more education. Well-being should thus be measured in terms of functionings or capabilities to achieve, not just in terms of their educational attainment. However, this is not to suggest that educational attainment is not an important constituent of well-being; it is very important because people without education have limited possibilities to function effectively in society.

The UNDP's concept of human development is not as narrow as the name suggests. It is defined in terms of achievements and focuses on the ends rather than the means of development and progress. According to this concept, the real objective of development is to create an enabling environment for people to enjoy long, healthy, and creative lives. Thus, the concept is very close to the ideas of "functionings" and "capabilities."

The UNDP developed the Human Development Index (HDI) to compare standards of living across countries. The idea of this index was conceived in order to focus on well-being rather than on GDP growth rates. It is a composite indicator reflecting three aspects of well-being: longevity, learning, and material standard of living.

Longevity is measured by life expectancy at birth, which indicates the number of years a new born infant would live if patterns of mortality prevailing for all people at the time of birth were to stay the same throughout his or her life. Life expectancy could be seen as an indicator of several other indicators of well-being such as nutrition, sanitation, and medical facilities. Moreover, since most people would prefer to live longer, life expectancy can be regarded as an indicator of achievement, and, therefore, becomes eligible for inclusion as an important component of well-being. On the other hand, learning is measured by an indicator that gives two-thirds of its weight to the literacy rate for adults and one-third to the combined gross primary and secondary school enrollment rate. Finally, the material standard of living is measured by real GDP per capita adjusted for purchasing power parity (PPP). The HDI is a single indicator of well-being that can be used to rank countries by the level of their well-being. Thus, we can compare each country's achievement in terms of the degree of well-being. These comparisons are obviously very important because they provide a basis for learning about policies that would enhance the well-being of the people, especially in countries where the level of well-being is low.

The HDI has the virtue of being simple because it is derived from a simple average of three important components of well-being. However, the index has been subject to considerable criticism because of its arbitrariness. There exists no rational justification for assigning equal weights to the different components of well-being. There is also arbitrariness in the selection of the minimum and maximum values used to normalize the various indicators.

How the different components of well-being should be weighted is a serious problem. If we insist on having a complete system of rankings of countries, then arbitrariness is unavoidable. An alternative approach suggested in the literature is that of principal components, where the component weights are proportional to the leading principal component of the correlation matrix. The rationale behind this approach is that the data should determine the "optimum" weights that capture the largest variations in the three indicators. The main difficulty with this approach lies in its extreme objectivity. The weight given to each component of well-being reflects our value judgments about how much importance we want to give to different aspects of well-being. These value judgments cannot be determined mechanically from the observed data.

Sen (1989) correctly argues that it is not necessary to convert several indicators of well-being into a single index. The concept of well-being has an inherent pluralism and should not be seen as a one-dimensional measure such as weight or height. Hence, we should adopt a partial approach under which we make comparisons of well-being using a small number of capabilities that are generally regarded as important.

Measuring poverty: income approach versus capability deprivation

One of the earlier studies on poverty was done by Rowntree (1901) who defined families as being in primary poverty if their total earnings are insufficient to obtain the "minimum necessities of merely physical efficiency." He estimated the minimum money costs for food that would satisfy the average nutritional needs of families of different sizes. To these costs he added the rent paid and certain minimum amounts for clothing, fuel, and sundries, to arrive at a poverty line for a family of given size. A family is then identified as poor if its total earnings are below the poverty line. This approach to measuring poverty may be called the "income approach," which identifies the poor on the basis of monetary income or consumption and measures the degree of poverty in society.

The income or consumption approach is widely used to measure poverty. Whether we should use income or consumption to measure poverty is an issue that is still debated. In general, consumption is believed to be a better indicator of a household's long-term welfare than income. Households tend to maintain a stable consumption level over time by saving when income levels are high and borrowing when income levels are low. Conversely, income tends to fluctuate more widely than consumption, and it is relatively more subject to measurement errors than consumption. Obtaining precise information on income is particularly difficult in developing countries, particularly countries that have large informal sectors. Households might also find it difficult to accurately recall income from various activities in the informal sector that allow immediate payments for the purchase of food and other necessities.

Regardless of how it is measured in practice, the income approach views poverty as the deprivation of income (or consumption). Poverty exists because some sections of society have such low incomes that they cannot satisfy their minimum basic needs as defined by the poverty line. But income is not the only deprivation people may suffer. Although income deprivation may give rise to several other deprivations, people may still suffer acute deprivation in many other areas, even if they possess adequate command over commodities. In this context, Sen (1999) correctly argues that poverty should be viewed as the deprivation of basic capabilities rather than merely as a low level of income.

Viewed in terms of capability deprivation, poverty encompasses not only material deprivation (as measured by income or consumption), but also many other forms of deprivation such as unemployment, ill health, lack of education, vulnerability, powerlessness, and social exclusion. Thus, poverty viewed from such a broad perspective opens up a wider range of policy options that governments may focus on to reduce poverty. For instance, if there is acute deprivation in health, then public policy should address the health aspects of poverty. Similarly, if poverty is only concerned about income deprivation, then policy needs to be geared toward increasing people's incomes. Hence, the most effective way of poverty alleviation would be to implement policies that deal directly with specific kinds of deprivation that have been identified. On the other hand, it is also possible that lack of income is the main cause of the specific deprivation. In this case, a combination of policies that enhance income and reduce the specific deprivation may be appropriate. Thus, using the capability deprivation approach should not imply that we abandon the income approach completely; rather, both approaches should complement each other.

Poverty as the lack of basic capabilities

Under the capability deprivation approach, an individual may be defined as poor if he or she lacks basic capabilities. But what are these basic capabilities and how do we identify them? These fundamental questions intrinsically involve value judgments. The answers to these questions depend on how a society prioritizes different capabilities. This prioritization may, in turn, depend on the economic resources that a country possesses. There is no clear-cut formula for determining basic capabilities. However, despite these complexities, it is still possible to get a consensus on some basic capabilities. For instance, if a person suffers from ill health and has a low life expectancy, he or she can surely be classified as poor. Similarly, an illiterate person can be defined as poor because he or she finds it difficult functioning independently in society. All those capabilities that relate to basic health, education, shelter, clothing, nutrition, and clean water may be regarded as basic capabilities.

In 1997, the UNDP developed a Human Poverty Indicator (HPI), which focused on five essential areas of human existence. The first component concerns the so-called "longevity deficit," which is defined as the percentage of the population that is at risk of dying at the age of 40. This indicator measures the health status of the population. The second component is related to deficiencies in education and is measured by the percentage of illiterate members of the population. The remaining three components are (i) the percentage of the population with no access to drinking water; (ii) the percentage of the population with no access to basic health services; and (iii) the percentage of children below five years old who suffer from malnutrition.

The HPI attempts to combine all these five components into a single indicator based on an ad-hoc weighting scheme. To formulate poverty reduction policies, it is unnecessary to produce a single human poverty indicator. Moreover, a composite index constructed from numerous indicators may not be viewed as desirable, given that each indicator reflects a different dimension of well-being. While a single composite index may have the virtue of being simple, and the advantage of providing cross-country rankings, measuring and monitoring deprivation separately is more useful for policymaking.

Poverty versus capability deprivation *per se*

Suppose that a millionaire, who has all the economic means to buy anything he or she wants, suffers from a disease that prevents him or her from achieving some basic functionings. Despite having access to the best medical facilities, this millionaire is surely suffering from a serious capability deprivation; however, it would be odd to call him or her "poor." This illustrates that poverty is only present when basic capability failure arises because a person has inadequate command over resources, whether from market or non-market sources. By examining capability deprivation alone, we cannot always identify persons who are poor in this specific sense.

Accordingly, there is a need to make a distinction between capability deprivation in general and poverty in particular. Poverty is concerned with the inadequacy of command over resources needed to generate socially determined basic capabilities, whereas capability deprivation is more general and may be caused by a host of factors, of which income or entitlement to resources may not be the most important. In that regard, a person may suffer capability deprivation but still not be poor.

Defining poverty from the capability perspective cannot be accomplished independently of income measurements. One should only be concerned with capabilities to function that are derivable from income. Income (or command over resources) and capability cannot be separated, but at the same time it must be recognized that the linkage between the two is far from being straightforward. As individuals have different needs, they are different in their ability to convert the incomes or resources they have into capabilities to function. Therefore, each individual will require different resources to achieve his or her basic capabilities.

Ideally, any proposed income measure of poverty should be constructed from capabilities. The choice of poverty line should reflect the cost of achieving basic human needs. However, the measure used most frequently internationally, that is, the US$1 (or $2) per person a day poverty line, is not in accordance with the capability approach to poverty: it does not reflect the inadequacy of command over the resources to achieve basic capabilities. A person can have income sufficient to be classified as non-poor according to the $1-a-day yardstick, but not to attain income-dependent basic capabilities. If poverty reduction, as properly understood, is to be achieved, then a new measure reflecting its extent and distribution in the world will be required. This new measure should reflect not only material dimensions of well-being, but also non-material dimensions such as education and health. In recent years, poverty has been increasingly viewed as multidimensional, so non-material dimensions of well-being have attracted substantial interest.

2   What is an equitable distribution?

Introduction

In this chapter we look at what an equitable distribution is and how equity can be measured. The main purpose of measuring equity is to understand how incomes generated in the economy affect people's welfare. Equity, therefore, does not just measure the dispersion in the distribution of income; rather, it is a normative concept and has to be linked with social welfare. Measures of equity discussed in this chapter are, therefore, linked to various social welfare functions proposed in the literature.

Equity is measured at the aggregate level, with the aggregation performed over all individuals in a society. To achieve this, we need to measure the economic welfare of each individual; ideally, this should incorporate all factors that contribute, directly and indirectly, to individual welfare. In practice, however, economic welfare is measured by either income or consumption, and there exists no consensus about which one to use. According to Deaton (2000), income and consumption are different concepts, not just two ways of measuring the same concept. Income measures the potential claims of an individual on an economy's output; in other words, it is a measure of the rights or entitlements each individual has within the economy. Consumption, on the other hand, measures actual consumption of goods and services and thus reflects current standards of living. While this is not the place to resolve this controversy, we note that in general income is used as a measure of welfare in developed countries, and consumption, largely, in developing countries.

Household surveys are the main source of information on household income and consumption, and estimates of individual economic welfare are derived from this data. Although further adjustments are required to account for differences in needs based on household size and composition, an index of economic welfare derived accordingly measures the economic welfare of each individual in society. This index is used to determine which individual is better off or worse off than others in the society. In this chapter, equality (or inequality) in the distribution of an individuals' economic welfare is referred to as equity (or inequity) in the distribution of economic welfare.

Lorenz curve and Gini index

The Lorenz curve, named after Max Otto Lorenz, is widely used to represent and analyze the distribution of income and wealth. Lorenz proposed this curve in 1905 to compare and analyze inequalities of income and wealth in a country during different periods, or in different countries during the same period. In this chapter, our main objective is to compare and analyze inequality in the distribution of individual economic welfare within a country. If we rank all individuals in ascending order of their economic welfare, the Lorenz curve can be described by a function, $L(p)$, which is interpreted as the fraction of total welfare enjoyed by the lowest pth fraction of population. Kakwani (1980) shows that $L(p)$ satisfies the following conditions:

(a)   If $p = 0$, $L(p) = 0$
(b)   If $p = 1$, $L(p) = 1$
(c) $L'(p) = \frac{x}{\mu} \geq 0$ and $L''(p) = \frac{1}{\mu f(x)} > 0$
(d) $L(p) \leq p$

where the welfare, x, of a person is a random variable with probability density function $f(x)$ and mean welfare, μ, and $L'(p)$ and $L''(p)$ are the first and second derivatives of $L(p)$ with respect to p.

These conditions imply that the Lorenz curve is represented in a unit square. In Figure 2.1, the diagonal OB line through the unit square is called the egalitarian line. The Lorenz curve lies below this line. If the curve coincides with the egalitarian line, this suggests that each person enjoys the same welfare; that is, the case of perfect equality. In the case of perfect inequality, the Lorenz curve coincides with OA and AB, implying that all economic welfare in society is enjoyed by only one person.

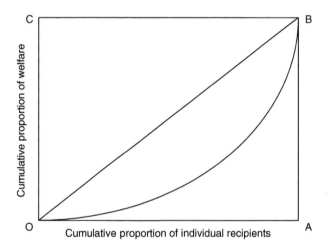

Figure 2.1 The Lorenz curve, $L(p)$.

Because the Lorenz curve displays the deviation of each person's welfare from perfect equality, it captures, in a sense, the essence of inequality. The nearer the Lorenz curve is to the egalitarian line, the more equal the distribution of welfare. Consequently, the Lorenz curve can be used as a criterion for ranking government policies or programs. Suppose there are two alternative government policies that result in two different welfare distributions, X_1 and X_2. If the Lorenz curve of X_1 is above that of X_2 at all points, then, from an equity point of view, the first policy is preferred over the second policy, or we may say that distribution X_1 is more equitable than distribution X_2. However, if the two Lorenz curves intersect, neither policy can be said to be more equitable than the other. Thus, the Lorenz curve only provides a partial ranking of distributions.

A complete ranking of distributions can be obtained with the Gini index, which measures the deviation of the Lorenz curve from the egalitarian line. It is defined as one minus twice the area under the Lorenz curve:

$$G = 1 - 2 \int_0^1 L(p) dp \tag{2.1}$$

The Gini index lies between 0 and 1: a value of 0 implies perfect equity (i.e., everyone receives the same welfare) and 1 implies perfect inequity (i.e., one person receives all the welfare). The values of the Gini index for different distributions inform us which distribution is more equitable than the other. The greater the Gini index, the lower the equity in the distribution of welfare. Thus, the Gini index is a well-known measure of inequity and represents the opposite of equity. So we may use $(1 - G)$ as a measure of equity in the distribution of welfare.

Bonferroni curve and Bonferroni index

In 1930, Carlo Emilio Bonferroni proposed a curve similar to the Lorenz curve derived from the cumulative means of an income distribution. Again, ranking individuals in ascending order of their economic welfare, we can construct a conditional mean welfare of the bottom p proportion of the population. Suppose μ_p is the mean welfare enjoyed by the bottom p proportion of the population and μ is the mean welfare enjoyed by individuals in the population, then the Bonferroni curve is defined as

$$B(p) = \frac{\mu_p}{\mu} \tag{2.2}$$

Note that $\mu_p = 0$ if $p = 0$ and $\mu_p = \mu$ if $p = 1$. This suggests that $B(p)$ lies between 0 and 1. The relationship between the Lorenz curve and the Bonferroni curve is then derived as

$$B(p) = \frac{L(p)}{p} \tag{2.3}$$

The higher the curve, the more equal the distribution. A distribution X will be more equitable than Y if the Bonferroni curve for X is higher than that for Y. Similar to the Lorenz curve, if the two Bonferroni curves intersect, we cannot infer whether X is more or less equitable than Y. The Bonferroni curve also provides a partial ranking of income distributions. A complete ranking of distributions is provided by the Bonferroni index that is defined as one minus the area under the Bonferroni curve:

$$B = 1 - \int_0^1 B(p)dp \tag{2.4}$$

which ranges between 0 for perfect equality and 1 for perfect inequality. Like the Gini index, B in equation (2.4) is a measure of inequity. So we may measure equity by $(1-B)$, the values of which for different distributions are able to indicate which distribution is more equitable compared to the other.

Relative and absolute equity

Equity can be measured in both relative and absolute terms. If a measure of equity remains unchanged when the welfare enjoyed by each individual in society is altered by the same proportion, then such a measure is called a relative measure of equity. The Lorenz curve gives a relative measure of equity because the curve remains unchanged when the welfare of each individual is increased or decreased by the same proportion. In a similar manner, the Gini and Bonferroni indices discussed above are relative measures of equity or inequity. However, according to Kolm (1976), an equi-proportional increase in all welfare must increase inequity, because richer persons will enjoy a higher incremental increase in their standards of living than poorer persons. So alternatively, we can define absolute measures of equity (or inequity) that do not show any changes in equity or inequity when everyone's welfare is increased or decreased by the same magnitude.

Although inequality is commonly perceived as a relative concept, an absolute concept of inequality can also be attractive, since government transfer policies are generally understood in terms of absolute benefits going to the poor. Suppose there are two people with incomes of $100 and $1,000, and the government implements a policy which gives $15 to the poorer individual and $100 to the richer. Such a policy may not be readily accepted as equitable even if the poor benefits proportionally more than the non-poor: this policy has actually increased the absolute difference in income between the rich and the poor even as it reduced the relative difference between them. Note that equity is a concept related to fairness and justice; as such, its measure in absolute terms is intuitively more appealing from the perspective of fairness and justice. The poor person in the hypothetical example above could still see that his income was lower by $900 than the rich person's.

To measure absolute inequity, we introduce an absolute inequity curve:

$$\varphi(p) = \mu[p - L(p)] \tag{2.5}$$

This curve has the following properties:

(a) If $p = 0$, $\varphi(p) = 0$
(b) If $p = 1$, $\varphi(p) = 0$
(c) $\varphi'(p) = -(\mu - x)$
(d) $\varphi''(p) = -\frac{1}{f(x)} < 0$

It can be shown that if the welfare of all people is increased or decreased by the same *absolute* amount, the curve will not change. In Figure 2.2, OA is the egalitarian line. If the curve coincides with the egalitarian line, this means that each person enjoys the same welfare, which is the case of perfect equity. The higher the absolute inequity curve, the greater is the absolute inequity in the distribution of welfare. The curve attains its maximum value at the point where $x = \mu$. A policy will be judged as absolutely equitable (or inequitable) if it causes $\varphi(p)$ to shift downward (or upward).

The area under the inequity curve multiplied by 2 gives

$$A_G = \mu G \qquad (2.6)$$

which is an absolute index of inequity; the larger the index, the greater the absolute inequity in the distribution. An alternative absolute inequity curve related to the Bonferroni curve is given by

$$\epsilon(p) = \mu(1 - B(p)) = (\mu - \mu_p) \qquad (2.7)$$

It can be easily shown that any absolute increase or decrease in welfare of all people does not shift the $\epsilon(p)$ curve either upward or downward. The area under

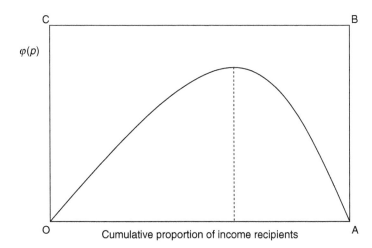

C   B

$\varphi(p)$

Cumulative proportion of income recipients

O   A

Figure 2.2 Absolute inequity curve $\varphi(p)$.

the Bonferroni absolute inequity curve is given by

$$A_B = \mu B \tag{2.8}$$

which is an alternative measure of absolute inequity related to the Bonferroni index and may be called the Bonferroni absolute inequity index.

There is another measure, called the relative mean deviation, which is defined as the maximum distance between p and $L(p)$. This maximum is attained when $x = \mu$ so that the relative mean deviation is given by

$$R = F(\mu) \left[\frac{\mu - \mu^*}{\mu} \right] \tag{2.9}$$

where $F(\mu)$ is the proportion of individuals who have per-capita welfare less than μ, and μ^* is the mean income of individuals who have per-capita welfare less than μ. R is a relative measure of inequity. It lies between 0 and 1, thus, $(1 - R)$ may be used as a measure of equity. An absolute measure of inequity related to the mean deviation is given by

$$R_A = F(\mu)[\mu - \mu^*] \tag{2.10}$$

It can be easily verified that the absolute measure of mean deviation in equation (2.10) is invariant when the welfare of all individuals is increased or decreased by the same amount, while the relative measure of mean deviation in equation (2.9) is invariant when the welfare of all individuals is increased by the same proportion.

The Lorenz curve and social welfare

Government policies should be judged based on their impact on social welfare, which is an aggregate measure of society's welfare derived from each individual's welfare levels. Following this view, a policy X_1 should be judged as superior to another policy X_2 when the social welfare derived from X_1 is greater than that derived from X_2. Fortunately, under certain conditions, the ranking of distributions according to the Lorenz curve is identical to the ranking implied by the social welfare function. In 1970, Anthony B. Atkinson proved a theorem showing that if social welfare is defined as the sum of individual utilities, and every individual has an identical utility function that is increasing in income and is concave, then the ranking of distributions according to the Lorenz curve criterion is identical to the ranking implied by the social welfare function, provided that the distributions have the same mean income and their Lorenz curves do not intersect. An important implication of this theorem is that one can evaluate alternative policies from the point of view of welfare without knowing the form of individuals' utility functions, except that they are increasing and concave, and provided that the Lorenz curves do not intersect. If the Lorenz curves do intersect, however, two utility functions that would rank the distributions differently can always be found.

Atkinson's theorem relies on the assumption that the social welfare function is equal to the sum of individual utilities and that every individual has the same utility function—assumptions that are rather restrictive. Fortunately, Dasgupta, Sen, and Starrett (1973) as well as Rothschild and Stiglitz (1973) demonstrated that the theorem is, in fact, more general and would hold for any symmetric welfare function that is quasi-concave.

The Lorenz curve makes distributional judgments under the assumption that the two distributions have the same mean incomes. In practice, we can never have any two distributions with the same mean incomes. As extensions of the Lorenz partial orderings, Shorrocks (1983) and Kakwani (1984) arrived at a criterion that would rank any two distributions with different means. The new ranking criterion they developed is given by $L(\mu,p)$, which is the product of the mean income μ and the Lorenz curve $L(p)$:

$$L(\mu,p) = \mu L(p) \qquad (2.11)$$

In comparison, the Lorenz ranking is based only on $L(p)$. Shorrocks and Kakwani proved a theorem saying that if the generalized Lorenz curve of distribution X_1 is higher than the generalized Lorenz curve of distribution X_2 at all points, then we can say unambiguously that the social welfare implied by distribution X_1 will always be higher than the social welfare implied by distribution X_2. In other words, distribution X_1 is welfare-superior to distribution X_2. This result holds for a wide range of social welfare functions. The only restriction on the social welfare function is that it should be symmetric and quasi-concave in individual incomes. Figure 2.3 presents the generalized Lorenz curves for two distributions X_1 and X_2.

Similar to the idea of the generalized Lorenz curve, we propose a generalized Bonferroni curve defined as

$$B(\mu,p) = \frac{\mu L(p)}{p} \qquad (2.12)$$

It can be easily shown that if the generalized Bonferroni curve of distribution X_1 is higher than the generalized Bonferroni curve of distribution X_2 at all points, we can say unambiguously that social welfare implied by distribution X_1 will always be higher than the social welfare implied by distribution X_2. In other words, distribution X_1 is welfare-superior to distribution X_2. Again this result holds for a wide range of social welfare functions.

Inequity indices and social welfare

In the previous section, we demonstrated that we can rank government policies from a welfare point of view using either the generalized Lorenz curve or the generalized Bonferroni curve, provided the curves do not intersect. If the curves

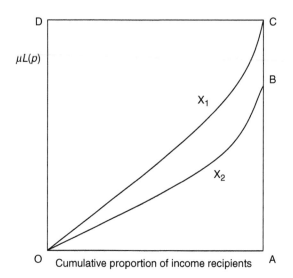

Figure 2.3 Generalized Lorenz curve $\mu L(p)$.

for different policies intersect, we cannot judge if one policy is welfare-superior to another. Thus, the two curves provide only a partial ranking of different policies. In such situations, we cannot rank policies without specifying social welfare functions.

Since a higher generalized curve implies greater social welfare, we can achieve a complete ordering of policies by calculating the area under the generalized Lorenz curve, which can be used as a measure of social welfare. The area under twice the generalized Lorenz curve is obtained as

$$W_G = 2 \int_0^1 L(p)dp = \mu(1 - G) = 2 \int_0^1 x_p(1 - p)dp \tag{2.13}$$

Equation (2.13) is the social welfare function implied by the Gini index that was proposed by Sen (1974). Note from the third term on the right hand side of equation (2.13) that the Gini social welfare function is the weighted average of individual welfare levels, with weight given by $w(p) = 2(1 - p)$. It can easily be shown that total weight adds up to 1. Furthermore, the weight is proportional to the welfare ranking of individuals: the poorest individual receives the maximum weight and the richest individual gets the minimum weight. If this pro-poor weighting of welfare is acceptable to policymakers, then it is a useful tool to analyze government policies.

From equation (2.13) we also note that G measures the loss of welfare in percentage terms due to the existence of inequity, while the absolute measure A_G measures the absolute loss of welfare due to the existence of inequity.

Alternatively, we can derive a new measure of social welfare that is equal to the area under the generalized Bonferroni curve as given in equation (2.12):

$$W_B = \mu \int_0^1 \frac{L(p)}{p} dp = \mu(1 - B) = -\int_0^1 x_p \ln(p) dp \tag{2.14}$$

which is the social welfare measure implied by the Bonferroni inequity index. Note that like the Gini welfare measure, the Bonferroni welfare measure is the weighted average of individual welfare levels with weight given by $v(p) = -\log(p)$. It can be shown that the total weight adds up to 1 and that weights decrease monotonically with p. This suggests that the poorest individual receives the maximum weight, while the richest person gets the minimum weight.

Based on our discussions so far, we now have two social welfare functions: one implied by the Gini index and the other implied by the Bonferroni index, both of which have all the desirable properties of a social welfare function—that is, increasing in individual welfare, quasi-concave, and weights decreasing monotonically as individual welfare increases. A pertinent question that subsequently arises is which index of inequity should be used in practice? The Gini index is most widely used, while hardly any studies use the Bonferroni index. It can easily be seen that weighting functions for the two indices have the following first and second derivatives:

$$w'(p) = -2 \quad \text{and} \quad w''(p) = 0 \tag{2.15}$$

and

$$v'(p) = -\frac{1}{p} \quad \text{and} \quad v''(p) = \frac{1}{p^2} \tag{2.16}$$

The equations in (2.15) show that weights in the Gini social welfare function decrease monotonically at a constant rate. On the other hand, the equations in (2.16) suggest that weights in the Bonferroni social welfare function decrease monotonically at an increasing rate. In short, the Bonferroni weight function declines more steeply than the Gini weight function. Since the total weight for both functions adds up to unity, this implies, as indicated by Figure 2.4, that the Bonferroni social welfare function gives a greater weight to the individuals at the bottom of the welfare distribution than the Gini social welfare function. Based on this result, it can be concluded that the Bonferroni social welfare function is more egalitarian (or pro-poor) than the Gini social welfare function.

The social welfare function implied by the relative or absolute mean deviations can be defined as

$$W_R = \mu - F(\mu)[\mu - \mu^*] \tag{2.17}$$

This social welfare function gives exactly the same weight to all individuals who have per-capita welfare less than μ, where the weight is proportional to $F(\mu)$;

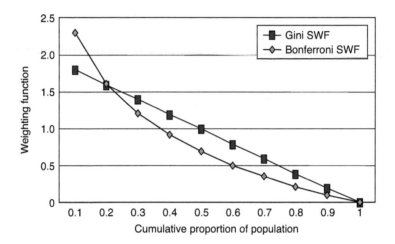

Figure 2.4 Weighting functions for Gini and Bonferroni social welfare functions (SWFs).

similarly, it gives exactly the same weight to all individuals whose per-capita welfare is greater than μ, with the weight being proportional to $[1 - F(\mu)]$. This suggests that the social welfare function is completely insensitive to any transfer of welfare among the individuals with per-capita welfare that is either less than or greater than μ. The social welfare function is only sensitive to transfers of welfare between the two groups of individuals: those with per-capita welfare less than μ and those with per-capita welfare greater than μ. Such social welfare functions are not regarded as desirable.

Empirical illustration

For empirical analysis, we use data from the Philippines' Annual Poverty Indicators Survey (APIS) conducted in 1998, 2002, 2004, and 2007 obtained from the National Statistical Office in Manila. The APIS is a nationwide household survey designed to provide poverty indicators at the provincial level.

APIS gathers information on various aspects of well-being for all 78 Philippine provinces, as well as for the cities and municipalities of Metropolitan Manila. It provides detailed information on demographic and economic characteristics; health status and education of family members; awareness and use of family planning methods; housing, water, and sanitation conditions and families; availability of credit to finance a family business or enterprise; and family income and expenditures. The APIS data sets for 1998, 2002, 2004, and 2007 collected such information from more than 38,000 households and 190,000 individuals across the Philippines.

Table 2.1 Measures of social welfare and equity in the Philippines

	1998	*2002*	*2004*	*2007*
Consumer price index (1998 = 100)	100.0	121.1	132.8	156.2
Nominal expenditure per capita	18,196	24,505	27,088	29,531
Real expenditure per capita in 1998 prices	18,196	20,228	20,395	18,910
Relative Gini index	46.29	47.64	45.64	45.24
Absolute Gini index	8,422	9,636	9,309	8,554
Relative Bonferroni index	56.93	58.11	56.26	55.82
Absolute Bonferroni index	10,359	11,754	11,474	10,555
Gini social welfare	9,774	10,591	11,086	10,356
Bonferroni social welfare	7,837	8,473	8,921	8,355

Source: Author's calculations.

Table 2.1 presents various measures of social welfare and equity in the Philippines, covering 1998–2007. As expected, nominal expenditure per capita increased from 18,196 pesos in 1998 to 29,531 pesos in 2007, an increase of over 62%. However, as shown in Table 2.1, inflation has run at 4.95% a year over the decade (using 1998 as the base year), so after adjusting for inflation we see that growth in real expenditure per capita was sluggish at 0.43% annually during 1998–2007.

Table 2.1 also presents the estimates for two alternative measures of relative inequality: the relative Gini index and the relative Bonferroni index. The two measures display the same pattern of inequality measured using per-capita expenditure: inequality initially increased from 1998 to 2002 and then decreased from 2002 onwards. The table also shows the social cost of inequality in terms of per-capita expenditure. Such monetized losses are estimated by means of absolute Gini and Bonferroni indices. According to the absolute Gini index, per-capita expenditures lost due to inequality were 8,422 pesos in 1998, 9,636 pesos in 2002, and down to 8,554 pesos in 2007. A similar pattern emerges from the absolute Bonferroni index; yet, its monetary loss in absolute terms is far higher than its counterpart Gini index because the former gives a greater weight to the poorer segment of the distribution compared with the latter. These findings clearly suggest a loss of social welfare due to inequality in society. This brings us to our next discussion on the estimates for Gini and Bonferroni social welfare.

Note that the Gini and Bonferroni social welfare are expressed in terms of per-capita real expenditure, but accounting for losses in social welfare due to inequality. In the Philippines, social welfare based on the Gini index was estimated at 10,356 pesos in 2007, while actual per-capita expenditure was 18,910 pesos; in other words, 8,554 pesos per capita were lost due to inequality. The story becomes even more dramatic when we place greater importance on the poorer segments of the society using the Bonferroni social welfare: in 2007, the social welfare losses due to inequality amounted to 10,555 pesos per capita in the country, resulting in social welfare of 8,355 pesos per capita.

Conclusion

Distribution is largely ignored in microeconomic theory, being relegated to two fundamental theories of welfare where nature or an omnipotent state will have to think of and implement distribution. However, in the real world, how the economic pie is distributed is not a peripheral but a central consideration, sometimes spelling the difference between social harmony and social unrest. Thus, measuring how economic gains are distributed in society is of utmost importance for both researchers and policymakers.

In this chapter, we discussed two measures of distribution—the Lorenz curve and the Bonferroni curve—and their related numerical indices—the Gini index and the Bonferroni index. Both indices are measures of inequality, such that a higher value (between zero and one) represents more inequality. Both indices are also relative measures of inequality; that is, an equiproportional increase in everyone's income (or expenditure) will not change the value of the indices, even if it has resulted in a wider gap in the income (or expenditure) between the rich and poor. This makes these indices inadequate from a policy and social justice point of view; thus, we develop absolute measures of inequality that would be sensitive to such increases in the gap between the rich and poor. In these absolute measures, which are modified from the Gini and Bonferroni indices, the values of the indices will not change if there is an equal increase in the magnitude of everyone's income (or expenditure). These absolute measures of inequality are more intuitive and useful from a policy and social justice point of view.

Policies often have the aim of improving social welfare, which in turn is the aggregate of individual welfare. However, evaluating the social welfare impacts of policies is easier said than done, since there is no way for a government to know with certainty what the underlying social welfare function is, much less the values of individual welfare. Fortunately, it is possible to rank distributions—say, before and after the implementation of a certain policy—without knowing the form of the social welfare function. Using the generalized Lorenz and generalized Bonferroni curves—and their related Gini social welfare and Bonferroni social welfare indices, respectively—it is possible to gauge whether a particular policy, or any other event for that matter, worsened or alleviated social welfare. However, given these alternative measures, which one should researchers and policymakers choose? Both measures are pro-poor—that is, poorer individuals are given greater weight than richer ones—but weights in the Gini welfare index decrease at a constant rate with income (or expenditure) while those for the Bonferroni welfare index decrease at an increasing rate. Thus, the latter index may be considered to be more pro-poor than the former.

Using data from the Philippines, the above measures of social welfare and equity show that inequality increased in 1998–2002 but decreased in 2002–07, even though real expenditure growth per capita was measured at 0.43% annually in 1998–2007. Data analysis also quantifies how much social welfare is lost due to inequality, assuming that social welfare functions are based on either the generalized Lorenz or Bonferroni curves. Even though real expenditure per capita in 2007 was measured at 18,910 pesos (at 1998 prices), an egalitarian society would consider itself poorer by 8,554 pesos (based on the Gini social welfare index) or 10,555 pesos (based on the Bonferroni social welfare index) per capita because of inequality. In other words, these measures of the social costs of inequality say that the misery of the poor is much greater than the affluence of the rich and, as a result, society is poorer.

3 On the concept of equity in opportunity

Introduction

It is now widely accepted that economic growth is necessary, but may not be sufficient to achieve economic development. Economic growth creates opportunities in the economy that enhance well-being. For instance, it generates employment, which allows people to consume goods and services. Yet the economic opportunities are not always equally available to all; circumstances or market failures generally bar the poor from availing them, and they generally benefit less.

Economic growth can directly create opportunities through market operations. More importantly, however, it generates resources in the form of tax revenues, fees, and fines, which governments use to create opportunity, particularly in education, health, housing, and so on. How equitably are people able to avail these opportunities? This is an important policy issue. We need to measure the equity of opportunity before the government can formulate policies and programs that facilitate the full participation of those who are less well off. In this chapter, we define and measure equity of opportunity, accomplished through the social opportunity function, which is similar to the idea of the social welfare function discussed extensively in Chapter 2.

Social opportunity function

Suppose there are n individuals in a society arranged in ascending order of their incomes, that is, $x_1, x_2, x_3, \ldots \ldots \ldots, x_n$. Given this, we may define a general social welfare function as

$$W = W(X) = W(x_1, x_2, x_3, \ldots \ldots \ldots, x_n) \tag{3.1}$$

where $X = (x_1, x_2, x_3, \ldots \ldots \ldots, x_n)$ is an ordered income distribution, which defines a specific ordering of the society.

This concept of a general social welfare function was introduced by Bergson in 1938 and subsequently developed by Samuelson in 1947. In Chapter 2, we discussed the relationship between the generalized Lorenz curve and social welfare function: if the generalized Lorenz curve of distribution X_1 is higher than the generalized Lorenz curve of distribution X_2 at all points, then we can say unambiguously that social welfare implied by distribution X_1 will always be higher than social welfare implied by distribution X_2. This relationship holds under three fairly general conditions, viz., that the social welfare function is (i) increasing, (ii) symmetric, and (iii) quasi-concave in individual incomes. The generalized Lorenz curve can be drawn using data on household income or consumption, which are widely available from household surveys. Based on such data, we can infer which social ordering is welfare-superior to another without knowing the form of the social welfare function.

Similar to the idea of the social welfare function, we may define a social opportunity function:

$$O = O(y_1, y_2, y_3, \ldots \ldots \ldots, y_n) \tag{3.2}$$

where y_i is the opportunity enjoyed by the ith person in society whose income is x_i, and i varies from 1 to n. Opportunities can be defined in terms of various services, for example, access to health or educational services or access to job opportunities in the labor market. The main objective of government policy is to maximize the social opportunity function to enhance social well-being.

The average opportunity for the population is defined as

$$\bar{y} = \frac{1}{n} \sum_{i=1}^{n} y_i \tag{3.3}$$

This is the average opportunity available, but it does not tell us how it is distributed across the population. To say how equitable or inequitable opportunity is, we need to know the social opportunity function as defined in equation (3.2). In practice, we cannot know the social opportunity function exactly, which raises the question of how to measure equity or inequity of opportunity in a society. Just as the social welfare function is related to the generalized Lorenz curve (discussed in Chapter 2), below we discuss the relationship between the social opportunity function and the concentration curve. The idea of the concentration curve can be used to measure equity or inequity of opportunity, which is discussed in the following section.

Concentration curve

As discussed in Chapter 2, the Lorenz curve describes the entire distribution of a single variable such as income or consumption in a society. Mahalanobis (1960) generalized the concept of the Lorenz curve to describe the consumption patterns of different commodities. Later Kakwani (1977, 1980) provided a more general and rigorous treatment of concentration curves in a study of relationships among the distributions of different economic variables. In this chapter, we use many of Kakwani's results to define and measure equity of opportunity.

Suppose $y(x)$ is an individual opportunity function, which is the opportunity enjoyed by an individual with income x. If x is a random variable with probability density function $f(x)$, then the average opportunity enjoyed by the whole society is given by

$$\bar{y} = \int_0^\infty y(x)f(x)dx = \int_0^1 y_p dp \qquad (3.4)$$

where $dp = f(x)dx$ and y_p is the opportunity enjoyed by an individual at the pth percentile, with p varying from 0 to 1. Equation (3.4) is similar to equation (3.3) but expressed in a continuous distribution. Suppose $C(p)$ is the proportion (or share) of opportunity enjoyed by the bottom p proportion of individuals in the population when individuals are arranged in ascending order of income and given by

$$C(p) = \frac{1}{\bar{y}} \int_0^p y_r dr \qquad (3.5)$$

where y_r is the opportunity enjoyed by an individual at the rth percentile. The function $C(p)$ is called the concentration curve. It has the following properties (Kakwani 1980):

(a) If $p = 0$, $C(p) = 0$
(b) If $p = 1$, $C(p) = 1$
(c) $C'(p) = \frac{y(x)}{\bar{y}} \geq 0$ and $C''(p) = \frac{y'(x)}{\bar{y}f(x)}$
(d) $C(p) < p$ for all p if $y'(x) > 0$ for all x and $C(p) \geq p$ for all p if $y'(x) \leq 0$ for all x

$C'(p)$ is the first derivative of $C(p)$ with respect to p and is always non-negative because the opportunity function $y(x)$ cannot be negative. This implies that the concentration curve increases with p: in other words, the curve is sloping upward. $C(p) = p$ is the egalitarian line where everyone in society enjoys the same opportunity.

The second derivative of the concentration curve, $C''(p)$, is positive (negative) if $y'(p)$ is positive (negative). If $y'(x) > 0$ for all x, the concentration curve is convex to the p-axis, implying $C(p) < p$ for all p. In this case, the concentration curve lies below the egalitarian line. On the other hand, if $y'(x) < 0$ for all x, then the concentration curve is concave to the p-axis; thus, $C(p) > p$ for all p, which implies that the concentration curve lies above the egalitarian line. If $y'(x) = 0$ for all x, the concentration curve coincides with the egalitarian line. Like the Lorenz curve, the concentration curve is represented in a unit square (Figure 3.1), but there is one difference between the two: while the Lorenz curve always lies below the egalitarian line, the concentration curve can either lie above or below the egalitarian line or can cross it several times.

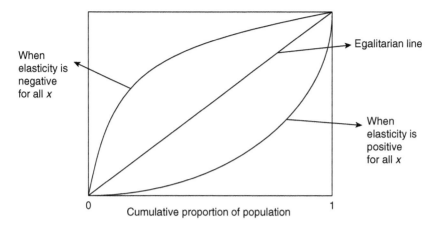

Figure 3.1 Two hypothetical concentration curves.

Defining equity of opportunity

Let us define the elasticity of the individual opportunity function as

$$\vartheta(x) = \frac{x}{y} \frac{dy(x)}{dx} \tag{3.6}$$

This elasticity can be both negative and positive. If the elasticity is 0 for all x, this means that each individual enjoys the same opportunities irrespective of income. In practice, the rich tend to enjoy greater opportunity than the poor. If $\vartheta(x) > 0$ for all x, this suggests that as the income of an individual increases, he/she has greater access to opportunity. This situation may be referred to as inequitable opportunity. If elasticity is negative for all x, then as an individual's income increases, his/her access to opportunity decreases: putting this differently, poorer people have greater access to opportunity than richer people. This may be characterized as equitable opportunity. The magnitude of elasticity in equation (3.6) can measure the degree of equity (or inequity) in society; the larger (smaller) the elasticity, the greater the inequity (equity) of opportunity.

Kakwani (1997) proved that the elasticity has a one-to-one relationship with the concentration curve; the lower (higher) the elasticity, the higher (lower) the concentration curve. This is a very powerful result. Suppose Y_1 and Y_2 are two distributions of opportunity. Distribution Y_1 will be more equitable (inequitable) than distribution Y_2 if the concentration curve for Y_1 is higher (lower) than the concentration curve for Y_2. If the two concentration curves cross, then we cannot say if one distribution is more equitable or inequitable than the other. Thus, like the Lorenz curve, the concentration curve provides a partial ranking of the opportunity distributions.

The complete ranking of distributions can be obtained with the concentration index. The concentration index measures the deviation of the concentration curve from the egalitarian line. It is defined as one minus twice the area under the concentration curve:

$$C = 1 - 2 \int_0^1 C(p)dp \qquad (3.7)$$

The concentration index lies between -1 and $+1$. Its value of 0 implies that all individuals enjoy the same opportunity irrespective of their income, and 1, being perfect inequity of opportunity, occurs when only the richest person in the society has access to opportunity. Similarly, if the concentration index is -1, then the poorest person enjoys all the opportunity. The values of the concentration index indicate which opportunity distribution is more equitable or inequitable than another. The concentration index is a measure of inequity of opportunity. Therefore, a measure of equity of opportunity can be defined as $E = (1 - C)$; the larger the value of E, the more equitable will be opportunity. E is equal to 1 if all individuals enjoy the same opportunities. This could be the benchmark: as such, opportunity is equitably (inequitably) distributed if E is greater (less) than 1.

Bonferroni concentration curve

In Chapter 2, we discussed the Bonferroni curve to describe income distribution. We may now generalize this curve to describe distribution of opportunity across individuals' incomes. When all individuals are ranked in ascending order of income, we can construct a conditional mean of opportunity enjoyed by the bottom p proportion of population. Suppose $\overline{y}_p$ is the mean opportunity enjoyed by the bottom p proportion of the population and $\overline{y}$ is the mean opportunity enjoyed by all individuals in the population. Given these definitions, the Bonferroni concentration curve is defined as[1]

$$C_E(p) = \frac{\overline{y}_p}{\overline{y}} \qquad (3.8)$$

Note that $\overline{y}_p = 0$ if $p = 0$ and $\overline{y}_p = \overline{y}$ if $p = 1$. The relationship between the concentration curve and the Bonferroni concentration curve can be derived as

$$C_B(p) = \frac{C(p)}{p} \qquad (3.9)$$

The higher the curve, the more equitable will be the distribution of opportunity. Suppose Y_1 and Y_2 are two distributions of opportunity, distribution Y_1 will be more equitable (inequitable) than distribution Y_2 if the Bonferroni concentration curve for Y_1 is higher (lower) than the Bonferroni concentration curve for Y_2. If the two Bonferroni concentration curves cross, then we cannot say unambiguously whether one distribution is more equitable or inequitable than the other. Therefore, the Bonferroni curve also provides partial rankings of distributions of opportunity.

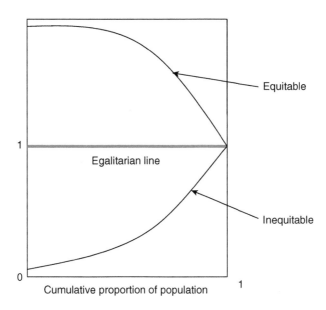

Figure 3.2 Two hypothetical Bonferroni concentration curves.

Figure 3.2 depicts two hypothetical Bonferroni concentration curves. The horizontal line at $C_B(p) = 1$ is the egalitarian line when everyone in society avails the same opportunities. The curve above the egalitarian line provides equitable opportunity while the curve below the egalitarian line provides inequitable opportunity.

A complete ranking of distributions is provided by the Bonferroni equity index proposed by Ali and Son (2007), which is defined as the area under the Bonferroni concentration curve:

$$E_B = \int_0^1 C_B(p)dp = \int_0^1 \frac{C(p)}{p} dp \qquad (3.10)$$

which is equal to 1 if all individuals in the society enjoy the same opportunities, in which case $C(p) = p$. There will be an extreme concentration of opportunities when the richest person enjoys them all, in which case $C(p) = 0$ for all p, which on substituting in equation (3.10) gives E_B equal to 0. If opportunities are concentrated mostly among individuals in the bottom of income distribution, $C_B(p) > 1$ for all p, which from equation (3.10) implies $E_B > 1$; the larger the value of E_B is, the more equitable opportunity will be. $E_B = 1$ is thus the benchmark that can be used to distinguish equitable and inequitable distribution of opportunity. Using this benchmark, it can be said that opportunities are equitably (inequitably) distributed if E_B is greater (less) than 1.

Relative and absolute measures of equity of opportunity

Equity in the distribution of opportunity may be measured in both the relative and absolute sense. If equity measures remain unchanged when the opportunity enjoyed by each person is altered by the same proportion, then such measures are called the relative measures of equity in opportunity. The concentration curve measures relative equity because the curve remains unchanged when opportunities are increased or decreased by the same proportion. Similarly, the equity indices E and E_B discussed in the previous sections are the relative measures of equity. Alternatively, following Kolm (1976), we may define absolute measures of equity of opportunity which show no change when the opportunities enjoyed by everyone are increased or decreased by the same absolute amount. Since richer people generally enjoy greater opportunity than poorer, an equi-proportional increase in all opportunity must decrease equity because the richer will enjoy greater absolute opportunity than the poorer. The relative measures of equity will show no change in equity, but the absolute measures of equity will show a decrease in equity as expected. The absolute measures of equity of opportunity may be more appealing from the perspective of justice and fairness.

To measure absolute equity, we begin by introducing an absolute equity curve:

$$\vartheta(p) = 2\overline{y}\,(C(p) - p) = 2p(\overline{y}_p - \overline{y}) \tag{3.11}$$

It can be seen that when the opportunities enjoyed by all are increased or decreased by the same absolute amount, the curve $\vartheta(p)$ does not change; the higher the curve, the more equitable the opportunities. The area under this curve is the measure of absolute equity of opportunity. This area is given by

$$E^* = \overline{y}\,(E - 1) \tag{3.12}$$

where E is the relative measure of equity, derived above, based on the concentration curve. Note that opportunity is absolutely equitable (inequitable) if E^* is positive (negative).

Similar to the absolute equity curve defined in equation (3.11), we may also define an absolute Bonferroni equity curve as

$$\omega(p) = \overline{y}\,[C_B(p) - 1] = (y_p - \overline{y}) \tag{3.13}$$

It can be seen that when the opportunities enjoyed by all persons in the society are increased or decreased by the same absolute amount, the curve $\omega(p)$ does not change; the higher this curve, the more equitable the opportunities. The area under the curve provides an alternative measure of absolute equity of opportunity. This area is given by

$$E_B^* = \overline{y}\,(E_B - 1) \tag{3.14}$$

where E_B is the relative measure of equity, derived above, based on Bonferroni's concentration curve. Note that opportunity is absolutely equitable (inequitable) if E_B^* is positive (negative).

Social opportunity index

We have introduced two basic ideas in this chapter: (i) the average opportunity available to the population and (ii) the equity of opportunity. There might be a trade-off between the two. For instance, a government in partnership with the private sector makes a large investment in higher education, which provides opportunities for people to enhance human capital. Consequently, average opportunity in the economy has increased, but at the same time the poor cannot access these opportunities because of the high costs of tertiary education. In this case, equity has become lower, and thus we have a trade-off between equity and efficiency. Efficiency relates to an increase in average opportunity, while equity pertains to how opportunity is distributed. We now turn to the issue of how to capture the trade-off between efficiency and equity. We attempt to address this issue by means of the social opportunity function defined above.

A general social opportunity function defined in equation (3.2) may be written as

$$O = O(y_1, y_2, \ldots \ldots \ldots \ldots, y_n) = O(\overline{y}, E) \tag{3.15}$$

which implies that a social opportunity function is a function of two factors: (i) average opportunity available to the society, and (ii) equity of opportunity (i.e., how opportunity is distributed). If the opportunity function defined in equation (3.15) is known, then the trade-off between efficiency and equity will also be known. Since the opportunity function is not known, we need to develop a proxy indicator that captures its basic properties.

The social opportunity function should be an increasing function of its arguments. If the opportunity of any person increases, then the social opportunity function must increase. This is a very basic property, which will generally be acceptable. This implies that the social opportunity function, O, will be an increasing function of $\overline{y}$: if we expand the average opportunity available to the society without reducing equity, the social opportunity function must increase. We may also increase the social opportunity function by making opportunity more equitable. To bring equity into consideration, we require a social opportunity function that satisfies the transfer principle: any transfer of opportunity from a poorer (richer) person to a richer (poorer) person must decrease (increase) the social opportunity function. This property also implies that the social opportunity function must be quasi-concave.[2] Thus, two basic properties of a social opportunity function include: (i) it is an increasing function of its arguments, and (ii) it is quasi-concave.

We may recall from Chapter 2 that the generalized Lorenz curve has a one-to-one relationship with the social welfare function: if the generalized Lorenz curve of distribution X_1 is higher than the generalized Lorenz curve of distribution X_2 at all points, then we can say unambiguously that social welfare implied by distribution X_1 will always be higher than the social welfare implied by distribution X_2. This result holds for a wide range of social welfare functions that are increasing and are quasi-concave in individual incomes. Similar to the idea of the generalized

Lorenz curve, we may propose a generalized concentration curve defined as

$$C(\mu, p) = \overline{y}C(p) \tag{3.16}$$

We can then show that the generalized concentration curve has a one-to-one relationship with the social opportunity function: if the generalized concentration curve of the distribution of opportunity Y_1 is higher than the generalized concentration curve of distribution of opportunity Y_2 at all points, then we can say unambiguously that the social opportunity function implied by distribution Y_1 will be always higher than the social opportunity function implied by distribution Y_2. This result holds for all social opportunity functions that are increasing and are quasi-concave in individual opportunity.

This result may have an important policy implication. Suppose a government has a targeted program of providing health insurance to its population and wants to know how this insurance program is performing over time. The program provides opportunity in terms of the utilization of healthcare services. We can say that the health insurance program is improving over time if the social opportunity function derived from the program has increased over the period. We cannot evaluate the program unless we have knowledge of the social opportunity function. Since there is a one-to-one relationship between the social opportunity function and generalized concentration curve of opportunity, we may be able to evaluate the program by calculating the generalized concentration curves of opportunity for each period. If the entire generalized concentration curve shifts upward over time, then we can unambiguously conclude that the program has expanded opportunity. This suggests that by looking at the generalized concentration curves of two distributions of opportunity, we can judge which distribution will provide greater social opportunity than the other, provided the two generalized concentration curves do not intersect. If they intersect, we cannot say which distribution is opportunity-superior. In such cases, we propose a proxy social opportunity index, which is obtained by twice the area under the generalized concentration curve:

$$\varphi = 2 \int_0^1 \overline{y}C(p)dp = \overline{y}E \tag{3.17}$$

where $E = (1 - C)$ is the relative measure of equity of opportunity, with C being the concentration of opportunity: opportunity is relatively equitable (inequitable) if E is greater (less) than 1. This equation shows that our proposed social opportunity index is the product of average opportunity and relative equity index of opportunity. This equation can also be written as

$$\varphi = \overline{y} + E^* \tag{3.18}$$

where $E^* = \overline{y}(E - 1)$ is the absolute equity index of opportunity, which is absolutely equitable (inequitable) if E^* is greater (less) than 0.

Similar to the idea of the generalized concentration curve, we may define the generalized Bonferroni concentration curve as

$$C_B[\overline{y}C_B(p)] = \overline{y}C_B(p) = \frac{\overline{y}C(p)}{p} \tag{3.19}$$

We can then show that the generalized Bonferroni concentration curve has a one-to-one relationship with the social opportunity function: if the generalized Bonferroni concentration curve of distribution of opportunity Y_1 is higher than the generalized Bonferroni concentration curve of distribution of opportunities Y_2 at all points, then we can say unambiguously that the social opportunity function implied by distribution Y_1 will be always higher than the social opportunity function implied by distribution Y_2. This result holds for all social opportunity functions that are increasing and quasi-concave. This leads to a definition of a new social opportunity index, which we call the "Bonferroni social opportunity index" and is equal to the area under the generalized Bonferroni concentration index:

$$\varphi_B = \overline{y}E_B \tag{3.20}$$

where E_B is the Bonferroni relative equity index defined in equation (3.10). This equation shows that the Bonferroni social opportunity index is the product of average opportunity available to society and the Bonferroni equity index. The government may increase social opportunity either by growth in average opportunity or by increasing the equity of opportunity (i.e., by increasing opportunity for the poor).

Equation (3.20) can also be written as

$$\varphi_B = \overline{y} + E_B^* \tag{3.21}$$

where $E_B^* = \overline{y}(E_B - 1)$ is the Bonferroni absolute equity index of opportunity as defined in equation (3.14): opportunity is absolutely equitable (inequitable) if E_B^* is greater (less) than 0.

We have now proposed two social opportunity indices, one based on the generalized concentration curve and the other on the generalized Bonferroni concentration curve. Which of the two indices should we use in practice? To answer, we write the two opportunity indices as the weighted average of individual opportunities as

$$\varphi = 2\int_0^1 y_p(1-p)dp \tag{3.22}$$

and

$$\varphi_B = -\int_0^1 y_p \ln(p)dp \tag{3.23}$$

The opportunity indices differ with respect to the weight given to individual opportunities. It is noted that weight in φ decreases monotonically at a constant rate

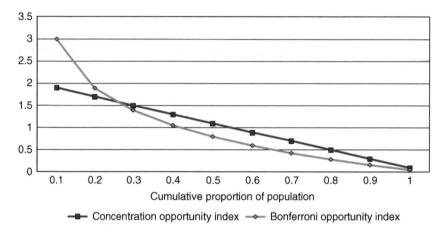

Figure 3.3 Weighting functions for concentration and Bonferroni opportunity index.

while weight in φ_B decreases monotonically at an increasing rate: the Bonferroni weight function declines more steeply than the concentration weight function. Since the total weights add up to 1, this implies that the Bonferroni index gives greater weight than the concentration index to the opportunities of individuals at the bottom of the welfare distribution (Figure 3.3). From this, we may conclude that the Bonferroni opportunity index is more egalitarian than the concentration opportunity index. If the policy focus is on providing greater opportunity to people at the bottom of the welfare distribution, then they should prefer to adopt Bonferroni's opportunity index for evaluating their policies.

Empirical illustration

The proposed methodologies outlined in the previous sections are applied to the Philippines. For this purpose, we have used the Annual Poverty Indicators Survey (APIS) conducted in 1998 and 2007, obtained from the National Statistics Office in Manila. Chapter 2 describes the APIS data in detail. The purpose of this application is to determine how equitable the delivery of education and health services is in the Philippines. We also want to know how much equity changed in education and health from 1998 to 2007.

A. Utilization and equity of education

All children in the school age groups must attend school, irrespective of their economic circumstances. If, somehow, children belonging to poor households are unable to attend school, we may say that there is inequity in the education system. We have calculated equity indices for school attendance for three age groups: (i) primary age 6–11 years; (ii) secondary age 12–17 years; and (iii) tertiary age 18–24 years (Table 3.1).

Table 3.1 Equity in school attendance in the Philippines

	Primary age 6–11 years		Secondary age 12–17 years		Tertiary age 18–24 years	
	1998	2007	1998	2007	1998	2007
Average attendance (%)	90.91	94.38	80.46	79.53	27.75	23.89
Concentration opportunity index	87.65	92.11	75.56	74.43	21.70	18.20
Bonferroni opportunity index	85.50	90.04	72.88	71.92	19.49	16.12
Relative concentration equity index	0.96	0.98	0.94	0.94	0.78	0.76
Relative Bonferroni equity index	0.94	0.95	0.91	0.90	0.70	0.67
Absolute concentration equity index	−3.3	−2.3	−4.9	−5.1	−6.0	−5.7
Absolute Bonferroni equity index	−5.4	−4.3	−7.6	−7.6	−8.3	−7.8

Source: Author's calculations.

As can be seen in Table 3.1, 90.91% of children aged 6–11 years attended a primary school in 1998, rising to 94.38% in 2007. This suggests that opportunity for primary-aged children has expanded over the decade. If all children in the primary school age group attended school, the relative equity index would equal 1. Our estimation shows that the relative concentration equity index was 0.96 in 1998, that is, less than 1, even though it increased to 0.98 by 2007. Inequity in attendance is also evident from the negative value of the absolute equity index, −3.3; inequity in attendance contributes to a loss of social opportunity of 3.3 percentage points, resulting in the social opportunity index equal to 87.65%.

School attendance among children aged 12–17 years was only 80.46% in 1998 and decreased to 79.53% in 2007. The relative concentration equity index for secondary school was estimated at 0.94 in 1998, holding steady in 2007. The relative Bonferroni index was even lower, equaling 0.91 in 1998 and holding steady in 2007. Thus, secondary school enrollment showed no significant improvement during almost a decade.

Attendance for those in the tertiary-age cohort was sharply lower, at only 27.75% in 1998 and 23.89% in 2007. The relative equity index for tertiary education was estimated at 0.78 in 1998 and decreased further to 0.76 in the subsequent period, suggesting that attendance in tertiary education was low and highly inequitable. More interestingly, the results reveal that while relative equity declined during 1998–2007, absolute equity improved over the same period. This suggests that because relative and absolute equity may not always move in the same direction, there can be different policy implications, depending on the equity defined in relative or absolute terms.

B. Utilization and equity of healthcare services

Table 3.2 shows the utilization and equity of healthcare services in the Philippines. The results suggest that in 1998–2007, about 42–45% of sick people sought treatment in one of the available healthcare facilities such as hospital, clinic, rural health unit (RHU), *barangay* health station (BHS), or other healthcare facilities.

Table 3.2 Equity in utilization of any health facility, 1998–2007

	Utilization when sick		Utilization when sick or not sick	
	1998	*2007*	*1998*	*2007*
Average utilization (%)	45.44	42.16	18.91	11.71
Concentration opportunity index	41.64	35.89	17.33	10.06
Bonferroni opportunity index	40.23	33.71	16.72	9.46
Relative concentration equity index	0.92	0.85	0.92	0.86
Relative Bonferroni equity index	0.89	0.80	0.88	0.81
Absolute concentration equity index	−3.80	−6.27	−1.57	−1.65
Absolute Bonferroni equity index	−5.21	−8.45	−2.19	−2.25

Source: Author's calculations.

When the utilization of a healthcare facility includes both those sick and not sick, its rate was estimated at 18.91% and 11.71% of the population in 1998 and 2007, respectively. Interestingly, the proportion of people who sought treatment in a healthcare facility, irrespective of sickness, declined during 1998–2007, as seen from the decline in the average utilization rate over the decade.

Furthermore, overall healthcare services in the Philippines appear to be inequitable in the sense that they are largely utilized by those at the top end of the income distribution. This is evident in the results in Table 3.2, which shows that the opportunity index—irrespective of concentration or Bonferroni type—is less than the average utilization rate throughout the period and that the equity index measured by either the concentration or Bonferroni method is less than the benchmark value of 1. When equity is evaluated based on the Bonferroni social welfare function, inequity in utilization of healthcare becomes more pronounced, because those at the bottom of the income distribution get a greater weight than when concentration-based social welfare is used. Inequity in utilization is also reflected in higher negative values of the absolute equity index of Bonferroni than its concentration counterpart; for example, in 2007 inequity in utilization contributed to a loss of social opportunity of 6.27 and 8.45 percentage points, resulting in concentration and Bonferroni social opportunity indices equal to 41.64% and 40.23%, respectively.

Table 3.3 presents selected types of healthcare facilities utilized by sick individuals during 1998–2007. The sick in the Philippines made heavy use of the health services at government hospitals, RHUs, and BHSs, for example, amounting to almost 64% of the sick who sought medical treatment in 2007. People also used private hospitals and private clinics. The quality of health services provided by private healthcare is expected to be better than public healthcare and thus is likely to be used mainly by the rich. While not presented here, our study has found that health services provided by private hospitals and private clinics tend to be highly inequitable and, moreover, became increasingly more inequitable over 1998–2007. Compared to private healthcare facilities, people

Table 3.3 Equity in utilization of selected health facilities when sick, 1998–2007

	Government hospital		Rural health unit		Barangay health station	
	1998	2007	1998	2007	1998	2007
Average utilization (%)	9.15	12.78	11.14	8.33	5.44	6.08
Concentration opportunity index	8.52	11.33	13.23	9.36	6.79	7.16
Bonferroni opportunity index	7.85	10.04	14.19	9.62	7.34	7.98
Relative concentration equity index	0.93	0.89	1.19	1.12	1.25	1.18
Relative Bonferroni equity index	0.86	0.79	1.27	1.15	1.35	1.31
Absolute concentration equity index	−0.62	−1.44	2.08	1.03	1.35	1.08
Absolute Bonferroni equity index	−1.29	−2.74	3.04	1.29	1.90	1.90

Source: Author's calculations.

tend to use government hospitals more: we found that the values of concentration and the Bonferroni opportunity indices are far greater for government hospitals than for private hospitals and clinics. Moreover, we also found that the value of the equity index for both concentration and Bonferroni types suggests that poor Filipinos more often sought treatment in government hospitals than in private healthcare, as expected. Unfortunately, the quality of healthcare in government hospitals remains severely wanting compared with private healthcare, especially in the capital, National Capital Region (NCR). This is particularly disconcerting since a large share of the national government budget for health is spent on NCR hospitals.

People who cannot afford private healthcare are the main users of public healthcare services. Compared to government healthcare, clients rank private healthcare as superior on all aspects of quality, such as care, facility, personnel, medicine, and convenience. Government healthcare caters to the poor because of low costs of treatment, cheaper medicines and supplies, and flexibility in paying health bills.

As expected, people at the lower end of the income distribution use healthcare provided by RHUs and BHSs. This is evident in the value of the opportunity index greater than the average utilization rate and becomes even clearer in the equity index surpassing 1. Further, the equity index derived from Bonferroni social welfare exceeds the benchmark value of 1 and, at the same time, is greater than the index based on the concentration social opportunity index.

While government hospitals are deemed tertiary public healthcare, both RHUs and BHSs are categorized as primary public healthcare. RHUs and BHSs are supposed to provide preventive healthcare and treatment for minor illnesses/accidents. Despite access to such primary healthcare, however, a sizable proportion of Filipinos still prefer to seek treatment in government hospitals and private clinics/hospitals. Thus, government hospitals end up providing the same services as primary healthcare. It is, therefore, critical to ensure that primary healthcare is delivered efficiently so that, through prevention, it can lower the incidence of diseases such as diarrhea, bronchitis, influenza, pneumonia, and tuberculosis. Preventive healthcare services do a lot more in the long run to protect health and require less funding than medical treatment.

Tables 3.4 and 3.5 pertain to healthcare use by the sick elderly. Table 3.4 suggests that 52% and 56% sought treatment in a healthcare facility in 1998 and 2007, respectively. Moreover, Table 3.5 shows that they mostly sought treatment in government hospitals, private hospitals, and private clinics, at almost 88% in 2007, with 12% using RHUs and BHSs. While the proportion of the sick elderly who sought treatment in a healthcare facility increased over the decade, its equity declined over the same period. The results reveal that overall healthcare services used by the sick elderly are inequitable, with the degree of inequity worsening during 1998–2007. Inequity in utilization contributed to a loss of social opportunity of 6.39 percentage points in 1998 and 9.14 in 2007. As a result, the social opportunity index was equivalent to 46.03% and 46.52% in the respective periods. As would be expected, the loss of social opportunity becomes even bigger when Bonferroni social welfare is used. These findings call for policies, such as free healthcare cards, that can help the elderly, particularly the poor, to access healthcare when needed.

As noted earlier, the elderly, when sick, mostly sought treatment in hospitals or private clinics during 1998–2007 (Table 3.5). We would expect that healthcare services provided by private hospitals and clinics to be used mainly by the rich elderly, but it is somewhat disconcerting to see that government hospitals are also inequitable. And yet, government hospitals are found to be less inequitable relative to private healthcare. Moreover, the equity index for government hospitals has increased over the period while the corresponding figure for its counterpart private healthcare has declined. In particular, inequity in the utilization of private hospitals contributed to a loss of social opportunity of 6.97 percentage points, leading to the social opportunity index equal to just 8.88% in 2007. Given that private hospitals provide better quality healthcare, the elderly, including the poor, should be able to seek treatment in a healthcare facility whenever needed.

Table 3.4 Equity in utilization of any health facility when sick among the elderly, 1998–2007

	1998	*2007*
Average utilization (%)	52.42	55.67
Concentration opportunity index	46.03	46.52
Bonferroni opportunity index	43.35	41.81
Relative concentration equity index	0.88	0.84
Relative Bonferroni equity index	0.83	0.75
Absolute concentration equity index	−6.39	−9.14
Absolute Bonferroni equity index	−9.07	−13.85

Source: Author's calculations.

Table 3.5 Equity in utilization of the sick elderly of selected healthcare, 1998–2007

	Government hospital		Private hospital		Private clinic	
	1998	*2007*	*1998*	*2007*	*1998*	*2007*
Average utilization (%)	13.29	19.10	12.47	15.85	16.01	14.05
Concentration opportunity index	11.98	18.01	8.06	8.88	12.46	9.25
Bonferroni opportunity index	10.69	16.19	7.20	6.74	10.85	7.20
Relative concentration equity index	0.90	0.94	0.65	0.56	0.78	0.66
Relative Bonferroni equity index	0.80	0.85	0.58	0.43	0.68	0.51
Absolute concentration equity index	−1.30	−1.09	−4.41	−6.97	−3.55	−4.80
Absolute Bonferroni equity index	−2.60	−2.91	−5.27	−9.11	−5.16	−6.85

Source: Author's calculations.

Conclusion

Measuring the amount and distribution of opportunities is of utmost importance to researchers and policymakers alike. Researchers need to measure opportunities in order to determine progress in human development and distill lessons that can be applied in similar settings. On the other hand, policymakers need to measure opportunities to formulate policies and programs that could help in sharing the "economic pie" among the most people, especially the poor. However, measuring opportunities in a society is difficult—even if one can assign a numerical value to the opportunity of every individual, mapping these values into a measurement of opportunities available in society is fraught with value judgments. For instance, how should we weigh the opportunities for the rich relative to the poor? Should all people be equal, or should we give preferential weight to those who have less in life? In other words, what social welfare function and, by extension, social opportunity function should we use to map individual opportunities into a measurement of their distribution in society?

The beauty of the discussion in the previous sections is that it is possible to measure and compare distributions of opportunity across societies and across time, even if we do not know the form of the social opportunity function. Using the properties of the generalized Lorenz curve and the Bonferroni curve as well as their related indices—that is, the concentration curve and the Bonferroni index of opportunity—it is possible to measure the distribution of opportunities in a society and compare them across societies or over time. This is an important result, because by using these measures we can determine whether one distribution is more equitable than another, or whether a policy intervention will worsen inequality. We can track progress in improving equity in opportunity over time, and it should be possible to find policies or programs that are successful in improving opportunities for the underprivileged.

These measurements, however, are still relative measures of opportunity: an equiproportional increase in the opportunity of all individuals will not change the values of the concentration or Bonferroni indices. In other words, given that the rich are already endowed with greater opportunities than the poor, a 10% increase in everyone's opportunities will not be seen as a deterioration of equity, even if the magnitude of increase was actually greater for the rich. To account for this anomaly, we develop absolute measures of equity based on the concentration and Bonferroni curves that will reflect the above situation as a deterioration of equity. These are then incorporated into the social opportunity index, which considers both the efficiency (i.e., average amount of opportunity available to everyone) and equity (i.e., distribution) of opportunity in society.

Again, the beauty of the social opportunity index is that we do not need to make value judgments on the relative weights of efficiency or equity in the social opportunity function—a reliable and comparable index of efficiency and equity is obtained even if the functional form is unknown. However, there is an important difference between using the social opportunity indices implied by the concentration and Bonferroni curves: while weights for individuals decrease with income for both indices, weights for the concentration-based social opportunity index decrease at a constant rate while that for the Bonferroni-based index decrease at an increasing rate. Thus, one may consider the Bonferroni-based social opportunity index to be more "pro-poor."

Applying the above methodologies to Philippine data, we found that access to education remains inequitable at all levels, with richer children more likely to attend school than those who are poor. Moreover, this inequity becomes more severe for older children—tertiary level education is the most inequitable because poorer children may not even get to finish primary or secondary school. Overall, equity in education did not changed between 1998 and 2007, but interestingly, relative and absolute measures of equity for tertiary education moved in the opposite direction during this time. On the other hand, access to healthcare remains inequitable in the Philippines, particularly access to private health facilities that provide superior quality. Poorer Filipinos are thus left to utilize primary healthcare facilities, as can be seen in the highly equitable (i.e., pro-poor) utilization of these facilities. Access to government hospitals, although still inequitable, is at least more equitable than access to private facilities. We also find that healthcare opportunities in the Philippines generally became more inequitable between 1998 and 2007.

Notes

1 Ali and Son (2007) used the Bonferroni concentration curve in connection with defining and measuring inclusive growth. They were not aware, however, that their proposed opportunity curve was in any way related to the Bonferroni curve. This relationship between the two has recently been established by Silber and Son (2010).
2 Quasi-concavity is a mathematical property of a general function with many arguments. For a detailed discussion on this see Kakwani (1980).

4　What is equitable growth?

Introduction

Poverty reduction is at the center of the development agenda. While sustained high growth can significantly reduce absolute income poverty, only a few countries—particularly in East Asia, Southeast Asia, and more recently South Asia—have enjoyed such growth levels. In many other economies, growth has been slow, highly volatile, or even negative for sustained periods, leading to little progress in poverty reduction. Even in many high-growth countries, growth has been associated with rising inequality, which can retard the impact of growth on poverty, so that the poverty impact of growth has been slower than what it could have been. As a consequence, inequality has received renewed attention because poverty reduction will be slower in countries that experience rising inequality as well as in countries with high initial inequality. Conversely, reducing inequality would directly abate poverty, increase the poverty impact of growth, and might even increase growth itself and thus accelerate poverty reduction (Klasen 2004).

To accelerate poverty reduction, it is thus crucial to devise strategies for equitable growth. The term "equitable growth" has been previously referred to as "pro-poor growth", thus these two terms are interchangeably used throughout this chapter. There has been a substantial amount of debate about what exactly constitutes equitable growth and how it can be measured (Kakwani and Pernia 2000; Ravallion and Chen 2003; Klasen 2004; Son 2004). This study adopts the definition proposed by Kakwani and Pernia (2000), which defines growth as equitable if it benefits the poor proportionally more than the non-poor. When there is a negative growth rate, growth is defined as equitable if the loss from growth is proportionally less for the poor than for the non-poor. Under this definition, an equitable growth scenario will reduce poverty more quickly than an inequitable growth scenario.

The pattern of growth is determined by its linkages with changes in poverty and inequality. This chapter examines this issue through a cross-country analysis of 25 developing countries in Asia for the period 1981–2005. This is thus an *ex post* analysis concerned with whether the growth process in a country has been equitable or inequitable. For this purpose, a measure called the "poverty equivalent growth rate" (PEGR) is used, which has been proposed by Kakwani and Son (2008). Using PEGR, this chapter studies how the benefits of growth have been distributed between the poor and the non-poor over time.

The poverty equivalent growth rate

The PEGR measure, introduced by Kakwani and Son (2008), takes into account both the growth rate in mean income and how the benefits from growth are distributed between the poor and the non-poor. This measure satisfies a basic requirement that a reduction in poverty is a monotonically increasing function of the PEGR: the larger the PEGR, the greater the reduction in poverty will be. Thus, the PEGR is an effective measure of poverty reduction such that maximization of PEGR implies a maximum reduction in poverty. If a government's objective is to achieve a maximum reduction in poverty, then its policies should be focused on maximizing the PEGR. Furthermore, the PEGR can be used as an important indicator to monitor poverty over time across socioeconomic and demographic groups. We will also see that the magnitude of PEGR determines the pattern of growth; that is, whether growth is pro-poor in a relative or absolute sense. Thus, the PEGR provides a conceptual framework for unifying the three alternative concepts of pro-poor growth.

The PEGR is derived for an entire class of additively decomposable poverty measures, including the Foster–Greer–Thorbecke (FGT) and Watts measures. Ravallion and Chen (2003) derived their measure of growth rate only for the Watts measure; thus, the PEGR is more general in the sense that it encompasses all additively decomposable poverty measures. Furthermore, while Ravallion and Chen's measure does not satisfy the basic axiom of monotonicity, the PEGR satisfies this axiom. The PEGR is derived as follows:

Suppose the income, x, of an individual is a random variable with a density function $f(x)$, and z is the poverty line, then a general class of additively decomposable poverty measures can be written as

$$\theta = \int_0^z P(z,x)f(x)dx \qquad (4.1)$$

where $P(z,x)$ is a homogenous function of degree zero in z and x such that

$$P(z,z) = 0, \quad \frac{\partial P(z,x)}{\partial x} < 0, \quad \text{and} \quad \frac{\partial^2 P(z,x)}{\partial x^2} > 0.$$

Foster, Greer, and Thorbecke (1983) proposed a class of poverty measures that is obtained by substituting $P(z,x) = \left(\frac{z-x}{z}\right)^\alpha$ in equation (4.1), where α is the parameter of inequality aversion. For $\alpha = 0$, $\theta = H$, which is the head-count ratio. For $\alpha = 1$, each of the poor is weighed by his or her distance from the poverty line: this measure is called the poverty gap ratio. For $\alpha = 2$, the weight given to each poor person is proportional to the square of his or her income shortfall from the poverty line. This measure is called the severity of poverty ratio and takes into account the distribution of income among the poor.

The growth elasticity of poverty is defined as the ratio of the proportional change in poverty to the proportional change in the mean income. This elasticity is obtained by the total differential of equation (4.1) as

$$\delta = \frac{d \ln(\theta)}{\gamma} = \frac{1}{\theta \gamma} \int_0^H \frac{\partial P}{\partial x} x(p) g(p) dp \tag{4.2}$$

where $\gamma = d \ln(\mu)$ is the growth rate of mean income and $g(p) = d \ln[x(p)]$ is the growth rate of the income of people at the pth percentile. δ is the percentage change in poverty resulting from a growth rate of 1% in mean income.

Poverty reduction depends on two factors. The first is the magnitude of the economic growth rate: the larger the growth rate, the greater the reduction in poverty. The second is the change in inequality. Growth is generally accompanied by changes in inequality; an increase in inequality reduces the impact of growth on poverty reduction. To measure these two impacts, we decompose the growth elasticity of poverty in equation (4.2) as the sum of two components, η and ρ:

$$\delta = \eta + \rho \tag{4.3}$$

where $\eta = \frac{1}{\theta} \int_0^H \frac{\partial P}{\partial x} x(p) dp$ is the neutral relative growth elasticity of poverty derived by Kakwani (1983), which measures the percentage change in poverty when there is a 1% growth in the mean income of society, provided that the growth process does not change relative inequality (i.e., when everyone in society receives the same proportional benefits of growth). This elasticity is always negative. On the other hand, ρ is given by

$$\rho = \frac{1}{\theta \gamma} \int_0^H \frac{\partial P}{\partial x} x(p) d \ln[L'(p)] dp \tag{4.4}$$

where $L'(p)$ measures the effect of inequality on poverty reduction. This tells us how poverty varies owing to changes in relative inequality that accompany the growth process. Growth is pro-poor (anti-poor) in a relative sense if the change in relative inequality that accompanies growth reduces (increases) total poverty. That is, growth is pro-poor (anti-poor) if the growth elasticity of poverty is greater (less) than the neutral relative growth elasticity of poverty.

Many studies measure the pro-poorness of growth by changes in the Gini index. However, the Gini index is not an appropriate measure of inequality that can measure pro-poorness because there is no monotonic relationship between changes in the Gini index and poverty reduction. Holding mean income constant, an increase or decrease in the Gini index can still leave poverty unchanged; similarly, any change in the Gini index can imply a reduction or an increase in poverty. Thus, a change in the Gini index will not always tell us whether or not growth is pro-poor. In this context, ρ, which was defined above, has a direct relationship with changes in poverty. This is derived from the part of the Lorenz curve that directly affects the poor.

Using the ideas outlined above, Kakwani and Pernia (2000) developed a relative pro-poor growth index, φ, defined as the ratio of the growth elasticity of poverty to the neutral relative growth elasticity of poverty:

$$\varphi = \frac{\delta}{\eta} \tag{4.5}$$

From this, a growth process is said to be pro-poor in a relative sense if φ is greater than 1. If the growth rate is negative, growth is defined as relatively pro-poor if φ is less than 1; that is, loss of income from negative growth is proportionally less for the poor than for the non-poor. In addition, a growth process is defined as neutral in relative distribution if $\varphi = 1$, which occurs when everyone enjoys the same proportional benefits from growth.

We define a growth process as "absolutely pro-poor" when the poor receive the absolute benefits of growth equal to or more than the absolute benefits received by the non-poor. Following this definition, absolute inequality would fall during the course of growth. Similar to the idea of neutral relative growth elasticity of poverty, we introduce the idea of neutral absolute growth elasticity of poverty, which is defined as the elasticity of poverty with respect to growth when the benefits of growth are equally shared by every individual in society. This elasticity is given by

$$\eta^* = \frac{\mu}{\theta} \int_0^H \frac{\partial P}{\partial x} dp \tag{4.6}$$

which is the proportional change in poverty given a 1% growth in the mean income of society, provided that the growth process does not change absolute inequality (i.e., when everyone in society receives the same absolute benefits of growth). It can be shown that the absolute magnitude of η^* is always greater than the absolute magnitude of η, which implies that poverty reduction will always be greater when people receive equal absolute benefits rather than equal proportional benefits from the same level of economic growth.

Similar to the idea of Kakwani and Pernia's (2000) relative pro-poor growth index, we define an absolute pro-poor growth index as

$$\varphi^* = \frac{\delta}{\eta^*} \tag{4.7}$$

A growth process will be pro-poor in the absolute sense if φ^* is greater than 1. If the growth rate is negative, growth is defined as absolutely pro-poor when φ^* is less than 1; that is, absolute loss of income from negative growth is less for the poor than for the non-poor. According to Ravallion and Chen (2003), growth is pro-poor if it reduces poverty, or when $d\ln(\theta) = \delta\gamma$ is negative, which we have identified as poverty-reducing pro-poor growth.

The two indices of pro-poor growth, φ^* and φ, measure how the benefits from growth are distributed across the population; however, they are not sufficient to determine any change in poverty. To determine how a growth process affects poverty, we need to have an indicator that accounts for both the growth rate in mean income and the distribution of benefits from growth.

To address this issue, the concept of a poverty equivalent growth rate is introduced. PEGR is the growth rate γ^* that would result in the same proportional change in poverty as the present growth rate γ if the growth process is not accompanied by any change in relative inequality (i.e., when everyone in society receives the same proportional benefits of growth). The actual proportional change in poverty is given by $\delta\gamma$, where δ is the growth elasticity of poverty. If growth were distribution-neutral in a relative sense (i.e., relative inequality did not change), then the growth rate γ^* would achieve a proportional change in poverty equal to $\eta\gamma^*$ which should be equivalent to γ. Thus, the PEGR denoted by γ is given by

$$\gamma^* = \left(\frac{\delta}{\eta}\right)\gamma = \varphi\gamma \tag{4.8}$$

which can also be written as

$$\gamma^* = \frac{\int_0^H \frac{\partial P}{\partial x} x(p) g(p) dp}{\int_0^H \frac{\partial P}{\partial x} x(p) dp} \tag{4.9}$$

which shows the PEGR as the weighted average of the growth rates of income at each percentile point, with the weight depending on the poverty measure used. For the FGT class of poverty measures, the PEGR is given by

$$\gamma^* = \frac{\int_0^H \left(\frac{z-x(p)}{z}\right)^{\alpha-1} x(p) g(p) dp}{\int_0^H \left(\frac{z-x(p)}{z}\right)^{\alpha-1} x(p) dp} \quad \text{for } \alpha \geq 1$$

On the other hand, the PEGR for the Watts measure is obtained by substituting $P(z,x) = \ln(z) - \ln(x)$ into equation (4.8) and can be defined as $\gamma_w^* = \frac{1}{H}\int_0^H g(p) dp$ which is, in fact, the pro-poor growth index proposed by Ravallion and Chen (2003).

Since η is always negative, equation (4.8) implies that if $\delta\gamma$ is negative (positive), γ^* will be positive (negative). Equivalently, the PEGR is consistent with the direction of the change in poverty: a positive (negative) value of the PEGR implies a reduction (increase) in poverty. The proposed measure thus satisfies a basic requirement that the reduction in poverty should be a monotonically increasing function of the PEGR; that is, the larger the PEGR, the greater the reduction in poverty. Thus, the PEGR is an effective measure of poverty reduction, and a maximization of PEGR implies a maximum reduction in poverty.

To determine whether growth is pro-poor or anti-poor in a relative sense, we can write

$$\gamma^* = \gamma + (\varphi - 1)\gamma \tag{4.10}$$

As noted earlier, growth is pro-poor in a relative sense when $\gamma > 0$ and $\varphi > 1$ or when $\gamma < 0$ and $\varphi < 1$. Each of these conditions implies that the second term in the right hand side of equation (4.10) is positive. Thus, growth will be pro-poor in a relative sense if $\gamma^* > \gamma$.

To determine whether growth is pro-poor in an absolute sense, we can write equation (4.10) as

$$\gamma^* = \gamma[1 + (\varphi - \varphi^*)] + (\varphi^* - 1)\gamma \tag{4.11}$$

As defined earlier, growth is pro-poor in the absolute sense when $\gamma > 0$ and $\varphi^* > 1$ or when $\gamma < 0$ and $\varphi^* < 1$. Each of these conditions implies that the second term in the right hand side of equation (4.11) is positive. Thus, growth will be pro-poor in the absolute sense if $\gamma^* > \gamma[1 + (\varphi - \varphi^*)]$. Since $\varphi > \varphi^*$ always holds, pro-poor growth in the absolute sense will always imply pro-poor growth in the relative sense, but not the other way around. Thus, absolute pro-poor growth is a higher standard than relative pro-poor growth, implying that with the same growth rate in mean income, an absolute pattern of growth will lead to a more rapid reduction in poverty than a relative pattern of growth.

Ravallion and Chen's (2003) definition of pro-poor growth implies that growth reduces poverty, which is satisfied when $\gamma^* > 0$. If growth rate $\gamma > 0$, then $\gamma^* > \gamma$ will always imply $\gamma^* > 0$, and thus the relative pro-poor growth always implies a poverty-reducing pro-poor growth. This demonstrates that poverty-reducing pro-poor growth is the weakest requirement, even weaker than either relative or absolute pro-poor growth, when the growth rate is positive. On the other hand, $\gamma^* > 0$ implies that $\gamma^* - \gamma > -\gamma$, which further implies $\gamma^* > \gamma$ and $\gamma < 0$. This demonstrates that poverty-reducing pro-poor growth is a stronger requirement than relative pro-poor growth when the growth rate in mean income is negative. Applying the same logic, we can show that poverty-reducing pro-poor growth is a stronger requirement than even the absolute pro-poor growth when the growth rate in mean income is negative. Thus, the PEGR provides a unifying framework to determine the patterns of growth defined by three alternative concepts of pro-poor growth.

Inequality is commonly perceived as a relative concept because few studies present absolute measures of inequality. We can thus expect that there will be a greater consensus on a relative, rather than an absolute, concept of pro-poor growth. However, an absolute concept of pro-poor growth can also be attractive, since government transfer policies are generally understood in terms of absolute benefits going to the poor. For instance, a policy that gives $5 to the poor and $1 to the rich will be readily accepted as pro-poor—such a policy will be absolutely pro-poor. On the other hand, a policy that gives $1 to the poor and $5 to the rich will never be regarded as pro-poor, even though it may reduce poverty. This suggests that the concept of poverty-reducing pro-poor growth may not be considered as an appropriate definition of pro-poor growth because it classifies growth as pro-poor even when the poor receive a tiny fraction of the benefits of growth that are enjoyed by the rich.

Son and Kakwani (2008) conducted a cross-country analysis of pro-poor growth in 80 countries in 237 growth spells during the period 1984–2001, and found 106 negative growth spells and 131 positive growth spells. The incidence of poverty fell in 86% of all positive growth spells and increased in 87% of all negative growth spells. These results show that most growth processes will be classified as equitable (inequitable) using the definition of poverty-reducing pro-poor growth, provided that the growth rate in mean income is positive (negative). This implies that governments can achieve equitable outcomes only by ensuring positive growth rates, but such outcomes may not guarantee a rapid reduction in poverty if the growth process leads to increases in relative and absolute inequalities. With this objective to the fore, the focus of government policies should be on both enhancing growth and improving relative and absolute inequality; that is, maximizing the PEGR.

Calculating the poverty equivalent growth rate

The general class of poverty measure, θ, given in equation (4.1) is fully characterized by the poverty line (z) and the vector of income distribution ($\tilde{x}$): $\theta = \theta(z, \tilde{x})$. Suppose the income distributions (adjusted for prices) in the initial and terminal years are $\tilde{x}_1$ and $\tilde{x}_2$, respectively, with mean incomes μ_1 and μ_2, then an estimate of the growth elasticity of poverty, δ, can be obtained by

$$\hat{\delta} = \frac{\ln[\theta(z, \tilde{x}_2)] - \ln[\theta(z, \tilde{x}_1)]}{\hat{\gamma}}$$

where $\hat{\gamma}$ is given by $\hat{\gamma} = \ln(\mu_2) - \ln(\mu_1)$, which is an estimate of the growth rate of mean income.

An estimate of PEGR is given by

$$\hat{\gamma}^* = \left(\frac{\hat{\delta}}{\hat{\eta}}\right)\hat{\gamma}$$

where $\hat{\eta}$ is an estimate of the neutral relative growth elasticity of poverty, which should satisfy equation (4.3):

$$\hat{\delta} = \hat{\eta} + \hat{\zeta}$$

where $\hat{\zeta}$ is an estimate of the effect of inequality on poverty reduction. Kakwani's (2000) poverty decomposition methodology can then be used to calculate $\hat{\eta}$ and

$\hat{\zeta}$ using the following formulae:

$$\hat{\eta} = \frac{\frac{1}{2}\left[\ln\left(\theta\left(z, \frac{\mu_2 \tilde{x}_1}{\mu_1}\right)\right) - \ln\left(\theta\left(z, \tilde{x}_1\right)\right) + \ln\left(\theta\left(z, \tilde{x}_2\right)\right) - \ln\left(z, \frac{\mu_1 \tilde{x}_2}{\mu_2}\right)\right]}{\hat{\gamma}}$$

and

$$\hat{\zeta} = \frac{\frac{1}{2}\left[\ln\left(\theta\left(z, \frac{\mu_1 \tilde{x}_2}{\mu_2}\right)\right) - \ln\left(\theta\left(z, \tilde{x}_1\right)\right) + \ln\left(\theta\left(z, \tilde{x}_2\right)\right) - \ln\left(z, \frac{\mu_2 \tilde{x}_1}{\mu_1}\right)\right]}{\hat{\gamma}}$$

This methodology can be used to estimate the PEGR for the entire class of poverty measures given in equation (4.1).

The proportional reduction in poverty is $\hat{\delta}\hat{\gamma}$, which is also equal to $\hat{\eta}\hat{\gamma}$ from equation (4.7). Since $\hat{\eta}$ is always negative (unless $\mu_1 = \mu_2$), the magnitude of poverty reduction will be a monotonically increasing function of $\hat{\gamma}^*$: the larger that $\hat{\gamma}^*$ is, the greater the percentage reduction in poverty will be between the two periods. Thus, maximizing $\hat{\gamma}^*$ will be equivalent to maximizing the percentage reduction in poverty.

To determine if growth is absolutely pro-poor, it will require a consistent estimate of $\hat{\eta}^*$, which can be estimated as

$$\hat{\eta}^* = \frac{\frac{1}{2}\left[\ln\left(\theta(z, \tilde{x}_1 + \mu_2 - \mu_1)\right) - \ln(\theta(z, \tilde{x}_1)) + \ln(\theta(z, \tilde{x}_2)) - \ln(z, \tilde{x}_2 - \mu_2 + \mu_1)\right]}{\hat{\gamma}}$$

Empirical analysis

Using the proposed methodology, we present a cross-country analysis of growth in 25 developing Asian countries in 400 growth spells during the period 1981–2005.[1] The data set utilized for this study is from the group data on income distribution, which are compiled by the World Bank mainly from household surveys from a number of countries.

Table 4.1 presents the level of mean expenditure and poverty for 25 developing Asian countries for the period 1981–2005. It is clear that developing Asian countries have seen improvements in their standard of living over the last 25 years: the per-capita monthly expenditure grew by more than 70% from 40.66 in 1981 to 84.16 in 2005.

Table 4.1 also presents results on poverty measured by the head-count ratio, poverty gap ratio, and severity of poverty. With rising per-capita mean expenditure, poverty declined sharply during 1981–2005. For instance, the proportion of people in developing Asia living below the $1.25-a-day poverty line more than halved over the years, falling from 68.61% in 1981 to 27.09% in 2005. Similarly, the poverty gap ratio and the severity of poverty fell substantially during the period. This suggests that growth has been more responsive to those living farther away from the poverty threshold, which leads us to the next discussion on the poverty elasticity of growth.

Table 4.1 Monthly per capita expenditure and poverty reduction in developing Asia

Period	Per capita expenditure at 2005 PPP	Poverty estimates		
		Head-count	Poverty gap	Severity
1981	40.66	68.61	28.37	14.75
1984	45.22	60.01	20.99	9.68
1987	49.27	52.88	17.42	7.75
1990	50.78	52.30	16.57	7.05
1993	53.52	48.35	14.68	6.07
1996	60.64	40.19	11.31	4.35
1999	63.09	38.86	11.05	4.31
2002	71.21	34.49	9.46	3.56
2005	84.16	27.09	6.79	2.40

PPP = purchasing power parity.

Note: Detailed estimates of growth rate in per-capita mean expenditure at 2005 PPP for 25 countries are presented in Appendix Table A.4.1.

Source: Author's calculations.

Table 4.2 Poverty elasticity of growth in developing Asia, 1981–2005

Growth spells	Poverty elasticity of growth		
	Head-count	Poverty gap	Severity
1981–1984	−1.26	−2.83	−3.96
1984–1987	−1.47	−2.18	−2.59
1987–1990	−0.36	−1.64	−3.14
1990–1993	−1.49	−2.30	−2.84
1993–1996	−1.48	−2.09	−2.66
1996–1999	−0.85	−0.58	−0.25
1999–2002	−0.99	−1.29	−1.58
2002–2005	−1.45	−1.98	−2.37

Source: Author's calculations.

Table 4.2 estimates the responsiveness of a 1% growth to changes in poverty for 25 countries in developing Asia. This responsiveness is captured through the poverty elasticity of growth, which provides a magnitude of poverty reduction that would be expected from a 1% growth. The results in Table 4.2 show that a 1% growth in per-capita mean expenditure led to a reduction in the poverty incidence of 1.45% during 2002–05 in developing Asian countries. The corresponding elasticities for the other two poverty measures are greater, which confirms our earlier argument that growth is more effective for poverty reduction among those far below the poverty line than those just below the poverty line.

It is interesting to compare the achievements of the People's Republic of China (PRC) and India on poverty. Table 4.3 presents the levels of mean expenditure and poverty estimates for the two large economies in 1981–2005. From the table, it is

Table 4.3 Monthly per-capita expenditure and poverty estimates in the People's Republic of China and India

Period	Mean expenditure		Head-count ratio		Poverty gap		Severity	
	PRC	India	PRC	India	PRC	India	PRC	India
1981	25.02	41.21	84.02	59.82	39.26	19.56	21.78	8.49
1984	33.17	42.77	69.43	55.49	25.56	17.23	12.16	7.19
1987	41.05	44.84	54.03	53.59	18.51	15.81	8.63	6.27
1990	40.79	45.98	60.18	51.27	20.72	14.59	9.36	5.62
1993	47.65	46.68	53.69	49.40	17.65	13.56	7.76	5.07
1996	60.17	48.75	36.37	46.56	10.73	12.40	4.30	4.54
1999	66.23	50.40	35.63	44.77	11.08	11.70	4.63	4.21
2002	84.09	51.52	28.36	43.91	8.66	11.39	3.54	4.08
2005	109.13	53.50	15.92	41.64	3.95	10.52	1.42	3.69

Source: Povcal database.

clear that the PRC is far better off than India. In terms of growth, the PRC outpaced India, with its per-capita mean expenditure jumping by 147.3% from 1981 to 2005, compared to India's 26.1%. Growth was particularly strong in the PRC during 1990–1993, which could have been largely due to the government's economic reforms which resulted in rapid globalization and privatization of state-owned enterprises (Liu 2006).

A similar story emerges for poverty, whereby poverty statistics for all three measures are lower in the PRC than in India. More importantly, poverty reduction in the PRC has been much faster than in India. For instance, the head-count ratio fell by 166.3% and 36.2% in the PRC and India, respectively, over the 25-year period. Furthermore, ultra-poor declined even faster in both countries.

Table 4.4 presents estimates of patterns of growth based on the $1.25-a-day poverty line. (Detailed estimates of patterns of growth are presented in Appendix Tables A.4.2–A.4.4.) The results show that all of the eight growth spells had positive growth rates in developing Asia. However, only in two spells have growth

Table 4.4 Patterns of growth in developing Asia, 1981–2005

Growth spells	Growth rate in mean expenditure	Poverty equivalent growth rate		
		Head-count	Poverty gap	Severity
1981–84	3.55	4.06	3.69	3.57
1984–87	2.86	2.75	2.49	2.32
1987–90	1.01	0.27	0.79	1.18
1990–93	1.75	1.63	1.77	1.81
1993–96	4.16	4.00	3.46	3.32
1996–99	1.32	0.87	0.49	0.19
1999–2002	4.03	3.49	3.11	2.97
2002–05	5.57	5.77	5.57	5.39

Source: Author's calculations.

Table 4.5 Gains and losses of growth rate

Growth spells	Gains/losses of growth rate (per annum)		
	Head-count	Poverty gap	Severity
1981–84	0.51	0.14	0.02
1984–87	−0.11	−0.37	−0.54
1987–90	−0.74	−0.22	0.17
1990–93	−0.12	0.02	0.06
1993–96	−0.16	−0.71	−0.84
1996–99	−0.46	−0.84	−1.13
1999–2002	−0.54	−0.92	−1.06
2002–05	0.20	−0.00	−0.18

Note: Detailed estimates of gains and losses in growth rates for 25 countries are presented in Appendix Tables A.4.5–A.4.7.

Source: Author's calculations.

processes in Asia been generally favorable to the poor. The findings suggest that poverty reduction in Asia has been generally contributed to by positive growth but hampered by the inequitable growth pattern. Note that these findings are true for the case where equitable growth is defined by the head-count ratio. The story remains more or less the same when patterns of growth are evaluated using the poverty gap ratio and severity of poverty measure. Results also show that growth processes in Asia have not been favorable to the extremely poor, who live far below the $1.25-a-day poverty line.

Based on detailed estimates of equitable growth, we further calculate the losses or gains of the economic growth rate resulting from inequitable or equitable growth patterns. As can be seen in Table 4.5, developing Asia's equitable growth pattern in 2002–05 led to a gain in the growth rate of 0.2% per annum during this spell. Conversely, the region's inequitable growth pattern in 1999–2002 led to a loss of growth of 0.54% per annum over the period. Thus, growth was not equitable until 2002 and became equitable only during 2002–05. Such results raise many questions, such as why growth became equitable or pro-poor in 2002–05 and whether it was attributable to governments' policies in Asia. And if so, what policies improved the equitability of growth in the region? While these are indeed pertinent questions, addressing these issues is beyond the scope of the current study. To address them appropriately, one needs to carry out detailed analyses of growth processes in individual countries of the region. This could be pursued in a future study.

Conclusions

This chapter has introduced an index that identifies whether economic growth is equitable or inequitable. This index—called the poverty equivalent growth rate— measures the gains or losses of the growth rate that result from changes in the distribution of income or consumption. The proposed methodology was applied to 25 developing countries in Asia and 200 growth spells, covering the period 1981–2005. Although the PEGR analytical tool is applied to cross-country data sets for 25 countries, data quality is often a major concern. Hence, one should be cautious when applying this tool for cross-country analysis. Instead, it is highly recommended to use micro unit record household surveys for such studies.

Our empirical results show that Asia enjoyed improvements in standards of living and rapid reduction in poverty during 1981–2005. However, the fruits of growth have not been shared equally among the poor and the non-poor: growth has benefited the non-poor proportionally more than the poor in six out of eight growth spells we investigated. Why, then, is growth generally inequitable or anti-poor? And how can it be made more equitable or pro-poor? Given the results emerging from this chapter, it appears that government policies in the region tend to favor the non-poor more than the poor. In the past a few decades, the region has learned well how to achieve rapid economic growth, yet a major challenge that the region is currently facing is how to make growth more broad-based so that it benefits the poor proportionally more than the non-poor. Rapid economic growth generates resources for the government to implement its policies; however, these policies still need to be designed in such a way that their implementation leads to improved equity that benefits society's vulnerable groups.

Note

1 Growth spells refer to the periods spanning two successive household surveys for a given country. In our data set, there are eight growth spells during 1981–2005. This means that the total number of growth spells for 25 countries should be 400.

Appendix

Table A.4.1 Growth rate in per-capita mean expenditure at 2005 purchasing power parity

	1981–84	1984–87	1987–90	1990–93	1993–96	1996–99	1999–2002	2002–05
Armenia	−0.80	−0.90	−15.73	−18.39	5.58	−10.15	1.12	6.53
Azerbaijan	−0.84	−0.90	−0.80	−0.52	−0.34	2.94	11.85	1.15
Bangladesh	−0.30	0.61	−0.74	0.48	2.61	−2.27	0.82	1.04
Bhutan	1.40	1.04	−4.83	2.17	−0.01	11.88	2.61	−0.40
Cambodia	4.97	6.33	−3.58	15.30	2.95	−0.30	−1.83	5.37
China, People's Rep. of – rural	11.08	6.75	−1.49	2.61	8.89	0.14	4.92	8.24
China, People's Rep. of – urban	4.55	6.45	0.56	7.31	5.20	5.07	9.00	7.02
Georgia	−0.85	−0.91	−0.80	−0.52	−6.20	−8.21	−6.55	3.05
India – rural	1.28	1.45	0.45	0.25	1.41	1.06	0.70	1.22
India – urban	0.98	1.75	1.62	0.92	1.37	1.04	0.65	1.22
Indonesia – rural	3.83	−1.84	5.10	−0.55	4.83	−3.68	8.06	5.95
Indonesia – urban	3.84	−2.66	7.73	0.81	5.90	−2.32	7.47	7.51
Kazakhstan	−0.61	−0.87	−10.16	−21.88	2.15	1.17	−4.43	8.39
Kyrgyz Republic	−0.85	−1.20	4.34	−8.26	−23.06	−0.52	−12.89	7.82
Lao People's Dem. Rep.	4.96	3.87	5.50	4.40	5.83	−0.46	0.14	3.71
Malaysia	1.56	−1.20	−0.74	3.48	5.19	−5.35	−4.08	−2.90
Mongolia	4.97	3.87	5.50	6.77	4.24	−10.23	12.41	−5.51
Nepal	3.27	2.98	2.73	2.19	3.27	6.22	4.99	1.79
Pakistan	2.16	0.90	3.29	13.97	−10.13	8.97	−3.76	6.16
Papua New Guinea	−2.63	0.26	−7.71	0.32	4.93	6.70	−1.77	−0.27
Philippines	−2.13	2.19	2.95	1.11	6.56	1.06	−0.93	−0.84
Sri Lanka	6.17	0.67	0.89	2.29	0.51	2.66	3.58	2.92
Tajikistan	−1.78	−0.71	1.39	−27.19	−22.28	9.23	4.96	9.16
Thailand	0.23	1.93	6.86	3.94	3.97	−1.67	1.99	3.58
Timor-Leste	2.28	0.92	5.37	4.15	5.98	−0.67	1.66	5.23
Turkmenistan	1.45	2.30	−7.47	−13.33	16.82	9.73	4.58	6.55
Uzbekistan	0.56	−1.89	−3.10	−10.22	9.15	−25.53	−9.32	2.79
Viet Nam	7.20	2.57	26.63	−14.83	2.65	5.17	5.48	10.42
Developing Asia	3.55	2.86	1.01	1.75	4.16	1.32	4.03	5.57

Source: Author's calculations.

Table A.4.2 Poverty equivalent growth rate for the head-count ratio

	1981–84	1984–87	1987–90	1990–93	1993–96	1996–99	1999–2002	2002–05
Armenia	−0.80	−0.90	−15.73	−18.41	5.59	−0.38	1.99	9.17
Azerbaijan	−0.84	−0.91	−0.80	−0.52	−1.11	3.69	12.80	63.31
Bangladesh	−0.67	−0.62	−0.75	−0.45	0.61	−2.28	0.82	1.04
Bhutan	1.61	1.04	−4.83	2.17	−0.00	11.89	2.61	−0.40
Cambodia	4.97	6.33	−3.58	15.31	2.69	−0.90	−2.96	5.37
China, People's Rep. of – rural	11.32	7.05	−3.34	1.69	8.67	−0.67	3.53	9.78
China, People's Rep. of – urban	4.66	4.99	−4.17	5.24	4.33	1.86	7.31	4.80
Georgia	−0.85	−0.91	−0.80	−0.55	−6.18	−9.01	−8.36	1.93
India – rural	1.95	0.88	0.66	0.56	1.15	0.75	0.39	0.96
India – urban	1.27	0.35	1.89	1.31	0.97	0.52	0.10	0.74
Indonesia – rural	3.84	−2.38	5.43	−0.38	4.23	−2.39	7.10	3.81
Indonesia – urban	3.84	−2.85	6.70	0.38	4.70	−0.85	7.31	3.23
Kazakhstan	−0.00	−0.00	−15.08	−10.36	−1.26	6.23	−6.13	9.75
Kyrgyz Republic	−0.00	−0.00	13.58	−43.99	−11.91	11.14	−11.08	6.75
Lao People's Dem. Rep.	4.97	3.87	5.50	4.40	4.67	−0.95	1.16	3.71
Malaysia	1.57	2.31	1.47	0.92	0.88	−2.02	2.67	3.32
Mongolia	4.97	3.87	5.50	6.76	4.25	−8.32	10.93	−5.56
Nepal	1.97	1.42	2.74	2.19	3.27	3.73	3.08	0.99
Pakistan	2.16	0.90	3.73	15.43	−9.05	6.92	−2.53	5.53
Papua New Guinea	−2.63	0.26	−7.72	0.32	4.93	6.70	−1.77	−0.28
Philippines	−2.14	2.07	1.18	0.65	4.82	0.05	−0.06	−0.50
Sri Lanka	6.18	1.18	1.78	0.20	−1.06	0.18	1.52	2.92
Tajikistan	−1.74	−0.71	1.39	−27.22	−22.29	9.23	3.90	8.54
Thailand	0.62	3.30	6.35	3.40	4.10	0.13	0.65	1.15
Timor-Leste	2.29	0.93	5.37	4.15	5.99	−0.67	1.66	5.24
Turkmenistan	1.45	2.79	−10.44	−15.41	12.54	11.22	4.57	6.55
Uzbekistan	1.11	−3.79	13.37	−31.05	10.97	−26.72	−3.26	1.67
Viet Nam	7.20	2.57	26.63	−14.84	2.47	4.86	4.50	9.65
Developing Asia	4.06	2.75	0.27	1.63	4.00	0.87	3.49	5.77

Source: Author's calculations.

Table A.4.3 Poverty equivalent growth rate for the poverty gap ratio

	1981–84	1984–87	1987–90	1990–93	1993–96	1996–99	1999–2002	2002–05
Armenia	−0.80	−0.90	−15.73	−18.39	5.60	1.41	2.73	9.72
Azerbaijan	−0.85	−0.91	−0.80	−0.52	−0.67	5.36	14.53	57.22
Bangladesh	−0.44	−0.46	−0.99	−0.66	0.25	−2.31	0.95	1.20
Bhutan	1.61	1.03	−4.83	2.18	−0.01	11.89	2.62	−0.41
Cambodia	4.97	6.33	−3.58	15.31	1.89	−1.68	−2.95	5.38
China, People's Rep. of – rural	10.32	5.56	−2.19	1.93	7.23	−1.16	2.85	9.49
China, People's Rep. of – urban	5.18	3.48	−4.87	4.89	4.68	1.04	6.64	4.07
Georgia	−0.85	−0.91	−0.68	−0.63	−6.20	−6.08	−9.15	1.27
India – rural	2.06	1.51	0.85	0.82	1.18	0.80	0.44	1.01
India – urban	1.54	0.19	1.91	1.33	0.74	0.28	−0.12	0.58
Indonesia – rural	3.83	−1.12	5.75	−0.27	3.86	−1.93	7.39	2.48
Indonesia – urban	3.85	−2.37	6.42	0.40	4.08	0.44	7.25	2.02
Kazakhstan	0.00	−20.00	−14.36	−35.88	−3.30	6.73	−6.10	10.29
Kyrgyz Republic	−0.00	−5.00	28.52	−40.02	−5.29	14.68	−9.48	6.81
Lao People's Dem. Rep.	4.96	3.87	5.50	4.40	3.20	−0.87	1.54	3.70
Malaysia	1.56	4.49	1.34	3.29	−0.24	−1.71	2.36	3.32
Mongolia	4.97	3.88	5.49	6.77	4.24	−9.28	12.16	−6.61
Nepal	1.77	1.08	2.73	2.19	3.27	3.00	2.49	0.70
Pakistan	2.16	0.90	3.30	17.73	−8.88	5.84	−2.03	5.15
Papua New Guinea	−2.64	0.26	−7.71	0.31	4.93	6.70	−1.76	−0.27
Philippines	−2.14	2.25	0.94	0.36	4.40	−0.00	−0.42	0.08
Sri Lanka	6.18	1.41	2.38	−0.22	−0.45	−0.63	1.58	2.91
Tajikistan	−1.95	−0.71	1.39	−27.18	−22.28	9.23	3.92	8.50
Thailand	0.93	3.64	6.94	3.54	3.49	1.80	0.44	−0.00
Timor-Leste	2.28	0.93	5.37	4.15	5.99	−0.67	1.66	5.24
Turkmenistan	1.45	2.79	−15.52	−16.13	11.08	12.13	4.57	6.57
Uzbekistan	−0.00	0.00	5.54	−30.50	10.17	−25.55	2.07	0.70
Viet Nam	7.20	2.58	26.62	−14.84	2.80	4.83	3.98	8.94
Developing Asia	3.69	2.49	0.79	1.77	3.46	0.49	3.11	5.57

Source: Author's calculations.

Table A.4.4 Poverty equivalent growth rate for the severity of poverty

	1981–84	1984–87	1987–90	1990–93	1993–96	1996–99	1999–2002	2002–05
Armenia	-0.00	-0.90	-15.73	-18.38	5.60	2.09	3.38	10.36
Azerbaijan	-0.84	-0.90	-0.77	-0.55	-0.06	7.12	17.30	52.06
Bangladesh	-0.23	-0.09	-1.18	-0.65	0.40	-2.33	1.01	1.26
Bhutan	1.61	1.03	-4.82	2.17	-0.00	11.87	2.63	-0.39
Cambodia	4.98	6.33	-3.57	15.30	1.33	-2.06	-2.57	5.37
China, People's Rep. of – rural	10.12	4.78	-1.40	1.95	6.87	-1.41	2.58	9.02
China, People's Rep. of – urban	5.74	1.48	-4.30	4.62	5.23	0.33	5.49	2.84
Georgia	-0.85	-0.00	-0.80	-0.52	-6.20	0.54	-10.28	0.73
India – rural	2.11	1.87	0.91	0.95	1.21	0.85	0.47	1.05
India – urban	1.74	0.41	1.91	1.34	0.62	0.17	-0.23	0.51
Indonesia – rural	3.84	-0.39	5.89	-0.25	3.69	-1.85	7.78	1.52
Indonesia – urban	3.84	-1.96	6.49	0.44	3.79	0.68	7.59	1.23
Kazakhstan	-10.00	-0.00	-5.00	-13.95	-5.17	7.13	-6.45	11.01
Kyrgyz Republic	0.00	-0.00	45.36	-37.51	-0.79	17.10	-7.92	6.88
Lao People's Dem. Rep.	4.97	3.87	5.50	4.40	2.13	-0.80	1.90	3.71
Malaysia	1.56	9.35	0.52	5.38	-3.50	-1.19	1.11	12.45
Mongolia	4.97	3.86	5.49	6.77	4.22	-10.09	13.90	-8.07
Nepal	1.68	0.98	2.73	2.19	3.28	2.82	2.38	0.64
Pakistan	2.16	0.91	3.02	19.13	-8.89	5.09	-1.62	4.97
Papua New Guinea	-2.62	0.27	-7.72	0.31	4.93	6.71	-1.77	-0.27
Philippines	-2.14	2.39	0.84	0.26	4.22	-0.00	-0.63	0.42
Sri Lanka	6.21	1.47	2.68	-0.09	0.08	-1.20	1.67	2.88
Tajikistan	-1.78	-0.71	1.39	-27.19	-22.27	9.21	4.79	8.46
Thailand	0.96	3.75	7.34	3.56	3.80	-0.00	ERR	-0.00
Timor-Leste	2.29	0.92	5.38	4.15	5.98	-0.67	1.66	5.24
Turkmenistan	1.49	2.78	-19.06	-15.72	10.27	12.96	4.56	6.60
Uzbekistan	0.18	-1.32	1.34	-33.31	6.91	-24.76	6.60	0.12
Viet Nam	7.20	2.57	26.64	-14.84	2.94	4.86	3.82	8.61
Developing Asia	3.57	2.32	1.18	1.81	3.32	0.19	2.97	5.39

Source: Author's calculations.

Table A.4.5 Gains and losses of growth rate for the head-count ratio

	1981–84	1984–87	1987–90	1990–93	1993–96	1996–99	1999–2002	2002–05
Armenia	0.00	0.00	0.01	−0.02	0.01	9.77	0.87	2.63
Azerbaijan	0.00	−0.00	−0.00	−0.00	−0.77	0.74	0.95	62.16
Bangladesh	−0.37	−1.23	−0.01	−0.92	−2.00	−0.02	0.00	0.00
Bhutan	0.21	0.00	0.00	−0.00	0.01	0.00	0.00	0.00
Cambodia	0.01	0.00	−0.00	0.01	−0.26	−0.60	−1.13	−0.00
China, People's Rep. of – rural	0.24	0.30	−1.85	−0.92	−0.22	−0.81	−1.39	1.55
China, People's Rep. of – urban	0.11	−1.46	−4.73	−2.08	−0.87	−3.21	−1.69	−2.22
Georgia	−0.00	−0.00	−0.00	−0.03	0.02	−0.80	−1.81	−1.12
India – rural	0.67	−0.56	0.22	0.31	−0.26	−0.31	−0.31	−0.26
India – urban	0.29	−1.41	0.28	0.40	−0.40	−0.52	−0.54	−0.48
Indonesia – rural	0.00	−0.54	0.32	0.17	−0.60	1.28	−0.96	−2.14
Indonesia – urban	0.00	−0.18	−1.03	−0.43	−1.20	1.47	−0.16	−4.29
Kazakhstan	0.61	0.87	−4.92	11.52	−3.41	5.06	−1.70	1.36
Kyrgyz Republic	0.85	1.20	9.24	−35.73	11.16	11.67	1.81	−1.06
Lao People's Dem. Rep.	0.01	0.00	0.00	−0.00	−1.16	−0.48	1.02	0.00
Malaysia	0.00	3.51	2.21	−2.55	−4.31	3.34	6.75	6.21
Mongolia	0.00	0.00	0.00	−0.01	0.01	1.91	−1.47	−0.05
Nepal	−1.30	−1.56	0.00	0.00	0.00	−2.48	−1.91	−0.80
Pakistan	0.00	−0.00	0.44	1.47	1.08	−2.06	1.23	−0.63
Papua New Guinea	−0.00	0.00	−0.01	−0.00	0.01	−0.00	−0.00	−0.00
Philippines	−0.00	−0.12	−1.78	−0.46	−1.74	−1.01	0.87	0.34
Sri Lanka	0.00	0.51	0.89	−2.09	−1.57	−2.48	−2.07	0.00
Tajikistan	0.04	−0.00	0.00	−0.03	−0.01	0.01	−1.05	−0.62
Thailand	0.39	1.37	−0.51	−0.55	0.13	1.80	−1.34	−2.43
Timor-Leste	0.00	0.00	0.00	−0.00	0.01	−0.00	0.00	0.00
Turkmenistan	−0.00	0.48	−2.96	−2.08	−4.28	1.50	−0.00	0.00
Uzbekistan	0.56	−1.89	16.47	−20.83	1.82	−1.19	6.05	−1.12
Viet Nam	0.00	0.00	0.01	−0.00	−0.17	−0.31	−0.99	−0.77
Developing Asia	0.51	−0.11	−0.74	−0.12	−0.16	−0.46	−0.54	0.20

Source: Author's calculations.

Table A.4.6 Gains and losses of growth rate for the poverty gap ratio

	1981–84	1984–87	1987–90	1990–93	1993–96	1996–99	1999–2002	2002–05
Armenia	0.00	0.00	−0.00	0.01	0.01	11.57	1.61	3.19
Azerbaijan	−0.00	−0.00	−0.00	−0.00	−0.34	2.42	2.67	56.07
Bangladesh	−0.13	−1.08	−0.25	−1.14	−2.36	−0.05	0.12	0.16
Bhutan	0.21	−0.01	−0.00	0.01	−0.00	0.00	0.01	−0.00
Cambodia	−0.00	0.00	−0.00	0.01	−1.06	−1.39	−1.12	0.00
China, People's Rep. of – rural	−0.76	−1.19	−0.70	−0.68	−1.66	−1.30	−2.07	1.25
China, People's Rep. of – urban	0.63	−2.97	−5.43	−2.42	−0.52	−4.03	−2.36	−2.95
Georgia	0.00	0.00	0.11	−0.11	−0.00	2.13	−2.60	−1.78
India – rural	0.78	0.07	0.40	0.56	−0.23	−0.26	−0.26	−0.21
India – urban	0.55	−1.57	0.30	0.42	−0.63	−0.76	−0.77	−0.64
Indonesia – rural	−0.00	0.71	0.65	0.28	−0.97	1.75	−0.67	−3.47
Indonesia – urban	0.01	0.30	−1.31	−0.41	−1.82	2.76	−0.22	−5.49
Kazakhstan	0.61	−19.13	−4.20	−14.00	−5.45	5.57	−1.68	1.90
Kyrgyz Republic	0.85	−3.80	24.18	−31.75	17.77	15.21	3.40	−1.01
Lao People's Dem. Rep.	0.00	0.00	−0.00	0.00	−2.63	−0.41	1.40	−0.00
Malaysia	0.00	5.69	2.09	−0.19	−5.43	3.64	6.44	6.22
Mongolia	0.00	0.01	−0.00	0.00	0.00	0.95	−0.25	−1.10
Nepal	−1.50	−1.90	0.00	0.00	−0.00	−3.22	−2.50	−1.09
Pakistan	0.00	−0.00	0.01	3.76	1.25	−3.13	1.73	−1.01
Papua New Guinea	−0.00	0.00	0.00	−0.01	0.01	−0.00	0.01	−0.00
Philippines	−0.00	0.07	−2.01	−0.75	−2.16	−1.06	0.50	0.92
Sri Lanka	0.01	0.74	1.49	−2.51	−0.96	−3.29	−2.01	−0.01
Tajikistan	−0.17	0.00	0.00	0.01	−0.01	0.00	−1.04	−0.67
Thailand	0.70	1.71	0.08	−0.40	−0.48	3.47	−1.55	−3.58
Timor-Leste	0.00	0.00	0.00	0.00	0.01	−0.00	−0.00	0.01
Turkmenistan	0.00	0.49	−8.05	−2.81	−5.74	2.40	−0.01	0.02
Uzbekistan	−0.56	1.90	8.64	−20.28	1.02	−0.01	11.39	−2.09
Viet Nam	0.00	0.00	−0.00	−0.00	0.16	−0.34	−1.50	−1.48
Developing Asia	0.14	−0.37	−0.22	0.02	−0.71	−0.84	−0.92	−0.00

Source: Author's calculations.

Table A.4.7 Gains and losses of growth rate for the severity of poverty

	1981–84	1984–87	1987–90	1990–93	1993–96	1996–99	1999–2002	2002–05
Armenia	0.80	0.00	0.00	0.02	0.01	12.24	2.26	3.83
Azerbaijan	0.00	0.00	0.03	-0.04	0.28	4.18	5.45	50.91
Bangladesh	0.07	-0.70	-0.44	-1.12	-2.21	-0.06	0.19	0.23
Bhutan	0.21	-0.01	0.01	0.00	0.01	-0.01	0.02	0.02
Cambodia	0.01	-0.00	0.00	0.00	-1.62	-1.76	-0.74	-0.00
China, People's Rep. of – rural	-0.96	-1.97	0.09	-0.66	-2.02	-1.54	-2.34	0.79
China, People's Rep. of – urban	1.19	-4.96	-4.85	-2.69	0.03	-4.74	-3.51	-4.18
Georgia	0.00	0.91	0.00	0.00	0.00	8.75	-3.73	-2.32
India – rural	0.83	0.42	0.47	0.70	-0.20	-0.22	-0.23	-0.17
India – urban	0.76	-1.35	0.30	0.43	-0.74	-0.87	-0.88	-0.70
Indonesia – rural	0.00	1.45	0.79	0.30	-1.14	1.83	-0.28	-4.43
Indonesia – urban	0.00	0.71	-1.24	-0.37	-2.11	3.00	0.12	-6.29
Kazakhstan	-9.39	0.87	5.16	7.93	-7.31	5.97	-2.02	2.62
Kyrgyz Republic	0.85	1.20	41.02	-29.24	22.27	17.63	4.97	-0.94
Lao People's Dem. Rep.	0.01	-0.00	-0.00	0.00	-3.70	-0.34	1.77	0.00
Malaysia	0.00	10.55	1.27	1.90	-8.69	4.16	5.19	15.35
Mongolia	0.00	-0.01	-0.01	0.00	-0.02	0.14	1.49	-2.56
Nepal	-1.59	-2.00	0.00	0.00	0.01	-3.40	-2.61	-1.15
Pakistan	0.01	0.00	-0.27	5.16	1.24	-3.89	2.14	-1.19
Papua New Guinea	0.01	0.01	-0.01	-0.01	0.00	0.01	-0.00	-0.00
Philippines	-0.00	0.20	-2.11	-0.85	-2.34	-1.06	0.29	1.26
Sri Lanka	0.03	0.80	1.79	-2.38	-0.43	-3.86	-1.91	-0.04
Tajikistan	0.00	0.00	0.00	0.00	0.01	-0.01	-0.17	-0.71
Thailand	0.73	1.82	0.48	-0.39	-0.16	1.67	–	-3.58
Timor-Leste	0.01	0.00	0.01	0.00	0.00	-0.00	0.00	0.00
Turkmenistan	0.04	0.48	-11.58	-2.39	-6.55	3.24	-0.02	0.05
Uzbekistan	-0.37	0.57	4.44	-23.09	-2.24	0.77	15.92	-2.67
Viet Nam	0.00	0.00	0.02	-0.01	0.29	-0.32	-1.66	-1.81
Developing Asia	0.02	-0.54	0.17	0.06	-0.84	-1.13	-1.06	-0.18

Source: Author's calculations.

5   Assessing fiscal policy from an equity perspective

Introduction

Governments collect revenues through taxes, user fees and charges, royalties from natural resources, and the sale of goods and services. They also receive income from investments and often from borrowing. These revenues are used to transfer payments to individuals and businesses, pay interest on accumulated debt, and finance general expenditures. Both the spending and revenue-raising activities tend to alter the relative economic position of individuals and families, often by design because income redistribution is one of the main functions of government activity.

Fiscal policy represents one of the key instruments by which government activity can affect poverty, through its impacts on growth and distribution. Fiscal policy is one of a number of important factors that influence economic growth rates and, subject to other conditions, a sustained higher growth rate will translate into faster poverty reduction (Gemmell 2001; McKay 2002). However, fiscal policy is also one of the main mechanisms by which government can have an impact on distribution. This can be achieved either through static redistribution, depending on the patterns of government spending and revenue collection, or through dynamic redistribution, through its influence on the distributional pattern of growth (Killick 2002). Indeed, fiscal policy is likely to play a central role in generating an equitable or pro-poor pattern of growth that benefits the poor proportionally more than the non-poor (Kakwani and Son 2008). Throughout this chapter, "equitable growth" is used interchangeably with "pro-poor growth": other things being equal, equitable growth or pro-poor growth will be much more effective at reducing poverty.

Government policy is said to be equitable or pro-poor if it benefits the poor proportionally more than the non-poor. Unfortunately, little is known about the precise role of fiscal policy from an equity perspective. This chapter aims to fill this gap by assessing the impact of fiscal policy on distribution and poverty. To that end, we introduce a methodology to assess the pro-poorness of fiscal policies in view of bringing about marginal reforms. We derive the poverty elasticity for a general class of poverty measures and, using this estimate of poverty elasticity, an index called the *pro-poor index* is introduced that can be utilized to assess government expenditure and tax policies from an equity perspective.

Methodology

Poverty measures

Income, x, of an individual is a random variable with distribution function given by $F(x)$. If we let z denote the poverty line, then $H = F(z)$ is the proportion of individuals whose income falls below the poverty line; that is, H is the proportion of poor individuals in society. H in this case is the head-count ratio and is the most popularly used measure of poverty.

A general class of a poverty measure that combines three characteristics of poverty—the percentage of poor, the aggregate poverty gap, and the distribution of income among the poor—can be written as

$$\theta = \int_0^z P(z,x)f(x)dx \tag{5.1}$$

where $f(x)$ is the density function of x and $\frac{\partial P}{\partial x} < 0$, $\frac{\partial^2 P}{\partial x^2} > 0$, $P(z,z) = 0$ and $P(z,x)$ is a homogenous function of degree zero in z and x. The Foster–Greer–Thorbecke class of poverty measures is obtained when we substitute $P(z,x) = \left(\frac{z-x}{z}\right)^\alpha$ in equation (5.1) to get

$$\theta_\alpha = \int_0^z \left(\frac{z-x}{z}\right)^\alpha f(x)dx \tag{5.2}$$

where α is the parameter of inequality aversion. For $\alpha = 0$, $\theta_0 = H$, which is the poverty head-count measure, while $\alpha = 1$ gives us the poverty gap ratio and $\alpha = 2$ gives us the severity of poverty. Note that the head-count measure is a crude index of poverty because it does not take into account the income gap among the poor. It is reasonable to argue that the farther the poor's income from the poverty line, the greater the incidence of poverty should be. In addition, the severity of poverty takes into account the distribution of income among the poor.

Growth elasticity of poverty

Any poverty measure can be written as

$$\theta = \theta(z, \mu, L(p)) \tag{5.3}$$

where μ is the mean income in society and $L(p)$ is the Lorenz function, which measures relative income distribution. Note that $L(p)$ is the percentage of income enjoyed by the bottom p percent of the population.

The growth elasticity of poverty measures the effect of a change in μ on θ when $L(p)$ remains constant. This elasticity, derived by Kakwani (1993), is given by

$$\eta_\theta = \frac{1}{\theta} \int_0^z x \frac{\partial P}{\partial x} f(x)dx \tag{5.4}$$

which is always negative because $\frac{\partial P}{\partial x} < 0$. For the head-count measure, $P(z,x) = 1$, so the elasticity is derived as

$$\eta_H = -\frac{zf(z)}{H} < 0$$

which is the percentage of the poor who will cross the poverty line as a result of 1% growth in society's mean income.

Substituting $P(z,x) = \left(\frac{z-x}{z}\right)^{\alpha}$ into equation (5.4) gives the elasticity of θ_{α} with respect to μ as

$$\eta_{\alpha} = \frac{\partial \theta_{\alpha}}{\partial \mu} \frac{\mu}{\theta_{\alpha}} = -\frac{\alpha(\theta_{\alpha-1} - \theta_{\alpha})}{\theta_{\alpha}} \tag{5.5}$$

for $\alpha \neq 0$, which will always be negative because θ_{α} is a monotonically decreasing function of α.

Growth elasticity of income components

The total (or net) income of an individual is the sum of several income components, which can consist of market income—such as wages and salaries, interest, dividends, and income from self-employment—and non-market income from private transfers and government transfers such as old-age pensions, family allowances, disability pensions, and unemployment benefits. Since poverty should be measured based on disposable income, we need to deduct personal income tax from gross income. That said, let x be the net or disposable income and $g_i(x)$ be the ith income component received by an individual or household with net income x. We can then express x as:

$$x = \sum_{i=1}^{m} g_i(x) \tag{5.6}$$

where m is the total number of income components, one of which is the income tax paid by the individual and which enters equation (5.6) as a negative component. Following Kakwani (1980), the concentration function of the ith income component—that is, $C_i(p)$—is defined as the percentage of the ith income component enjoyed by the bottom p percent of the population.

The first derivative of $C_i(p)$ with respect to p is given by $C_i'(p) = \frac{g_i(x)}{\mu_i}$, where μ_i is the mean of the ith income component. Substituting this into equation (5.6) gives

$$x = \sum_{i=1}^{m} \mu_i C_i'(p) \tag{5.7}$$

Our objective is to measure the responsiveness of θ to the mean of the ith income component, μ_i. This is accomplished by deriving the elasticity of θ with respect to μ_i, which we can call the ith income component elasticity. To derive this elasticity, we assume that a change in μ_i does not affect the distribution of the ith income component across net income. The concentration function $C_i(p)$ measures the distribution of the ith income component across the total (net) income. In deriving income component elasticity, we therefore assume that $C_i(p)$ does not change when μ_i changes. Thus, differentiating equation (5.7) with respect to μ_i and keeping $C_i'(p)$ constant gives us

$$\mu_i \frac{\partial x}{\partial \mu_i} = \mu_i C_i'(p) = g_i(x) \tag{5.8}$$

Differentiating equation (5.1) and using equation (5.8) gives the elasticity of θ with respect to μ_i as

$$\eta_{\theta_i} = \frac{\partial \theta}{\partial \mu_i} \frac{\mu_i}{\theta} = \frac{1}{\theta} \int_0^z \frac{\partial P}{\partial x} g_i(x) f(x) dx \tag{5.9}$$

For the Foster–Greer–Thorbecke class of poverty measures, the ith income component elasticity is derived from equation (5.8) as

$$\eta_{\alpha_i} = -\frac{\alpha}{\theta_\alpha} \int_0^z \frac{1}{z} \left(\frac{z-x}{z} \right)^{\alpha-1} g_i(x) f(x) dx \tag{5.10}$$

for $a \neq 0$, which can easily be computed given the data on income components and the net income x. The mean income component elasticity for the head-count ratio is given by

$$\eta_{Hi} = \frac{\partial H}{\partial \mu_i} \frac{\mu_i}{H} = -\frac{g_i(z) f(z)}{H}$$

where $g_i(z)$ is the value of the ith income component when an individual has an income equal to the poverty line.

Pro-poor index of income components

The income components method above can also provide information on the components of a fiscal system. From a policy point of view, it is important to know to what degree a particular income component is pro-poor (equitable) or anti-poor (inequitable). In this section, we derive a pro-poor index for the ith income component.

Based on equations (5.4), (5.6), and (5.9), it can easily be seen that

$$\sum_{i=1}^m \eta_{\theta i} = \eta_\theta \tag{5.11}$$

which implies that if all income components grow at the same rate of 1 percent, then poverty will change by η_θ percent.

When μ_i changes, it has two effects: first, μ_i changes the mean income μ and, second, μ_i shifts the Lorenz curve. To see the effect of a change in μ_i on the Lorenz curve, we follow Kakwani (1980) and write

$$L(p) = \sum_{i=1}^{m} \frac{\mu_i}{\mu} C_i(p)$$

which, on differentiating with respect to μ_i, gives us

$$\frac{\partial L(p)}{\partial \mu_i} \frac{\mu_i}{L(p)} = \frac{\mu_i}{\mu} \frac{[C_i(p) - L(p)]}{L(p)}$$

This expression defines the elasticity of $L(p)$ with respect to μ_i. It shows that if $C_i(p) > L(p)$ for all p, the Lorenz curve will shift upward as a result of an increase in μ_i. This will have the effect of reducing poverty. When the Lorenz curve shifts downward (which occurs when $C_i(p) < L(p)$ for all p), poverty increases. When the two curves $C_i(p)$ and $L(p)$ cross, it is not possible to say *a priori* whether an increase in μ_i redistributes income in favor of the rich or the poor. In this case, we must compute the redistribution effect of an income component on poverty. This is accomplished by decomposing the poverty elasticity $\eta_{\theta i}$ into two components:

$$\eta_{\theta i} = \frac{\mu_i}{\mu} \eta_\theta + \left(\eta_{\theta i} - \frac{\mu_i}{u} \eta_\theta \right) \tag{5.12}$$

The first term on the right-hand side is the income effect, and the second term is the redistribution effect. It is the redistribution effect that tells us whether an increase in μ_i favors the rich or the poor. If this component is negative (positive), it means that the redistribution effect of the ith income component reduces (increases) poverty, implying that the ith income component is pro-poor (anti-poor). This leads us to suggest a pro-poor index of the ith component as

$$\phi_i = \frac{\eta_{\theta i} \mu}{\eta_\theta \mu_i} \tag{5.13}$$

which implies that the ith component is pro-poor (anti-poor) if ϕ_i is greater (less) than 1.

The pro-poor index, ϕ_i, measures the marginal benefit from an extra dollar spent on the ith income component in terms of reducing poverty. Suppose i and j are two different government transfer programs. If $\phi_i > \phi_j$, then one dollar spent on the ith program will lead to a greater reduction in poverty than one dollar spent on the jth program. In other words, we reduce poverty by cutting down expenditure on the jth program and increasing the expenditure by the same amount on the ith program.

Indirect taxes and subsidies

Indirect taxes and subsidies have direct impacts on prices. The production side of the economy is not considered here, and the incidence of taxes is assumed to be borne solely by consumers. What would be the impact on poverty if one indirect tax were increased and another indirect tax decreased, with the government's tax revenue unchanged? To analyze the effect of indirect taxes and subsidies *at the margin*, we can measure the impact of price changes due to indirect taxes or subsidies on poverty. This is accomplished by deriving a measure of poverty elasticity with respect to prices of individual commodities.

To derive the elasticity, let us write the demand equations of k commodities as

$$\mathbf{q} = \mathbf{q}(x, \mathbf{p})$$

where $\mathbf{p}$ and $\mathbf{q}$ are the $k \times 1$ vectors of prices and quantities of k commodities, and x is disposable income. It is reasonable to assume that all individuals face the same price vector, which means that prices are fixed across individuals. Thus, we write the demand equation as $\mathbf{q} = \mathbf{q}(x)$, which are the quantities consumed by an individual with disposable income x.[1] Utilizing these demand equations, let us write the disposable income as

$$x = \sum_{i=1}^{k} p_i q_i(x) + S(x) \tag{5.14}$$

where p_i is the price of the ith commodity and $q_i(x)$ is the quantity of the ith commodity consumed by an individual whose disposable income is x, where $i = 1, 2, \ldots \ldots, m$. $S(x)$ is the savings of the individual with income x.

Suppose that due to indirect taxes and subsidies, the price vector $\mathbf{p}$ changes to $\mathbf{p}^*$. How will this change affect the individual's real income? To answer this question, we consider the cost function $e(u, \mathbf{p})$ that is the minimum cost required to obtain the u level of utility when the price vector is $\mathbf{p}$. The real income of the individual with income x will have to change by[2] $\Delta x = -[e(u, \mathbf{p}^*) - e(u, \mathbf{p})]$ which, on using the Taylor expansion, gives us

$$\Delta x = -\sum_{i=1}^{m}(p_i^* - p_i)q_i(x)$$

This equation immediately gives us

$$\frac{\partial x}{\partial p_i} = -q_i(x) \tag{5.15}$$

Differentiating equation (5.1) with respect to p_i and using equation (5.15) gives the elasticity of θ with respect to p_i as

$$\varepsilon_{\theta i} = \frac{\partial \theta}{\partial p_i} \frac{p_i}{\theta} = -\frac{1}{\theta} \int_0^z \frac{\partial P}{\partial x} v_i(x) f(x) dx \tag{5.16}$$

where $v_i(x) = p_i q_i(x)$ is the expenditure on the ith commodity. Note that this elasticity is positive because an increase in any price will increase poverty.

This elasticity can be written as the sum of two components:

$$\varepsilon_{\theta i} = -\frac{p_i \bar{q}_i \eta_\theta}{\mu} + \left(\varepsilon_{\theta i} + \frac{p_i \bar{q}_i \eta_\theta}{\mu} \right) \qquad (5.17)$$

where μ is the mean disposable income and $p_i \bar{q}_i$ is the mean expenditure on the ith commodity. The first term in equation (5.17) is the income effect of the price increase, which is always positive because η_θ, as given in equation (5.4), is negative. The second term is the redistribution or inequality effect of price changes. It is the redistribution effect that tells us whether an increase in price p_i hurts the poor proportionally more than the non-poor. If this component is positive, then the increase in the price of the ith commodity hurts the poor proportionally more than the non-poor. This leads us to suggest a pro-poor price index defined as

$$\phi_i = -\frac{\varepsilon_{\theta i}}{s_i \eta_\theta} \qquad (5.18)$$

where $s_i = \frac{p_i \bar{q}_i}{\mu}$ is the expenditure on the ith commodity as a proportion of the mean income of the total disposable income. If φ_i is greater (less) than 1, an increase in the price of the ith commodity hurts the poor more (less) than the non-poor. Thus, if φ_i is greater than 1, then the ith commodity should be subsidized so that the poor benefit more relative to the non-poor. Conversely, if φ_i is less than 1, a tax increase on the ith commodity will hurt the non-poor more than the poor. Thus, we can use φ_i as a tool to improve a tax or subsidy scheme that maximizes poverty reduction.

An overview of the fiscal system in Thailand

As in many Asian countries, the Thai fiscal system is highly centralized. The national government collects most tax revenues and also spends most of them. Local governments collect a very small share of revenue through taxation. Table 5.1 presents the overall revenue structure of the national government. It can be seen that the major source of government revenue comes from taxation— non-tax revenue is only 12.03% of total revenue. Although Thailand's revenue collection efforts is similar to those in the Philippines and Indonesia, they are lower than in Malaysia and the Republic of Korea.

The revenue share of direct taxes is about 43% in Thailand, which could be considered relatively low; for instance, the corresponding figure for the Philippines was 58% as of 2009–10, up from 43% in 2005–06. Individual income tax contributes only 11.84% to total government revenue, while corporate income tax, which is levied on the net income of companies, provides the major share of government revenue at 30.66% of the total.

Two taxes dominate the indirect tax system: the value added tax (VAT) and the excise or selective sales taxes. The most dominant indirect tax is the excise tax, accounting for 19.21% of total revenue. This tax is imposed on goods such

Table 5.1 Fiscal system in Thailand, 2009

Different types of taxes	Actual revenue in baht (million)	Distribution of taxes (%)	Tax as % of GNP
Taxes on income, profits, and capital gains	**638,395.78**	**42.50**	**7.65**
Payable by individuals	177,896.15	11.84	2.13
Payable by corporations and other enterprises	460,499.63	30.66	5.52
Unallocable	–	–	–
Taxes on goods and services	**595,695.06**	**39.66**	**7.14**
Value added taxes	277,241.97	18.46	3.32
Excises	288,561.62	19.21	3.46
Profits of fiscal monopolies	10,169.54	0.68	0.12
Taxes on specific services	17,548.53	1.17	0.21
Taxes on use of goods, permission to use goods	2,173.40	0.14	0.03
Taxes on international trade and transactions	**76,882.23**	**5.12**	**0.92**
Customs and other import duties	76,482.05	5.09	0.92
Taxes on exports	400.18	0.03	0.00
Other taxes	**10,300.02**	**0.69**	**0.12**
Total tax revenue	**1,321,273.09**	**87.97**	**15.84**
Non-tax revenue	**180,753.84**	**12.03**	**2.17**
Total revenues	**1,502,026.93**	**100.00**	**18.00**

GNP = gross national product.

Source: Government fiscal management information system, Ministry of Finance, Thailand.

as gasoline and petroleum products, tobacco, alcoholic beverages, and soft drinks as well as luxury items such as playing cards, crystal glasses, etc. Excise tax is computed according to the excise tax tariff on an ad valorem basis or at a specific rate, whichever is higher. VAT is the other dominant indirect tax, which is a sales tax levied on goods and services produced in or imported into Thailand. VAT includes municipal tax, which is charged at the rate of one-ninth of the VAT rate. The VAT on domestically consumed goods and services contributes 18.46% of total revenues.

Total government revenue as a percentage of gross national product (GNP) in Thailand is 18%, while government expenditure is 22.5% of GNP (Table 5.2). Thus, the government is running a budget deficit of 4.5% of GNP.

Table 5.2 shows the distribution of government expenditure classified by function. Of the six major functions—economic services, social services, environmental protection, defense, public order and safety, and general public services—social services has the largest share of total expenditure, at 43.60%. Further breakdown of social services shows that education is the major item of social spending, accounting for 21.15% of total expenditure. By contrast, the share of health expenditure is rather small, less than 10% of the total, perhaps because health services are provided on a user-fee principle; as such,

Table 5.2 Government expenditures by functional classification

Functional classification	Actual expenditure in baht (million)	Distribution of expenditure (%)	Expenditure as % of GNP
Economic services	**369,285.41**	**19.67**	**4.43**
Social services	**818,592.25**	**43.60**	**9.81**
Health	183,725.95	9.79	2.20
Education	397,153.75	21.15	4.76
Social protection	167,363.48	8.91	2.01
Housing and community amenities	49,958.73	2.66	0.60
Recreation, culture and religion	20,390.34	1.09	0.24
Environmental protection	**4,086.53**	**0.22**	**0.05**
Defense	**150,023.35**	**7.99**	**1.80**
Public order and safety	**118,407.24**	**6.31**	**1.42**
General public services	**417,169.14**	**22.22**	**5.00**
Total government expenditure	**1,877,563.92**	**100.00**	**22.50**

GNP = gross national product.

Source: Government fiscal management information system, Ministry of Finance, Thailand.

the poor may not be receiving adequate health services because they cannot afford to pay.

Economic services is also a major item in government expenditure: almost one-fifth of the budget is devoted to this item, which includes spending on agricultural and natural resources, transportation and communications, commerce and industry, and other economic development activities. In addition, the Government of Thailand spends a significant proportion of its budget on general public services, of which public debt transactions account for 5.19% of total expenditure, or 1.17% of GNP.

Empirical results

The proposed methodology for assessing the pro-poorness of fiscal policy is applied to Thailand using data from the Socio-Economic Survey (SES) conducted in 1998. Table 5.3 presents estimates of poverty elasticity and the pro-poor index for different income components, which we will use to assess the impact of public policies on various measures of poverty. The head-count ratio is a crude measure of poverty because it completely ignores the gap between the poverty line and income of the poor. On the other hand, the poverty gap ratio and the severity of poverty index have the more desirable properties of being sensitive to this gap. As such, this study only focuses on two poverty measures: the poverty gap and severity of poverty measure. Compared with the poverty gap ratio, the severity of poverty index gives a greater weight to poorer individuals. Thus, if our concern were specifically with the ultra-poor, then we should choose the severity of poverty rather than the poverty gap ratio as the measure of poverty.

Table 5.3 Pro-poor index for income components

Income components	Percentage share	Poverty gap ratio		Severity of poverty	
		Poverty elasticity	Pro-poor index	Poverty elasticity	Pro-poor index
Wage and salary	42.1	−0.684	0.60	−0.707	0.57
Entrepreneurial income	19.2	−0.190	0.36	−0.184	0.32
Farm income	10.8	−0.449	1.54	−0.482	1.52
Rent from boarders	0.6	−0.001	0.05	−0.001	0.06
Land rent from farming	0.2	−0.003	0.64	−0.003	0.66
Other rent from non-farming	0.1	−0.003	1.54	−0.002	0.66
Interest and dividends	1.1	−0.005	0.16	−0.006	0.19
Remittances	6.5	−0.182	1.03	−0.186	0.97
Pensions and annuities	1.3	−0.001	0.02	−0.000	0.01
Terminal pay and others	0.1	−0.001	0.28	−0.001	0.20
Food as part of pay	0.4	−0.005	0.48	−0.005	0.41
Rent received as pay	0.6	−0.006	0.34	−0.006	0.32
Other goods as pay	0.8	−0.004	0.19	−0.003	0.11
Home produced food	4.0	−0.506	4.71	−0.575	4.93
Owner occupied home	9.8	−0.494	1.86	−0.587	2.04
Other home goods	0.6	−0.065	4.13	−0.080	4.64
Crops received as rent	0.1	−0.003	0.94	−0.001	0.40
Food received free	1.0	−0.055	2.12	−0.059	2.08
Rent received free	0.5	−0.013	1.05	−0.016	1.21
Other goods free	1.0	−0.044	1.64	−0.051	1.74
Total money income	82.0	−1.519	0.68	−1.572	0.65
Total in-kind income	18.6	−1.194	2.36	−1.382	2.51
Taxes	−0.6	0.001	0.08	0.001	0.07
Income tax	−0.60	0.001	0.04	0.001	0.08
House and land tax	−0.02	0.001	1.18	0.000	0.76
Fine rate	−0.00	0.000	0.63	0.000	0.58
Other taxes	−0.00	0.000	0.03	0.000	0.50
Total current disposable income	100.0	−2.71	1.00	−2.95	1.00

Source: Author's calculation based on the 1998 Socio-Economic Survey.

As can be seen from the results in Table 5.3, poverty elasticities vary widely for different income components. As any increase in income reduces poverty, the poverty elasticities of income components take negative values. If, for instance, wage and salary incomes increase by 1%, then poverty measured by poverty gap and severity of poverty will fall by 0.684% and 0.707%, respectively. Thus, the percentage reduction in poverty is greater for any increase in wages and salaries when the ultra-poor receive a greater weight than the rest of the poor. Note, however, that these measures assume that the distribution of the income component is unchanged, so in this case all individuals get a 1% increase in their wages and salaries, regardless of poverty status.

As pointed out earlier, the pro-poor index can be used to make fiscal policy more pro-poor. An income component is said to be equitable or pro-poor (inequitable or anti-poor) if the pro-poor index is greater (less) than unity. The higher the value of the index, the greater will be the proportional benefits accrued to the poor. For example, home-produced goods has the highest pro-poor index, at 4.71, which means that any subsidy given to households whose main income is generated from home-produced goods will help the poor much more than the non-poor. Similar results could be seen for other income components such as other home-produced goods, free in-kind income, imputed rent from owner-occupied homes, and farming income (see also Figure 5.1).

It is generally believed that the major source of income among the poor is wages and salaries. This may lead to a recommendation that any policy that increases wages and salaries will be equitable or pro-poor. However, this proposition is not substantiated by empirical results. The pro-poor index for wage and salary income is 0.60 for the poverty gap ratio, implying that any increase in wage and salary will benefit the non-poor proportionally more than the poor. Other income components that do not favor the poor include entrepreneurial income, rent from property, interest and dividends, and pensions and annuities.

The SES data record only direct taxes collected from households, and the pro-poor index for direct taxes is only 0.08 for the poverty gap ratio. This suggests that direct taxes are largely paid by the non-poor and have almost negligible impact on poverty, as indicated by the pro-poor index. The pro-poor index for the personal income tax is 0.04, implying that this tax is largely paid by non-poor and is thus highly equitable or pro-poor.

The Thai government collected only 13.11% of revenue from corporate income taxes in 1998, but this rose rapidly to 22% in 2003 and 31% in 2009. In an open

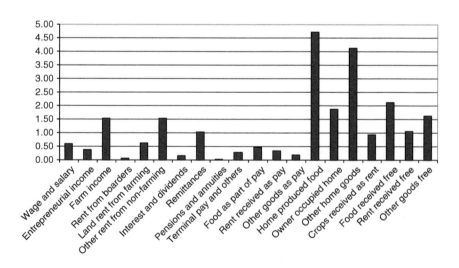

Figure 5.1 Pro-poor index for income components, poverty gap ratio.

economy such as Thailand's, it is reasonable to assume that the burden of corporate taxes is mostly borne by wage and salary earners. The pro-poor index for wage and salary income is 0.60 for the poverty gap ratio, suggesting that any tax burden borne by wage and salary earners will fall mainly on the non-poor. Given this magnitude, corporate income tax can be said to be equitable or pro-poor, but its degree of pro-poorness is much smaller than that of personal income tax.

Surprisingly, the pro-poor index for house and land tax is 1.18, which means that the poor pay proportionally more of these taxes than the non-poor. In 1998, the government was able to collect only 0.70% of its revenue from house and land tax. As the share of this tax is fairly small, it will have little impact on poverty, even if it is equitable or pro-poor. However, this finding suggests that there is scope for the government to improve or redesign the house and land tax in a way that the non-poor will pay proportionally more than the poor.

Pensions and annuities contribute 1.3% to total personal income. These income sources are found to be highly anti-poor, as indicated by the value of the pro-poor index, equivalent to 0.02 for the poverty gap ratio. This suggests that the poor do not have much access to pensions and annuities, which are mainly given to retired public servants. The Thai government does not have a welfare assistance program specifically designed to help vulnerable groups such as the poor. Instead, there are informal safety nets provided by family members that can take the form of domestic or overseas remittances. As can be seen in Table 5.3, remittances contribute around 6.5% of disposable income, and its pro-poor index is equal to 1.03 for the poverty gap ratio. Thus, remittances are indeed pro-poor and benefit the poor proportionally more than the non-poor. However, the index falls to 0.97 when it is calculated for the severity of poverty measure: the ultra-poor get less of a proportion of the remittances than the rest of the poor. This could indicate that while poor households are more likely to receive remittances than the non-poor, the ultra-poor nevertheless do not receive much remittance income. It is quite possible that remittances are able to lift households from being ultra-poor, but are unable to lift them completely out of poverty.

Table 5.4 presents the values of poverty elasticity with respect to prices. Since price increases reduce people's real income and thus increase poverty, all the elasticities take positive values. Values of the pro-poor index can be either greater or less than 1. A pro-poor index that is larger (smaller) than unity suggests that the increase in prices would hurt the poor more (less) than the non-poor. For instance, the index is highly anti-poor for grains and cereal products: its index value is 4.43 for the poverty gap ratio and further increases to 5.07 for the severity of poverty. This indicates that subsidizing (taxing) these items will benefit (hurt) the poor much more than the non-poor. A similar conclusion emerges from other food items, which implies that indirect taxes on food items are likely to be anti-poor. For this reason, to partially correct the anti-poorness of the indirect tax burden, basic necessities such as unprocessed foodstuffs, medical and health services, and educational materials should be exempted from the VAT.

Table 5.4 Pro-poor index for consumption expenditure components

Expenditure items	Percent share	Poverty gap ratio		Severity of poverty	
		Poverty elasticity	Pro-poor index	Poverty elasticity	Pro-poor index
Grains and cereal products	4.95	0.595	4.43	0.741	5.07
Meat and poultry	3.46	0.307	3.28	0.384	3.77
Fish and seafood	2.80	0.284	3.74	0.366	4.44
Milk, cheese and eggs	1.95	0.136	2.57	0.166	2.89
Oils and fats	0.48	0.048	3.70	0.064	4.56
Fruits and nuts	1.72	0.079	1.69	0.103	2.04
Vegetables	2.49	0.249	3.68	0.310	4.22
Sugar and sweets	0.71	0.062	3.23	0.089	4.23
Spices, coffees and teas	0.91	0.068	2.75	0.091	3.41
Prepared meals taken home	3.30	0.148	1.65	0.184	1.89
Non-alcoholic beverage at home	0.66	0.024	1.31	0.032	1.64
Alcoholic beverage at home	0.80	0.035	1.59	0.041	1.74
Alcoholic beverage drunk outside	0.45	0.010	0.81	0.011	0.82
Meals eaten away from home	5.97	0.194	1.20	0.259	1.47
Tobacco products	0.98	0.054	2.02	0.070	2.40
Clothing	2.35	0.116	1.83	0.148	2.15
Footwear	0.58	0.037	2.31	0.047	2.74
Shelter	13.07	0.575	1.62	0.698	1.81
Fuel and light	3.64	0.222	2.25	0.277	2.58
Textile house furnishings	0.20	0.013	2.46	0.018	3.19
Minor house equipment	0.12	0.006	2.05	0.009	2.59
Major house equipment	0.24	0.009	1.32	0.012	1.76
Cleaning supplies	0.91	0.053	2.16	0.070	2.61
Servants	0.19	0.000	0.03	0.000	0.01
Personal care items	1.58	0.103	2.40	0.132	2.83
Personal services	0.41	0.020	1.80	0.026	2.11
Local transportation	1.52	0.062	1.49	0.084	1.86
Travel out of area	0.64	0.018	1.06	0.029	1.55
Vehicle operation	4.75	0.194	1.51	0.247	1.76
Vehicle purchase	2.82	0.084	1.09	0.107	1.28
Communication services	1.56	0.017	0.41	0.021	0.46
Communication equipment	0.05	0.000	0.30	0.000	0.23
Admissions	0.12	0.002	0.56	0.003	0.83
Recreation and sport equipment	0.42	0.007	0.63	0.009	0.70
Musical equipment	0.18	0.006	1.31	0.009	1.69
Reading materials	0.24	0.002	0.33	0.003	0.47
Religious activities	0.55	0.025	1.68	0.032	1.96
Ceremonies	0.88	0.064	2.69	0.098	3.80
Miscellaneous services	0.09	0.001	0.52	0.002	0.59
Education expenses	**4.04**	**0.237**	**2.16**	**0.304**	**2.55**
Private school fees	0.49	0.008	0.62	0.009	0.62
Public school fees	0.23	0.017	2.67	0.022	3.13
Private vocational tuition fees	0.20	0.004	0.73	0.005	0.75
Public vocational tuition fees	0.08	0.004	1.70	0.006	2.60
Private university tuition fees	0.24	0.003	0.48	0.001	0.21
Public university tuition fees	0.18	0.002	0.41	0.003	0.58

(Continued)

Table 5.4 Cont'd

Expenditure items	Percent share	Poverty gap ratio		Severity of poverty	
		Poverty elasticity	*Pro-poor index*	*Poverty elasticity*	*Pro-poor index*
Text books	0.33	0.030	3.45	0.039	4.09
School equipment	0.19	0.017	3.29	0.023	3.96
Special lessons	0.08	0.001	0.69	0.001	0.52
Student lunch	0.26	0.007	1.01	0.010	1.38
Pocket money	1.74	0.140	2.97	0.182	3.55
Other education expenses	0.02	0.003	3.89	0.003	4.31
Medicine	**0.39**	**0.028**	**2.68**	**0.036**	**3.16**
Cough remedies	0.03	0.003	4.41	0.004	5.38
Antipyretics and Analgesics	0.09	0.009	3.73	0.012	4.34
Cold remedies	0.03	0.002	2.73	0.003	3.27
Anti-inflammatory analgesics	0.03	0.003	3.53	0.004	4.30
Antimicrobials	0.01	0.001	3.43	0.001	3.58
Anti venom	0.01	0.000	2.62	0.000	2.96
Anti fungal	0.01	0.000	1.79	0.000	2.06
Antiseptics	0.00	0.000	2.15	0.000	3.03
Laxatives	0.00	0.000	2.59	0.000	2.29
Anthelmintics	0.00	0.000	4.33	0.000	5.72
Antacids and digestives	0.02	0.001	2.43	0.001	2.62
Anti diarrheas	0.01	0.001	3.19	0.001	3.81
Contraceptives	0.02	0.001	3.02	0.002	3.50
Inhalant	0.00	0.000	2.18	0.000	2.80
Vitamins	0.02	0.001	1.45	0.001	1.94
Other modern drugs	0.06	0.003	1.74	0.004	2.07
Traditional and herbal drugs	0.05	0.001	1.03	0.002	1.36
First aid kits	0.01	0.000	1.67	0.000	0.88
Medical services	**1.51**	**0.065**	**1.58**	**0.086**	**1.94**
Outpatients					
Government hospital and health center	0.62	0.028	1.68	0.036	1.96
Private hospital and health center	0.32	0.006	0.70	0.009	0.94
Doctor fees	0.02	0.003	4.19	0.004	5.38
Nursing fees	0.00	0.000	3.56	0.000	1.16
Eye examination and eyeglasses	0.01	0.000	1.11	0.000	0.17
Dental services	0.08	0.000	0.23	0.001	0.24
X-ray and lab fees	0.02	0.003	6.40	0.004	8.08
Healthcare card	0.01	0.001	2.37	0.001	2.32
Inpatients					
Government hospital and health center	0.22	0.014	2.39	0.020	3.09
Private hospital and health center	0.19	0.008	1.48	0.007	1.21
Other government medical services	0.00	0.000	3.63	0.000	1.81
Other private medical services	0.01	0.000	0.61	0.000	0.07
Total per-capita expenditure	**74.68**	**4.26**	**2.10**	**5.42**	**2.46**
Savings	**25.32**	**−1.55**	**−2.26**	**−2.48**	**−3.32**

Source: Author's calculation based on the 1998 Socio-Economic Survey.

By comparison, the value of the pro-poor index for alcoholic beverages consumed outside the home is shown to be less than 1, namely 0.80 and 0.81 for the poverty gap and severity of poverty, respectively. This suggests that any indirect tax on alcoholic beverages consumed outside the home will hurt the poor less than the non-poor. This conclusion, however, is reversed if we look at alcoholic beverages consumed at home—its pro-poor index is 1.59, suggesting that any tax on alcohol consumed at home is likely to hurt the poor proportionally more than the non-poor. To achieve the maximum reduction in poverty, therefore, alcohol can be taxed more heavily when it is sold and consumed at bars or restaurants.

Government often grants exemptions in implementing indirect taxes such as VAT due to various social, political, and administrative reasons. Exemptions may be given for basic necessities and services (e.g., unprocessed food), social welfare services such as medical and health services, goods or services related to culture (e.g., education, books, newspapers, and artistic works), and so forth. In this regard, the results in Table 5.4 show that tax exemptions or subsidies on education and health would benefit the poor (particularly the ultra-poor) more than the non-poor.

The Thai government plays an important role in providing educational services to its people. Nevertheless, the pro-poor index for private expenditure on education is 2.16 for poverty gap and 2.55 for severity of poverty, indicating that the poor tend to pay proportionally much more for schooling than the non-poor. This suggests that ultra-poor people pay proportionally more than the rest of the poor. Analyzing components of educational expenses, we calculate the pro-poor indices for detailed items which are shown in Table 5.2. The results show that the burden of price increases on items such as textbooks, school equipment, or public primary and secondary school fees, which may stem from the VAT, will be borne more heavily by the poor rather than by the non-poor. On the other hand, price reductions in tuition fees for private vocational institutes and private and public universities, which may stem from the government subsidies on education, will benefit students from non-poor households proportionally more than those from poor ones.

A similar story emerges when we look at private expenditure on health. As health services in Thailand are generally provided on a user-fee principle, the poor are likely to bear a proportionally greater financial burden from price increases in these services compared to the non-poor. The pro-poor index for private expenditure on medicine and medical services takes a value far greater than 1 (see also Figure 5.2), suggesting that the poor will bear a proportionally heavier burden than the non-poor from any price increase in health services. Specifically, a price increase in certain medicines (e.g., cough remedies) will have a more detrimental effect on the poor compared to other drugs (e.g., traditional herbal drugs or first aid kits). Similarly, government subsidies for certain medical services (e.g., X-ray and laboratory fees) will be more beneficial to the poor compared with other medical services (e.g., outpatient care in private hospitals and health centers).

Overall, the value of the pro-poor index indicates that the incidence of indirect taxes will be borne more heavily by the poor rather than by the non-poor; in other

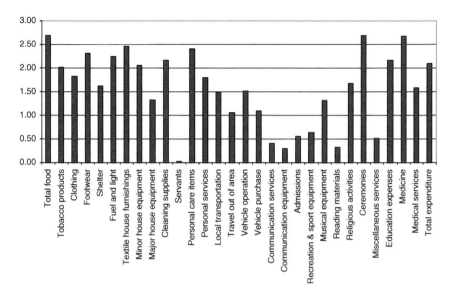

Figure 5.2 Pro-poor index for prices, poverty gap ratio.

words, indirect taxes in this case are regressive. The ultra-poor will be hurt even more by an increase in indirect taxes, as suggested by the index value of 2.46 for the severity of poverty. This finding confirms a number of empirical studies which find that indirect taxes are proportional to income or even somewhat regressive (Heller 1981; Oh 1982).

This study also finds that although the incidence of the special excise tax burden is estimated to be significantly less adverse to the poor compared with the VAT, it may not really be improving income distribution. Even though excise taxes on items such as liquor and tobacco levy higher rates on higher quality products consumed by the middle and upper income classes, the average tax amount tends to rise less than proportionately with income, which results in a greater proportional tax burden on the poor.

In general, the VAT is considered to be a regressive tax because poorer taxpayers consume a greater proportion of their income than do richer taxpayers. This suggests that the incidence of the VAT on food items and other essential commodities is likely to be borne more heavily by the poor than the non-poor. This conclusion is supported by our empirical results.

Furthermore, the pro-poor index reveals that savings in Thailand are highly inequitable or anti-poor, suggesting that savings are mainly enjoyed by rich people, a finding that reflects the similar results of Kakwani and Son (2002). The study argues that household savings in Thailand mainly come from the richest 20% of the population, while the rest tend to dissave.

The inability to effectively tax personal and corporate income and wealth has obliged the Thai government to rely largely on indirect taxes, despite the common observation that heavy taxation of consumption contravenes the objectives of improving equity and reducing poverty. The central government currently depends heavily on two indirect taxes: the VAT and the excise tax. To achieve a more progressive tax system, it is important for the government to moderate the anti-poorness of the indirect tax system in general and the VAT in particular, and to move toward greater reliance on direct taxes. Equally important is the careful consideration of the population's consumption patterns in the selection of items to be taxed and setting of tax rates, giving due attention to variables such as the income and price elasticities of taxable goods.

Conclusion

In this chapter, we evaluate equity in tax policies and public spending by investigating their marginal impacts on poverty. This task is carried out using the pro-poor index proposed in the study, which provides a tool to assess the impact of fiscal policy on poverty. The index, which is based on the income and price elasticities of poverty, measures the impact of fiscal policy on both prices and income components and reflects a country's consumption patterns. While the pro-poor index for income components can be used to assess government expenditure policy, the index for prices can be useful in evaluating the impact of indirect taxes and subsidies.

While the methodology introduced in this chapter is able to provide some important policy implications, it also has several limitations. First of all, since our analysis is carried out at the margin, in some cases it may not account for the full impacts of tax policies and public spending. Nevertheless, the impact at the margin would provide a fairly good idea of the distributional and poverty impact of any shift in policy, and would thus be informative enough to guide policies. Another limitation of the study is that it does not account for externalities stemming from public policies or other indirect effects. This limitation is largely due to the fact that in practice externalities are not easy to observe, much less satisfactorily estimate using survey data.

Notes

1 Note that in this case expressing the demand equations in the form of $q = q(x)$ is not meant to imply that all own-price and cross-price elasticities of demand are zero. This merely implies that prices do not vary across individuals.
2 $CV = [e(u, p^*) - e(u, p)]$ is the compensation variation, or the compensation that should be given to an individual to maintain his or her utility at the same level as before the price change.

6 A new approach to evaluating and designing targeted social protection

Measurement of targeting performance

The main objective of targeted government intervention is to reduce the deprivation suffered by the poor, who may suffer from poor health, chronic unemployment, or low levels of education, and many other kinds of deprivations. Projects or programs may be designed so that the poor get greater access to various government services, but the main binding constraint in designing such targeted programs is identifying the genuine poor. If we have information on incomes or expenditures of individual families, then we can easily assess their poverty by comparing their income or expenditure against a predetermined poverty line. Such detailed information and administrative ability to use it are not present in most developing countries (Haddad and Kanbur 1991). But despite the absence of such information, targeted program methods have been implemented to reach the poorest and most vulnerable members of society.

The number of targeted programs has increased in developing countries.[1] Coady, Grosh, and Hoddinott (2004) have listed 85 targeted programs in 36 countries. As these programs follow different procedures to identify beneficiaries, it is important to know how well different programs perform. Most of these social assistance programs have the sole objective of reducing poverty; thus, measurements of targeting efficiency should be closely related to this objective of poverty reduction. Not only should social assistance programs reach the poor, but they should also cover enough of the poor to actually have an impact on poverty while not wasting resources on other policy priorities. Thus, an ideal targeted program will cover all the poor and benefit only the poor, thereby maximizing its impacts on poverty reduction.

Many measures of targeting efficiency have been devised in the literature. In a recent paper, Ravallion (2009) provides a synthesis of almost all the measures proposed so far. The main message of his paper is that all the targeting measures are quite uninformative regarding their poverty impacts. In this chapter, however, we demonstrate that most of the targeting measures are closely linked with poverty reduction. This linkage is established through the poverty gap ratio, which measures the amount by which households (or individuals) are poor as well as the number of households that are poor.

Targeting efficiency is mainly concerned with the selection of beneficiaries in the program. Since targeted programs are usually not based on the actual incomes or expenditures of households, there is the danger of committing two types of error in the process of selecting beneficiaries. Type I error occurs when someone who deserves the benefits is denied them, and Type II when benefits are paid to someone who does not deserve them. Often, these two types of errors move in opposite directions: attempts to reduce Type II errors lead to an increase in Type I errors.

To tackle this problem, we derive a new targeting indicator, which is a function of four factors: percent of poor targeted by the program, percent of population that can be covered by the program, Type I errors, and Type II errors. The indicator is derived using Cramer's *phi* statistic, which measures the association between the poverty status of households or individuals and the selection of beneficiary households or individuals. The higher the value of this indicator, the better the targeting ability of the program. The indicator has also been shown to be closely linked with poverty reduction.

On the issue of coverage, a program is said to be mismatched if the number of beneficiaries is not equal to the number of poor people in the population. Although this issue is distinct from the targeting issue mentioned above, it informs us about the program's efficiency and impacts on poverty reduction: too many beneficiaries means resources are being wasted and too few means poverty impacts are minimal. Most targeted programs suffer from a severe mismatch that reduces the targeting power of the programs—even if we have perfect information about the poor, the program can still suffer from a mismatch if by design not all the poor can be reached. In practice, however, the issue of mismatch is somehow ignored. In this chapter, we develop an indicator of mismatch that informs us about the extent to which the mismatch reduces targeting efficiency. The issue of mismatch should be tackled right at the design stage of any program.

A proxy means-testing, which is now widely used in developing countries, enables us to identify beneficiaries on the basis of easily identifiable variables that accurately predict a household to be in poverty. A nationally representative household survey makes it possible to conduct such a proxy means-test. In this chapter, we illustrate how the new targeting indicator developed here can be used to design a targeted program. Data from the Philippines' Family Income and Expenditure Survey conducted in 2006 will be used to illustrate this capability.

The first step in designing a proxy means-testing is to identify a set of variables that are highly correlated with the poverty status of households. These selected variables must be easy to measure but at the same time should be able to predict with reasonable accuracy whether or not a household is poor. To accomplish this, we have developed a formula to calculate the correlation coefficient between any proxy variable with the poverty status of households. This correlation coefficient helps to identify the proxy variables.

We have also used this methodology to evaluate the targeting efficiency of three large-scale social protection programs: *Bolsa Familia* in Brazil, *Di Bao* in the People's Republic of China (PRC), and *Progresa* in Mexico. These programs have very complex procedures for targeting the poor, and each program has two or three stages of selecting the beneficiaries. The administrative costs of selecting beneficiaries can be very high because of their complex criteria. More importantly, the programs suffer from severe mismatch. The proxy means-test developed here based on the Philippines data is relatively very simple and does not suffer from mismatch and at the same time has much better targeting efficiency.

Deriving the targeting indicator

Suppose N is the total population of households, and among them N_p are poor, then the head-count ratio of poverty is given by

$$H = \frac{N_p}{N} \tag{6.1}$$

Suppose that N_b are the households who benefit from the program, then the probability of selecting a beneficiary household is given by

$$B = \frac{N_b}{N} \tag{6.2}$$

If we had perfect information about the poor, then all beneficiaries of the program would be poor; however, we know that this is not the case in practice. Suppose among N_b beneficiaries, N_{bp} are poor and the remaining $(N_b - N_{bp})$ are the non-poor beneficiaries. The probability of selecting a beneficiary among the poor is given by

$$B_p = \frac{N_{bp}}{N_p} \tag{6.3}$$

Similarly, the probability of selecting a beneficiary among the non-poor is given by

$$B_n = \frac{(N_b - N_{bp})}{N - N_p} \tag{6.4}$$

If there is no association between the actual poor and selection of a beneficiary, such as when beneficiaries are randomly selected from the population, then the probability of selecting a beneficiary from among the poor must be equal to the probability of selecting a beneficiary from among the non-poor, or $B_p = B_n$. This situation may be characterized as having no information as to who the poor are, so everyone has the same probability of being selected into the program. Conversely, a program can be classified as pro-poor if the probability of selecting a beneficiary among the poor is greater than that among the non-poor, that is, when $B_p - B_n > 0$.

However, proxy means-testing can never identify the poor perfectly because two kinds of errors are committed. Type I error is defined as the probability of not selecting a poor household as beneficiary[2] and can be written as

$$\alpha = (1 - B_p) \tag{6.5}$$

Type II error is the probability of selecting a non-poor household as beneficiary and can be expressed as

$$\beta = B_n \tag{6.6}$$

which gives

$$(1 - \alpha - \beta) = B_p - B_n \tag{6.7}$$

A good social assistance program should be designed so that it is pro-poor, that is, the poor are more likely to be selected into the program than the non-poor. The degree of pro-poorness can be measured by how much higher the probability is of selecting a poor person for the program is to the probability of selecting a non-poor person for the program, which is measured by $(B_p - B_n)$. Thus, the efficiency of the proxy means-testing can be measured by the magnitude of $(1 - \alpha - B)$.

We can measure the association between poverty status and selection of beneficiaries by Cramer's *phi* statistic as

$$\varphi = (1 - \alpha - B)\sqrt{\frac{H(1 - H)}{B(1 - B)}} \tag{6.8}$$

When $\varphi = 0$, the statistic implies that there is no association between poverty and selection of beneficiaries, that is, the poor are as likely to be selected in the program as the non-poor. It can be seen that $N\varphi^2$ is distributed as a χ^2 distribution with one degree of freedom. This result allows us to test the null hypothesis of no association between poverty status and selection of beneficiaries.

The larger the value of φ, the greater the association between poverty status and selection of beneficiaries will be. As we showed above, this statistic is also related to the degree of pro-poorness of the program; the larger the φ, the greater the pro-poorness of the program. In the case of perfect targeting, all the poor are selected as beneficiaries and all non-poor are completely left out, which can happen only when $\alpha = 0$, $\beta = 0$ and $B = H$, which from equation (6.8) gives us $\varphi = 1$. Conversely, in the case of perfect "anti-poor" targeting, where all the poor are left out of the program and all non-poor are included (i.e., $\alpha = 1$, $\beta = 1$ and $B = 1 - H$), then $\varphi = -1$. Thus, our proposed targeting indicator, φ, lies between -1 and $+1$, and its magnitude gives an indication of how good a given program is in targeting the poor. Any program that gives negative values of φ should not be implemented because it is anti-poor (i.e., the poor have lesser chance of being selected than the non-poor). On the other hand, φ^2 is similar to the coefficient of determination in regression analysis: proportion of total variation that is explained by the proxy means-test. In designing a program, we should aim to maximize φ^2.

Mismatch between beneficiary and poor households

As can be seen in equation (6.8), targeting efficiency is not only dependent on the likelihood of Type I and II errors, but also on the scope and coverage of the program (i.e., B and H). Why is this so? If $B < H$, we are likely to exclude more poor and also more non-poor households from the program because of under-capacity, which implies higher Type I error and lower Type II error. On the other hand, if $B > H$, we are likely to include more of both poor and non-poor households in the program because of over-capacity, resulting in lower Type I error and higher Type II error. However, in almost all targeted programs we have encountered, B is never equal to H. An important implication of this is that even if we have perfect information on which household is poor and which is not poor, the two types of errors can never be eliminated. In other words, we can never have perfect targeting if B is not equal to H.

If there is no mismatch and if we have perfect information about households' poverty status, we will naturally ensure that all poor households are included in the program and all non-poor households are excluded, which implies $\alpha = 0$ and $\beta = 0$, which on substituting in equation (6.8) gives us $\varphi = 1$. Thus, we will have a perfect correlation between poor and beneficiary households. This is the ideal situation. The targeting efficiency of a program can thus be judged by how far below its φ value is from 1. For instance, if $\varphi = 0.4$, this suggests that the program is 40% efficient in targeting the poor. When there is no mismatch, the targeting indicator in equation (6.8) is given by

$$\varphi = 1 - \alpha - \beta \tag{6.9}$$

which coincidentally is the targeting differential measure proposed by Ravallion (2000). His measure thus informs us how high the probability of selecting poor households in the program is over that of the non-poor households. However, this measure is only suitable for ranking programs that have no mismatch, that is, if the number of beneficiary households is exactly equal to the number of poor households. Most targeting programs in developing countries do not meet this condition.[3]

Given that mismatch is so common, it is important to assess its impact in designing a targeted program. We have two kinds of mismatch. The most common mismatch is when $B < H$. The cost of any targeted program depends on what proportion of beneficiary households are included in the program; the larger B is, the greater the cost of the program will be. Most governments in developing countries have limited budgets, so there is always a tendency to design programs that have B as small as possible. Suppose that we have perfect information on the poverty status of households, all beneficiaries will then be among the poor households so that Type II error (β) will be equal to 0. Type I error will occur because the program does not include all poor households; hence $\alpha = (H - B)/H$, which on substituting in equation (6.8) gives the upper limit of φ as

$$\varphi_u = \sqrt{\frac{B(1-H)}{H(1-B)}} \quad \text{if} \quad B < H \tag{6.10}$$

A mismatch may also occur when $B > H$. If we have perfect information, this mismatch implies that $\alpha = 0$ and $\beta = (B - H)/(1 - H)$, which on substituting in (6.8) gives the upper limit for φ as

$$\varphi_u = \sqrt{\frac{H(1-B)}{B(1-H)}} \quad \text{if} \quad B > H \tag{6.11}$$

The expression $\varphi_m = 1 - \varphi_u \leq 1$ is the measure of mismatch; the larger (smaller) the value, the larger (smaller) the mismatch and $\varphi_m = 0$ when $B = H$, that is, there is no mismatch.

Every targeted program has a decision rule that distinguishes a poor household from a non-poor household. The targeting efficiency of a program should be judged on the basis of how effective the decision rule is. If we have perfect information about the poverty status of households, the decision rule will be able to pick only the poor households for inclusion in the program. In practice we do not possess perfect information on households' poverty status, so we judge the targeting efficiency of a program by measuring how far below the targeting indicator is from the counterfactual situation of having the perfect information. Equations (6.10) and (6.11) give the upper limits of the targeting indicator under perfect information. We can thus define the targeting efficiency of a program as the ratio of targeting indicator, φ, to its upper limit φ_u as defined in equations (6.10) and (6.11):

$$\varphi^* = \frac{(1-\alpha-\beta)H}{B} \quad \text{if} \quad B < H$$

$$= \frac{(1-\alpha-\beta)(1-H)}{(1-B)} \quad \text{if} \quad B > H \tag{6.12}$$

Therefore, the targeting indicator can be written as product of two components:

$$\varphi = \varphi^*(1 - \varphi_m) \tag{6.13}$$

This decomposition allows us to determine how effective a program is in identifying the poor, and how much the mismatch is in the program.

It will be useful to explain the idea of mismatch with an example. We have taken a hypothetical example of two programs operating in two cities, which is discussed by Ravallion (2009). In city A, 50% of the population is poor but the program has selected only the poorest 20% as beneficiaries. In city B, 10% of the population is poor but the program has selected the poorest 40% of the population as beneficiaries. City A has 20% beneficiaries but 50% poor, whereas city B has 40% beneficiaries but only 10% poor. It is quite obvious that both programs have severe mismatch problems. Given this information, the measure of mismatch gives the values of 0.50 for city A and 0.59 for city B. Thus, both cities have severe mismatches, even more so in city B.

There would not have been any mismatch if the program in city A had chosen 50% beneficiaries, whereas in city B, only 10% beneficiaries would have been sufficient. Further, in city A, 40% of the poor are selected as beneficiaries, whereas in city B, 100% of the poor are selected as beneficiaries. The target indicator is calculated as 0.50 in city A and 0.41 in city B, which means the program in city A is better targeted than in city B, even though 100% poor are covered by the program in city B. The targeting efficiency in both cities is computed to be equal to 1. This is the result we expected to obtain because in both cities, we have perfect information about the poverty status of individuals, that is, which household belonged to which percentile. Thus, even if we have perfect information on the poor, we can have a poorly designed program if the number of beneficiaries is not in line with the number of the poor. In practice, the issue of mismatch is somehow ignored, yet this example demonstrates it should not be. It should be addressed right at the design stage of any program.

Linkage with poverty reduction

In this section, we attempt to link the targeting indicator developed above with poverty reduction. Many poverty measures that reflect the different facets of poverty exist in the literature. In designing a targeted program, we have to choose a poverty measure with which the program should be linked. The head-count ratio is a crude measure of poverty because it completely ignores the gap in incomes from the poverty line. The poverty gap ratio, which is adopted here, is more attractive because it measures the amount by which households (or individuals) are poor, as well as the number of households that are poor.[4]

A social protection program may be defined as pro-poor if it provides greater absolute benefits to the poor compared to the non-poor. Obviously, with a given fixed cost, a pro-poor program will lead to greater poverty reduction than a non-pro-poor program. Using this framework, Kakwani and Son (2007) derived the pro-poor policy index for a wide range of poverty measures. Assuming that all beneficiaries receive exactly the same benefits from the program, the pro-poor policy index for the poverty gap ratio is obtained as

$$\delta = \frac{B_p}{B} \tag{6.14}$$

where B_p is the percentage of beneficiaries among the poor and B is the percentage of beneficiaries in the whole population. The program will be pro-poor if the percentage of beneficiaries among the poor is greater than that of beneficiaries in the whole population, or when $\delta > 1$. The larger the value of δ, the greater the degree of pro-poorness of the program will be.

Note that the value of δ does not depend on the size of the program in terms of its budget, which means that δ alone cannot tell us the poverty impact of different programs with different budgets. The magnitude of the reduction in the poverty gap ratio is fully captured by the product of H, B and δ, which means that for given values of B and H, the magnitude of poverty reduction has a positive monotonic relationship with δ; the larger the value of δ, the greater the poverty reduction will be.

The targeting indicator φ defined in equation (6.8) can also be written as

$$\varphi = (\delta - 1)\sqrt{\frac{HB}{(1-H)(1-B)}} \qquad (6.15)$$

which shows that given H and B, φ has a positive monotonic relationship with δ. Since δ has a positive monotonic relationship with poverty reduction, so will φ. Thus, our proposed targeting indicator is closely linked with poverty reduction: given H and B, the higher the value of φ, the greater the poverty reduction. From a policy perspective, it will be useful to consider poverty reduction per unit cost. This indicator is important because our objective is to maximize poverty reduction given a budget constraint. The reduction in poverty gap ratio per unit cost is captured by $\delta^* = H\delta$, which on substituting in equation (6.15) shows that for given H and B, φ has a positive monotonic relationship with δ^*; that is, the larger the value of φ, the greater the reduction in the poverty gap ratio, with fixed cost.

Evaluating welfare programs in three countries

Brazilian welfare programs

We apply our methodology to see how well different programs in Brazil are targeted. Brazil has many welfare programs, the largest of which is *Bolsa Escola*, which benefits 10.9% of the total population. All of Brazil's welfare programs together benefit about 22.6% of the total population. Note that these different programs are not mutually exclusive—some families may receive benefits from more than one program.

A striking feature of the Brazilian welfare system is that Type I error is very high and Type II error is very small. This means that programs are efficient with respect to preventing leakage to the non-poor, but as a consequence a large proportion of the poor is left out of these programs. Except for unemployment insurance, all programs are pro-poor; that is, the probability of selecting a poor person in the program is much higher than the probability of selecting a non-poor person in the program. This is indicated by the positive values of the targeting indicator (Table 6.1).

Table 6.1 Targeting efficiency of welfare programs in Brazil

Welfare program	Proportion of beneficiaries	Errors		Targeting indicator	Targeting efficiency	Mismatch index
		Type I	Type II			
Bolsa Familia	0.058	0.836	0.017	0.28	0.71	0.60
Fome Zero	0.020	0.940	0.005	0.18	0.76	0.77
Bolsa Alimentacao	0.015	0.960	0.005	0.13	0.64	0.80
Bolsa Escola	0.109	0.742	0.051	0.30	0.53	0.44
Peti-child labor	0.011	0.971	0.004	0.10	0.61	0.83
Unemployment insurance	0.015	0.991	0.017	−0.03	−0.16	0.80
Beneficio de Prestacao Continuada	0.018	0.962	0.010	0.09	0.44	0.79
Fuel subsidy	0.093	0.782	0.044	0.27	0.52	0.49
Other benefits	0.010	0.978	0.005	0.08	0.47	0.84
Proportion of poor	0.280					

Source: Author's calculations based on the Brazilian National Household Survey 2004.

Comparing different programs, we find that three programs—*Bolsa Familia, Bolsa Escola*,[5] and the fuel subsidy—stand out as the best targeted programs, with targeting indicators equal to 0.28, 0.30, and 0.27, respectively. The least efficient program is unemployment insurance, which is not even pro-poor. The *Beneficio de Prestacao Continuada* (BPC) is an unconditional cash transfer to the elderly or to extremely poor individuals with disabilities. Its targeting indicator value is only 0.09, so it cannot be regarded as a well-targeted program.

The maximum value of the targeting indicator for Brazil's welfare programs is 0.30, which means that the criteria used for identifying the poor explains only about 9% of the poor population; that is, other variables which cumulatively account for and can predict poverty in the population are not captured by the criteria. These results suggest that welfare programs in Brazil, despite their fame, are not well targeted. This, however, may be a misleading conclusion because it ignores the loss of predictive power of the programs due to mismatch.

Targeting efficiency is the product of the targeting and mismatch indicators (as in equation 6.13). The targeting indicator measures how well the decision rule identifies the poor population, or how far the actual situation is from the ideal of having perfect information about the poverty status of households. Mismatch, on the other hand, can occur even if we have perfect information. The targeting efficiency of *Bolsa Familia* is 0.71, which we regard as a reasonably good targeting system. The mismatch index is 0.6, which reduces the predictive power of targeting by about 60%. Thus, the major Brazilian welfare programs have reasonable targeting efficiency, but they suffer from severe mismatch between the number of poor who are the intended beneficiaries of the programs and the number of beneficiaries who are included in the programs.

Minimum Livelihood Guarantee Scheme in the People's Republic of China

The PRC's "Minimum Livelihood Guarantee Scheme," popularly known as *Di Bao*, is one of the largest social protection programs in the developing world. It was started in 1999 and has expanded rapidly. According to Ravallion (2009), the program covers 2.2 million people representing 6% of urban residents. Beneficiaries are determined on the basis of income reported by the persons seeking assistance. A person is included if his or her reported income is less than a stipulated "poverty line." Municipalities run the program, each locality determining its own poverty line. Although local authorities conduct eligibility checks, it is difficult to believe that potential beneficiaries do not underreport their incomes. Furthermore, Ravallion (2009) points out that local authorities have considerable power over the program, including setting the *Di Bao* poverty lines, funding, and implementation. This means that the process of selecting beneficiaries is subjective, which can cause horizontal inequity when the program is implemented at the national level. Suppose there are two persons, A and B, who belong to two different municipalities but have exactly the same standard of living. It is possible that person A is classified as poor and person B is classified as non-poor. This can happen because the two municipalities are not using exactly the same criteria for selecting beneficiaries and there is no consistency across the country.

Ravallion (2009) conducted a thorough evaluation of *Di Bao* using the PRC's Urban Household Short Survey for 2003–04, covering 35 of the country's largest cities with a total sample of 76,000. He concluded that targeting performance was excellent by international standards, and the program is a clear outlier in targeting performance internationally.

Across the 35 cities, 7.7% of the total population had a net income of less than the *Di Bao* poverty line. The percentage of beneficiaries among the poor was found to be only 29%, which means that 71% of the poor were excluded from the program. This figure does not suggest that the *Di Bao* can be considered an outlier in targeting performance internationally. However, the percentage of beneficiaries among the non-poor was only 1.83%, which is very small. Thus, the program has a high under-coverage rate but low leakage rate. The targeting indicator, φ, proposed here is calculated at 0.37, which falls well short of perfect targeting ($\varphi = 1$). Still, *Di Bao* performs better than Brazil's well-known *Bolsa Familia*, for which the value of φ is equal to 0.28. This result is surprising because the *Bolsa Familia* is based on sophisticated objective criteria to identify the beneficiaries, whereas *Di Bao* uses subjective judgments by municipalities. To explain this anomaly, we calculated the mismatch index for *Di Bao*, which was found to be 0.30, and which resulted in targeting efficiency of 0.53. The *Bolsa Familia*, on the other hand, has a much larger degree of mismatch, with an index value equal to 0.60.

The targeting efficiency of *Bolsa Familia* was calculated to be equal to 0.71 as against the value of 0.53 for *Di Bao*. Thus, *Bolsa Familia* has much greater power than *Di Bao* in identifying the beneficiaries, but suffers from a more severe mismatch. If *Bolsa Familia* had avoided a mismatch, it would have been much superior to *Di Bao*. Later in this chapter we will discuss how mismatches can be avoided.

Mexico's health, education, and nutrition program (Progresa)

Conditional cash transfer (CCT) programs are regarded as the modern way to reconcile safety nets (or more generally social protection policies) with investments in human capital among the poor. The basic idea behind these programs is that they reduce poverty in both the short and long run. Latin American countries such as Mexico and Brazil have been pioneers in implementing large-scale CCT programs. Mexico pioneered the first national CCT program in 1997, a comprehensive program on education, health, and nutrition, called *Progresa* (detailed discussions on CCTs are provided in Chapter 7). It is useful to evaluate the targeting efficiency of this program because it follows statistically rigorous methods of identifying the beneficiary households who are supposed to be extremely poor.

The selection of beneficiary households is accomplished in three stages. At the first stage, communities are selected using a marginality index based on census data. The marginality index was developed for each locality in Mexico using the method of principal components based on seven variables:

- Share of illiterate population aged 15 years or more
- Share of dwellings without running water
- Share of household dwellings without drainage
- Share of household dwellings without electricity
- Average number of occupants per room
- Share of dwellings with earthen floor
- Percentage of labor force working in agricultural sector

The marginality index was divided into five categories. It is not known how good these indicators are in identifying the poor localities. Ideally, we could rank the localities if we knew the percentage of poor households in each locality, but such information is not available. Skoufias, Davis, and Vega (2001) have attempted to assess the efficacy of selecting localities against consumption-based poverty maps, but these poverty maps are themselves subject to large errors and therefore we cannot properly assess how good the marginality index really is.

At the second stage, households are chosen within the selected communities. It involves a rather complicated procedure, which we do not need to discuss here. At the third stage, the communities are presented with a list of potential beneficiaries, and the final list is prepared. These three stages are so complicated we cannot assess the overall targeting efficiency of the program. We can, however, make an

Table 6.2 Targeting indicator at the second stage of selection by *Progresa*

	Percentage poor	*Percentage beneficiaries*	*Type I error*	*Type II error*	*Targeting indicator*	*Mismatch indicator*	*Targeting efficiency*
Progresa targeting	25	78	6.63	72.97	0.21	0.69	0.70
Progresa targeting	50	78	10.80	66.94	0.27	0.47	0.51
Progresa targeting	78	78	16.27	57.98	0.26	0.00	0.26
Locality-level targeting	78	78	18.96	67.28	0.14	0.00	0.14

Source: Skoufias et al. (2001).

assessment of the program at the second stage of selection using the information provided by Skoufias et al. (2001). They used the data collected by *Progresa* in 1997 for 24,077 households residing in a sample of 506 marginal communities. On average, 78% of the households in the sample were *Progresa* beneficiaries. Table 6.2 presents the results on targeting indicator using three poverty lines.

Type I error was 6.63% when extreme poverty of 25% was used, which means that 6.63% of extremely poor households were excluded by *Progresa*. As the poverty line increased, the exclusion error increased to 10.8% at the 50th percentile and 16.27% at the 78th percentile. On the other hand, Type II error was very high, which means that a large proportion of non-poor were included in the program. The targeting indicator has a value of only 0.21 for the extremely poor at the 25th percentile.

Compared to the other programs we have looked at, these results clearly indicate that *Progresa* has very poor targeting performance. The value of the targeting indicator when targeting is done at the local level using the marginality index is only 0.14. Thus, targeting is much more inferior at the local level. This should be qualified, however, because it provides only a partial assessment at the stage of selection among the households residing in the poorest communities.

Designing a social protection program

Income is difficult to measure in most low-income countries. Moreover, many households consume from their own production, which makes it difficult to use income as a measure for identifying poor households. A proxy means-test, which is now widely used in developing countries, enables us to identify beneficiaries on the basis of easily identifiable variables that accurately predict whether a household is poor. In this section, we design a hypothetical social protection program applying the proposed methodology above. To illustrate its applicability, we use household data from the Philippines to evaluate the design capabilities of our methodology.

Proxy variables

The first step in designing a proxy means-testing is to identify a set of variables that are highly correlated with the poverty status of households. These variables generally include household characteristics such as household composition, dwelling characteristics (e.g., type of roof, toilet, electricity connection, water supply, sanitation, etc.), households' labor force characteristics, land owned and operated, ownership of durables, and so on. The variables selected must be easy to observe and measure, but at the same time must be able to predict the poverty status of households with reasonable accuracy. To accomplish this objective, we should look at how a particular variable is correlated with poverty. Suppose, for instance, we believe that female-headed households have more severe poverty than male-headed households. Then we can choose female-headed households as one of the selection criteria in designing the program. This variable will be a good selection criterion if a large proportion of female-headed households are indeed poor.

Suppose B_j is the proportion of beneficiary households based on the jth proxy variable in the population, H is the proportion of poor households in the population, and B_j^p is the proportion of beneficiary households among the poor, then the correlation coefficient between the ith proxy variable and the poverty status of households is given by

$$\rho_j = \frac{(B_j^p - B_j)}{B_j} \sqrt{\frac{HB_j}{(1-H)(1-B_j)}} \tag{6.16}$$

Using the Philippines' 2006 Family Income and Expenditure Survey (FIES) and the official poverty line, we calculate that 24.23% of Philippine households are poor. In the whole country, 18.67% of households are female-headed, but only 10.6% of poor households. This means that poverty is less severe among the female-headed households than among male-headed households. Using equation (6.16), the correlation between female-headed households and the poverty status of households is calculated to be -0.12. From this result, we can conclude that a female-headed household is not a good proxy variable for poverty. On the other hand, variables related to the ownership of assets generally have high correlation coefficient. For instance, possession of television has a correlation coefficient of -0.44, which implies that poor households generally do not own a television. The proxy variables are generally determined on an ad-hoc basis, and the correlation coefficient given in equation (6.16) can be used to develop a set of proxy variables in a more objective way.

If the proxy variable is not a binary (i.e., dummy) variable, then the formula for the correlation coefficient in equation (6.16) will not be valid. Suppose the proxy variable Z_j is a continuous variable with mean μ_j and variance σ_j^2, then the correlation coefficient between Z_j and the poverty status of households will be given by

$$\rho_j = (\mu_j^p - \mu_j)\sqrt{\frac{H}{(1-H)\sigma_j^2}} \tag{6.17}$$

where μ_j^p is the mean of Z_j among the poor households.

The household size is often used as a proxy variable because generally poor households have a larger household size than non-poor households. In the case of the Philippines, we find that the average household size in the population is 4.82, whereas poor households have an average household size equal to 5.88. The correlation coefficient from equation (6.17) for household size is computed at 0.28, which is quite high and significant. Thus, household size can be regarded as a good proxy variable for poverty status.

The complete list of proxy variables along with their correlation with poverty is presented in Table A.6.1 in the Appendix. The correlations of the selected variables are all statistically significant.

The model used

Having determined the proxy variables, the next step is to combine them into a composite index that can be used as the basis for identifying beneficiary households. We should combine them in such a way that they provide the maximum probability of a household being identified as poor; the larger the probability, the better the targeting efficiency.

A household is defined as poor if its per-capita income is less than the per-capita poverty line. Suppose y_i^* is a variable that determines the poverty status of the ith household and can be determined by a set of k proxy variables, X_i, by means of the following model:

$$y_i^* = X_i\beta + \epsilon_i \tag{6.18}$$

where β is the vector of k coefficients and ϵ_i is the stochastic error term, which has 0 mean and constant variance. Although y_i^* is not observable, we can still relate it to the observed poverty status of ith households z_i (which takes value 1 if the ith household is poor, otherwise it takes value 0) defined as

$$z_i = 1 \text{ if } y_i^* > 0$$
$$= 0 \text{ if } y_i^* < 0 \tag{6.19}$$

It can be easily seen that $E(z_i) = \pi_i = P(z_i = 1) = P(y_i^* > 0)$ where π_i is the probability that the ith household is poor. Our objective is to estimate π_i based on k proxy variables. To do this we use the logit model:

$$\pi_i = \frac{e^{X_i\beta}}{1 + e^{X_i\beta}} \tag{6.20}$$

This model can be estimated using the maximum likelihood method. Table A.6.2 in the Appendix presents the estimates of the k coefficients in β. The table also gives the t-values, which indicate whether a given proxy variable is statistically significant. If the t-value is greater than 1.96, we can say that the proxy variable is statistically significant at the 5% level of significance. It is noted that the coefficients corresponding to almost all proxy variables are statistically significant. This means that the proxy variables chosen have a significant impact on determining the poverty status of households. By substituting the estimates of β from Table A.6.2 into equation (6.20), we obtain the estimate of each household's probability of being poor.

Decision rules

Having estimated each household's probability of being poor, we can now design a decision rule to determine which household should or should not be included in the program. We can have a decision rule where the ith household is a beneficiary for the program if its estimated probability of being poor, denoted by $\hat{\pi}_i$, is greater than π, which is an exogenously determined cutoff point. Suppose B is the percentage of beneficiary households selected by this decision rule. Obviously, B will depend on the value of π; the larger the value of π, the smaller B will be. Using the household survey data from the Philippines we obtained the proportion of beneficiaries among the households in the entire population and also among the poor for different values of π. The results are presented in Table 6.3.

Based on the official poverty line, 24.23% of Philippine households are poor. This program has been designed to target all these households. If $\pi = 0.8931$, the beneficiary households in the population are only 5%, which means there will be a high degree of mismatch. The percentage of beneficiaries among the poor and non-poor households is equal to 19.2 and 0.46, respectively, and the targeting indicator is 0.37 and mismatch index is 0.59.

Note that our objective is to maximize the targeting efficiency of the program. Figure 6.1 shows the targeting efficiency for different values of beneficiaries and shows an inverted U-shaped curve. Targeting efficiency achieves the maximum value of 0.63 when the percentage of beneficiaries is equal to the percentage of poor households in the population. At this point, the mismatch index is equal to zero and, obviously, targeting efficiency will then be equal to the targeting index, which is 0.63. This is the maximum degree of targeting we can achieve with the proxy variables selected in the design of this program. The percentage of beneficiaries for this program is 24.23, which is exactly equal to the percentage of target households. The percentage of beneficiaries among the poor is almost 72%, which means that 28% of the poor are left out of the program. The percentage of beneficiaries among the non-poor households is about 9%. Comparing the targeting efficiency of three major programs evaluated here we find that this program is far superior. For instance, the value of the targeting indicator for Brazil's *Bolsa Familia* was only 0.28 and for the PRC's *Di Bao* it was 0.37.

Table 6.3 Targeting indicator for different proportion of beneficiaries

Cutoff point for probability	Proportion of beneficiaries		Proportion of beneficiaries among non-poor	Targeting indicator	Mismatch index	Targeting efficiency
	in population	among poor				
0.8931	5	19.20	0.46	0.37	0.59	0.91
0.788	10	36.35	1.58	0.50	0.41	0.84
0.6682	15	51.01	3.48	0.57	0.26	0.77
0.5376	20	63.30	6.15	0.61	0.12	0.69
0.4293	24	71.94	8.98	0.63	0.00	0.63
0.3139	30	81.00	13.69	0.63	0.14	0.73
0.2282	35	87.03	18.36	0.62	0.23	0.80
0.1641	40	91.23	23.61	0.59	0.31	0.85
0.1191	45	94.29	29.24	0.56	0.37	0.90
0.084	50	96.56	35.11	0.53	0.43	0.93
0.0571	55	98.10	41.22	0.49	0.49	0.96
0.0384	60	99.00	47.53	0.45	0.54	0.97
0.0254	65	99.51	53.97	0.41	0.59	0.99
0.0162	70	99.72	60.50	0.37	0.63	0.99
0.0102	75	99.86	67.05	0.32	0.67	0.99
0.0057	80	99.95	73.62	0.28	0.72	1.00
0.003	85	99.98	80.21	0.24	0.76	1.00
0.0013	90	100.00	86.81	0.19	0.81	1.00
0.0003	95	100.00	93.40	0.13	0.87	1.00

Source: Author's calculations based on the Philippines' Household Income and Expenditure Survey (FIES) 2006.

Implementation

It should be noted that the well-known social assistance programs discussed above have very complex procedures for targeting the poor. Each program has two or three stages for selecting the beneficiaries, and the administrative costs of selecting beneficiaries can be very high because of complex eligibility criteria. In comparison, the proxy means-test developed here is very simple and at the same time has better targeting efficiency. We have used about 20 well-defined proxy variables, and the information required can easily be collected. One can then design a two-page questionnaire that seeks information from households that want to be included in the program. On the basis of this information, the decision rule developed here will indicate whether the household should be included in the program. The beneficiary households may be required to fill out this form every year so that the decision can be made as to whether the household should continue or cease to be in the program. To prevent potential exclusion errors caused by not assessing those who do not apply for assistance, the program could be widely advertised nationwide and within communities so that households who are in real need of assistance are not left out because of lack of awareness.

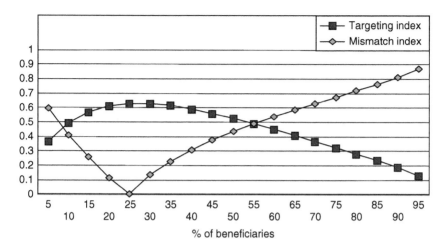

Figure 6.1 Targeting and mismatch indices.

The proxy means-test developed here targeted the poorest 24.23% of households because these are the households regarded as officially poor in the Philippines. To avoid a mismatch, the percentage of beneficiary households should also be 24.23%, which will require large resources that many governments in developing countries may not be able to afford. The proxy means-test developed could provide flexibility to the government with respect to the percentage of households that should be targeted. For instance, government resources might only allow targeting the bottom 10% of the poorest households. If so, the decision rule could then be designed to identify only the poorest 10% of households. Thus mismatch can be avoided by selecting the percent of target population equal to the percent of beneficiaries. This methodology would allow such flexibility.

Once the beneficiaries have been selected, the levels of payments should be determined so that we achieve a maximum reduction in poverty with given budget constraints. This can be achieved if payments are linked to meeting the minimum basic needs of households, which are determined by the poverty line. The rules governing payments can then be devised using the national household survey.

Community-based monitoring system

The community-based monitoring system is a poverty monitoring system that began in the Philippines in the early 1990s under the leadership of the Philippine Institute of Development Studies, and is now being implemented in 14 countries in Asia and Africa. It is becoming an increasingly important tool for fighting poverty.[6] It is an organized way of collecting ongoing or recurring information by communities, with its core indicators designed to capture multiple dimensions of poverty. The information collected is used by "local governments, national governments, non-governmental organizations and civil society for planning, budgeting, implementing local development programs as well as monitoring and evaluating their performance" (Reyes and Due 2009).

Using the proxy variables, one can design a short questionnaire that accurately gathers data for the proxy variables from the households. Communities can conduct this survey on a regular basis and may identify poor households using the decision rule as designed here. This procedure can also provide poverty maps that are comparable across the country. The communities can do some fine-tuning if there are obvious odd cases. Thus, one can have a community-based monitoring as well as targeting system that has greater consistency across the country.

Conclusion

This chapter has developed a new targeting indicator, which is a function of four factors:

- The percentage of poor targeted by the program
- The percentage of beneficiaries in the program
- Type I error: percentage of poor not included in the program
- Type II error: percentage of non-poor included in the program

The main objective of targeted social protection programs is to reduce poverty. Most national programs target households identified as poor on the basis of a certain poverty line. In order that no poor household is left out of the program, the percentage of beneficiary households must be at least equal to the percentage of poor households. However, each additional beneficiary in the program involves additional costs; thus, the poorer a country, the greater the program costs will be. As many governments cannot afford these, most social programs have a small proportion of beneficiaries relative to the target population. This creates a mismatch in the programs, which reduces the targeting efficiency of programs. This chapter has presented a mismatch index to measure the extent to which a mismatch reduces the targeting efficiency.

Regarding Type I and II errors, these do not move in the same direction: attempts to reduce Type II error lead to increased commitment of Type I error and *vice versa*. There is always a tradeoff. The targeting indicator derived here addresses this tradeoff by combining the two types of errors in a composite index. The indicator is derived using Cramer's *phi* statistic, which measures the association between poverty status of households or individuals and selection of beneficiary households or individuals: the higher the value of this indicator, the better the power of targeting. This indicator has been shown to be closely linked with poverty reduction. Our empirical illustration based on the Philippine data shows that the proposed targeting can be useful to designing a well-targeted program.

Computations on targeting efficiency show that three very popular social protection programs—*Bolsa Familia* in Brazil, *Di Bao* in the PRC, and *Progresa* in Mexico—suffer from severe mismatches, resulting in a huge loss of targeting efficiency. The issue of mismatch should be tackled, as suggested above, right at the design stage of any program. These well-known social assistance programs have very complex procedures for targeting the poor. Each program has two or three stages of selecting the beneficiaries, and the administrative costs of selecting beneficiaries can be very high because of complex eligibility criteria. The proxy means-test developed here is relatively simple and at the same time has better targeting efficiency. This chapter has shown that designing complex selection procedures does not guarantee higher targeting efficiency.

In many African countries, 50%–60% of the population lives in poverty, so governments cannot afford to target all the poor. The proxy means-test developed here could provide flexibility with respect to the percentage of households that should be targeted. For instance, government resources might only allow targeting of the bottom 10% of the poorest households. If so, the decision rule could then be designed to identify only the poorest 10% of the households. This methodology would allow such flexibility.

Using the proxy variables, one can design a short questionnaire that accurately provides information on households for proxy means-testing. Communities can conduct this survey on a regular basis and to identify poor households using the decision rule as designed here. This procedure, while carried out by communities, will provide poverty maps that are comparable across the country. Communities can also fine-tune in obviously odd cases. Thus, one can have a community-based monitoring as well as targeting system that has greater consistency across the country.

This chapter has covered a wide range of issues relating to evaluating and designing social protection programs in developing countries. It has developed simple techniques to tackle the complex targeting issues. Future work should look into applying these techniques to designing social protection programs in as many developing countries as possible.

Notes

1 For an extensive review of cross-country experiences in cash transfer programs, see Subbarao, Bonnerjee, Braithwaite, et al. (1997).
2 Some studies refer to this as Type II error (Ravallion 2009). According to the standard statistical literature, Type I error is the probability of rejecting a null hypothesis. If our null hypothesis is that a household selected is poor, then the probability of not selecting this household in the program should be Type I error. Thus, we are following the statistical convention in defining Type I and Type II errors.
3 An excellent discussion of targeted programs in developing countries is given in two books: (i) Coady, Gosh, and Hoddinott (2004) and (ii) Subbarao, Bonnerjee, Braithwaite, et al. (1997). It is interesting to note that almost all the programs synthesized in those books are mismatched.

4 There is a third measure called the severity of poverty, which has more attractive properties than the poverty gap ratio. However, this measure is somewhat more complex so we have chosen the poverty gap ratio.

5 *Bolsa Familia* is a new program that provides transfers to families with children. *Bolsa Escola* is an old program designed to enhance school attendance of children coming from poor families.

6 For an excellent description of community-based monitoring system see the recent book by Reyes and Due (2009).

Appendix

Table A.6.1 Correlation coefficients of proxy variables

Variables	Percentage of beneficiary in population	Percentage of beneficiary among poor	Correlation coefficient
Ownership of assets			
Television	69.6	33.5	−0.44
DVD/VCR	45.0	12.8	−0.37
Refrigerator	39.5	5.5	−0.39
Washing machine	29.6	2.6	−0.33
Air conditioner	7.1	0.2	−0.15
Car	6.9	0.3	−0.15
Telephone	52.7	15.6	−0.42
Computer	6.6	0.1	−0.15
Microwave	6.0	0.1	−0.14
Electricity	82.1	54.5	−0.41
Sanitary toilet facilities			
No toilet	9.0	21.9	0.26
Others	1.5	3.0	0.07
Open pit	4.9	11.3	0.17
Closed pit	8.9	15.2	0.13
Water sealed	75.8	48.7	−0.36
Household size			
Household size 1	3.9	0.7	−0.09
Household size 2	8.6	3.4	−0.11
Household size 3	14.0	6.7	−0.12
Household size 4	19.2	13.4	−0.08
Household size 5	18.9	19.1	0.00
household size 6	14.3	19.3	0.08
Household size more than 6	21.1	37.4	0.23
Age of household head			
less than 30	7.1	7.0	−0.00
30–39	22.6	28.6	0.08
40–49	27.0	30.2	0.04
50–59	21.6	17.6	−0.05
60+	21.7	16.5	−0.07

Continued

Table A.6.1 Cont'd

Variables	Percentage of beneficiary in population	Percentage of beneficiary among poor	Correlation coefficient
Education of household head			
Less than elementary	24.7	44.4	0.26
Elementary	18.9	25.5	0.10
High school incomplete	12.4	13.1	0.01
High school complete	21.8	13.0	−0.12
College incomplete	11.8	3.5	−0.14
Complete college	10.5	0.5	−0.18
Household headed by female	18.7	10.7	−0.12
Head not engaged in agriculture	75.8	44.5	−0.41
Urban households	49.6	20.2	−0.33
Dependency ratio	41.2	66.8	0.29
Percentage of poor households	24.2		

Source: Author's calculations.

Table A.6.2 Estimates of logit model

Variables	Coefficient	t-value
Ownership of assets		
Television	−0.534	−11.3
DVD/VCR	−0.438	−9.1
Refrigerator	−0.839	−14.4
Washing machine	−1.105	−14.1
Air conditioner	−0.752	−3.5
Car	−0.965	−4.1
Telephone	−0.940	−21.9
Computer	−1.377	−3.8
Microwave	−1.384	−3.3
Electricity	−0.320	−6.6
Sanitary toilet facilities (Ref. water sealed)		
No toilet	0.613	11.2
Others	0.305	2.6
Open pit	0.246	3.8
Closed pit	0.235	4.5

Continued

Table A.6.2 Cont'd

Variables	Coefficient	t-value
Household size (Ref. Household size 1)		
Household size 2	1.043	7.3
Household size 3	1.395	9.9
Household size 4	1.898	13.8
Household size 5	2.374	17.2
household size 6	2.888	20.3
Household size more than 6	3.437	24.4
Age of household head (years) (Ref. less than 30 years)		
30–39	0.079	1.1
40–49	0.193	2.7
50–59	0.218	2.8
60+	0.479	6.0
Education of household head (Ref. college completed)		
Less than elementary	1.669	10.7
Elementary	1.434	9.1
High school incompleted	1.276	8.1
High school completed	1.057	6.7
College incompleted	0.949	5.7
Household headed by female	−0.032	0.6
Head not engaged in agriculture	−0.690	−17.7
Urban households	−0.778	−19.2
Dependency ratio	2.263	14.0
Pseudo R^2	0.466	

Source: Author's calculations.

7 *Ex ante* impact of conditional cash transfer program on school attendance and poverty

Introduction

Conditional cash transfer (CCT) programs have been regarded as an effective way to reconcile safety nets—or more generally social assistance policies—with investments in human development benefitting the poor. Simply handing over cash to poor families will not be sufficient to tackle poverty in the long run. Hence, the idea is to transfer cash to the poor "on condition" that the poor will commit to empower themselves and help to bring future generations of poor families out of poverty.

CCT programs have been shown to be quite successful in Latin American countries. While there is no guarantee that the success of CCT programs in some countries can be replicated in others, the previous cases present a strong case for the effectiveness of CCT. The experiences learned in the various forms of CCT implemented by other countries provide an array of good practices from which other countries can learn. Alternatively, a good starting point from which to investigate CCT programs is to perform a detailed *ex ante* evaluation of the possible impact of such programs. However, one should always be aware that many relevant questions about the design of the program can only be answered by *ex post* impact evaluations.

An *ex ante* evaluation may help policymakers decide on key design elements of the CCT, such as the order of magnitude of the necessary transfers for the desired impact, and the targeted areas and population. It also offers an idea of the potential impact one can expect given the design of the program. This study aims to contribute in this area, offering a first approximation of the impacts of a CCT program on school attendance and poverty in the Philippines by exploring different budget scenarios and targeting strategies. This study is limited to demand aspects. Due to a lack of readily available information, we do not look into the availability and quality of schooling facilities. Therefore, we have no choice but to assume that supply-side constraints, including quality of schools, are already resolved.

The first section of this chapter is devoted to describing the CCT program in the Philippines, called *Pantawid Pamilyang Pilipino* (*PPP*). The second section presents the methodology for an *ex ante* simulation exercise. In section three, the empirical results are discussed.

The *Pantawid Pamilyang Pilipino* program

The *PPP* program has been running since January 2008 and was launched nationwide after going through a pilot program in June–December 2007. It is estimated that 300,000 households are currently targeted under the *PPP* program, which aims to provide money to extremely poor households to help family members meet government-set human development goals. Its prime focus is to build human capital—health/nutrition and education—of children aged below 15 years from the poorest families. In the Philippines, studies have found a strong correlation between low schooling and high malnutrition and poverty. The main objectives of the *PPP* program include (i) increasing enrollment/attendance of children at the elementary level, and (ii) reducing poverty.[1] This study evaluates the CCT program on these two objectives.

The targeting involves three steps. In the first step, the poorest 36 provinces are selected based on official poverty lines. Following this, the poorest municipalities from the selected provinces are further chosen using the small area estimation method. The second step involves the administration of total enumeration of households in identified municipalities. In the third step, the poorest households are finally selected using a proxy means-testing that assesses household socioeconomic characteristics such as ownership of assets, type of housing units, level of educational attainment of household head, and access to water and sanitation facilities. The poorest households with children aged 6–14 years qualify for the *PPP* program provided that their children are enrolled in schools and regularly attend classes. The minimum school attendance rate is 85% and schools are supposed to report the attendance rate of program beneficiaries to the respective municipal governments. The monthly benefit is 300 pesos (P) per child attending school for 10 months, up to a maximum of three children per household. Transfers are generally handed to the most responsible adult in the household, and are credited to the cash card facility of the Land Bank of the Philippines. According to the experience of the *Bolsa Escola* in Brazil, the presence of banking facilities such as magnetic cards greatly facilitates the monitoring of the whole program.

In addition to the education component, the *PPP* program also has a health component, under which the selected households are given cash grants on the condition that (i) pregnant women get prenatal care starting from the first trimester and get postnatal care thereafter; (ii) childbirth is attended by a skilled/trained professional; (iii) parents/guardians attend family planning sessions/mother's class, parent effectiveness service, and other services; and (iv) children under 5 years old get regular preventive health check-ups and vaccines. The health package provides a beneficiary household with P6,000 per year. In this study we have not considered the impact of the health component of the *PPP* program on health and nutritional status, due mainly to the unavailability of appropriate data.

Since the CCT program is relatively recent in the Philippines, it may be hard to estimate the total costs of administrating the program. Yet, the CCT programs are not inexpensive to administer, particularly during the initial period of implementation. Much of the budget is spent on undertaking the targeting of transfers and monitoring the recipients' actions. However, administrative costs will spread over the implementation of the programs, and their ratio to total transfers is expected to fall rapidly over the years.

To reduce administrative costs, program designers may opt to reduce expenditures on targeting. Yet, severely weakened targeting performance may result in large leakage of benefits to the non-poor, and thus may endanger achieving the prime objective of the program. The importance of targeting should not be overlooked for the *PPP* program, which targets the poorest of the poor. In addition, monitoring conditionality is part of the administrative costs of implementing a CCT program. Of the total administrative costs of CCT programs, about 9% was devoted to monitoring in Honduras, and roughly 2% in Mexico. Determining optimal levels of resources to monitor conditionality is a difficult task, and will vary with local circumstances.

To illustrate the magnitude of administrative costs, the experiences of *Progresa* and *Bolsa Escola* could be useful. In Mexico, during the first year of implementation of the *Progresa* in 1997, the cost of targeting represented 65% of the total cost of the program, followed by monitoring at 8%, and actual delivery of transfers at 8% of the total. By 2000, the major component was the actual transfers (41%), followed by monitoring of conditionality (24%), then targeting costs (down to 11%).

Methodology

Conceptual framework

In this chapter it is assumed that the decision to send children to school is made through the household decision process. The analysis here is based on three alternative choices. Let C_i be a qualitative variable representing the alternative choice made for a child in the ith household such that:

$C_i = 1$ if the child does not attend school
$C_i = 2$ if the child goes to school and also works in the labor market
$C_i = 3$ if the child goes to school but does not work in the labor market

When $C_i = 3$, it does not preclude the possibility that the child makes a contribution to unpaid domestic work at home. We make an assumption that the variable C_i is determined on the basis of household socioeconomic and demographic circumstances. However, we do not account for how decisions about these occupational choices are made within households. There can be cultural factors that determine whether or not a child should study full-time or part-time, or not study at all. We focus only on some observable factors that are likely to impact on household behavior regarding children's education.

It is further assumed that the household decision to send children to school (C_i) is made based on a utility function that is determined by household socioeconomic and demographic characteristics. Suppose u_{ij} is the utility of the ith household when it makes a choice that $C_i = j$, where j varies from 1 to 3. A household makes a choice on the basis of maximum utility it derives from that choice. For instance, the ith household will choose $C_i = 2$ in preference to $C_i = 1$ if $u_{i2} > u_{i1}$.

The utility function depends on a number of factors including characteristics of children such as age, gender, previous schooling, and their potential earnings. Certain household characteristics also influence the utility function, including age and gender of the household head, education of parents, household size and composition, and presence of younger siblings in the household. We can put all these variables together into a row vector z_i.

The most important variable that affects the occupational choice of a child is the household income, which is the sum of household income (net of the child's earnings) and the child's potential income. Suppose X_i is the household income (without the child's earnings) and x_i is the potential income of the child. Accordingly, the household choice will depend on the sum ($X_i + x_i$). Therefore, the utility function of the ith household making the jth choice can be written as

$$u_{ij} = z_i \gamma_j + (X_i + x_i)\alpha_j + e_{ij} \qquad (7.1)$$

The potential child contribution to the household income, denoted by x_i, is an important variable that determines the household decision about child occupational choice. This contribution depends on how much he/she can earn in the labor market and also how much he/she can contribute to household domestic work. The child contribution to domestic work is not known, and needs to be imputed. The imputation of the monetary value of domestic work has many pitfalls and requires strong assumptions. We have used the following methodology.[2]

Suppose w_i is the actual earning of the child in the ith household and A_i is a row vector of the child characteristic. Following the Becker–Mincer human capital model, the earnings function is estimated by

$$\log(w_i) = A_i \delta + D_i m + \varepsilon_i \qquad (7.2)$$

where D_i is a dummy variable that takes the value 1 when $C_i = 2$, and 0 otherwise (i.e., when $C_i = 1$). Note that children who are studying full-time and not working in the labor market—for which $C_i = 3$—have been excluded because they do not earn any income in the labor market. Further note that the parameter m is expected to be negative because with given individual characteristics of the child (A_i), a child who is studying and working is expected to earn less than a child who is not studying but only working. This implies $M = \exp(m) < 1$.

The potential earnings of a child are determined by the expected or predicted value of w_i obtained from equation (7.2), which gives us the following:

$$\hat{w}_i = \exp(A_i\hat{\delta}) \quad \text{if} \quad C_i = 1$$
$$= \hat{M} \exp(A_i\hat{\delta}) \quad \text{if} \quad C_i = 2$$
$$= K \exp(A_i\hat{\delta}) \quad \text{if} \quad C_i = 3 \tag{7.3}$$

where $\hat{M} = \exp(\hat{m})$. For $C_i = 3$, while a child is studying full-time and not working in the labor market, he/she may be performing domestic work. Given the individual characteristic vector A_i, the child has the potential to earn $\exp(A_i\delta)$ income if he/she is working in the labor market. Since the child is performing only domestic work, his/her domestic work is assumed to be valued at $K \exp(A_i\delta)$, where K is greater than 0 but less than 1.

Substituting $x_i = \hat{w}_i$ from equation (7.3) into (7.1) gives

$$u_{ij} = z_i\gamma_j + X_i\alpha_j + \hat{x}_i\beta_j + e_{ij} \tag{7.4}$$

where

$$\hat{x}_i = \exp(A_i\delta), \quad \beta_1 = \alpha_1, \quad \beta_2 = \alpha_2 M \quad \text{and} \quad \beta_3 = \alpha_3 K \tag{7.5}$$

Equation (7.4) provides the utility of the ith household under different occupational choices made for its children. If the values of parameters α, β, γ and residuals are known, we can determine the household choices using equation (7.4).

Estimating the model

As mentioned earlier, the ith household will make a choice 2 in preference to choice 1 if $u_{i2} > u_{i1}$. Let us define a dummy variable $y_{i2} = 1$ if $u_{i2} > u_{i1}$, and 0 otherwise. Thus,

$$Pr(y_{i2} = 1) = Pr(u_{i2} > u_{i1}) = Pr[(e_{i1} - e_{i2}) < z_i(\gamma_2 - \gamma_1) + X_i(\alpha_2 - \alpha_1)$$
$$+ x_i(\beta_2 - \beta_1)]$$
$$= F[z_i(\gamma_2 - \gamma_1) + X_i(\alpha_2 - \alpha_1) + x_i(\beta_2 - \beta_1)] \tag{7.6}$$

where $F(\,.\,)$ is the probability distribution function. Similarly, if the ith household makes a choice 3, then we have

$$Pr(y_{i3} = 1) = Pr(u_{i3} > u_{i1}) = Pr[(e_{i1} - e_{i3}) < z_i(\gamma_3 - \gamma_1) + X_i(\alpha_3 - \alpha_1)$$
$$+ x_i(\beta_3 - \beta_1)]$$
$$= F[z_i(\gamma_3 - \gamma_1) + X_i(\alpha_3 - \alpha_1) + x_i(\beta_3 - \beta_1)] \tag{7.7}$$

Equations (7.6) and (7.7) imply that multinomial Logit estimation permits identification of only differences $(\gamma_j - \gamma_1)$, $(\alpha_j - \alpha_1)$, and $(\beta_j - \beta_1)$, where $j = 2$

and 3. We can also estimate the residuals $(e_{i1} - e_{i2})$ and $(e_{i1} - e_{i3})$. The choice 1 is assumed to be the reference choice. These equations provide links between the probability of a choice with the utility of the choice: the larger the $Pr(y_{ij} = 1)$, the greater the household utility u_{ij}. While utility cannot be measured directly, we can still say if the household utility would be maximized when the household makes a choice.

The following parameters can be estimated directly by applying a multinomial logit model to equations (7.6) and (7.7):

$$\hat{a}_2 = \alpha_2 - \alpha_1 \quad \text{and} \quad \hat{a}_3 = \alpha_3 - \alpha_1 \tag{7.8}$$

$$\hat{b}_2 = \beta_2 - \beta_1 \quad \text{and} \quad \hat{b}_3 = \beta_3 - \beta_1 \tag{7.9}$$

$$\hat{c}_2 = \gamma_2 - \gamma_1 \quad \text{and} \quad \hat{c}_3 = \gamma_3 - \gamma_1 \tag{7.10}$$

$$\hat{v}_{i2} = (e_{i2} - e_{i1}) \quad \text{and} \quad \hat{v}_{i3} = (e_{i3} - e_{i1}) \tag{7.11}$$

Using the equations (7.8) to (7.11) in conjunction with equations in (7.5) gives rise to $\hat{\alpha}_1 = (M\hat{a}_2 - \hat{b}_2)/(1 - M)$, $\hat{\alpha}_2 = (\hat{a}_2 - \hat{b}_2)/(1 - M)$, and $\hat{\alpha}_3 = \hat{a}_3 + \hat{\alpha}_1$. To perform various simulations, the estimates required are $\hat{\alpha}_1, \hat{\alpha}_2, \hat{\alpha}_3, \hat{b}_2, \hat{b}_3, \hat{c}_2, \hat{c}_3$, $\hat{v}_{i2}$ and $\hat{v}_{i3}$, which can be obtained from the above equations.

Simulations

Having estimated the model, we can now perform alternative simulations using the utility function given in equation (7.4). Given that a household makes its three alternative choices based on the utility function, we can write the following:

$$u_{i1} = z_i \hat{\gamma}_1 + X_i \hat{\alpha}_1 + \hat{x}_i \hat{\beta}_1 + \hat{e}_{i1}$$

$$u_{i2} = z_i \hat{\gamma}_2 + X_i \hat{\alpha}_2 + \hat{x}_i \hat{\beta}_2 + \hat{e}_{i2}$$

$$u_{i3} = z_i \hat{\gamma}_3 + X_i \hat{\alpha}_3 + \hat{x}_i \hat{\beta}_3 + \hat{e}_{i3}$$

The ith household will choose j if the utility obtained from this choice is greater than that obtained from other choices:

$$C_i = 1 \quad \text{if} \quad u_{i1} > u_{i2} \quad \text{and} \quad u_{i1} > u_{i3}$$

$$C_i = 2 \quad \text{if} \quad u_{i2} > u_{i1} \quad \text{and} \quad u_{i2} > u_{i3}$$

$$C_i = 3 \quad \text{if} \quad u_{i3} > u_{i1} \quad \text{and} \quad u_{i3} > u_{i2}$$

Suppose we want to simulate the impact of giving transfer T to all children who are studying and also working in the labor market. The income of households with children studying and working in the labor market increases by amount T, which changes the utility u_{i2} to u_{i2}^*:

$$u_{i2}^* = z_i \hat{\gamma}_2 + (X_i + T)\hat{\alpha}_2 + \hat{x}_i \hat{\beta}_2 + \hat{e}_{i2}$$

With this policy, all households will change their behavior and make new choices denoted by C_i^* in such a way that

$$C_i^* = 1 \text{ if } u_{i1} > u_{i2}^* \text{ and } u_{i1} > u_{i3}$$

$$C_i^* = 2 \text{ if } u_{i2}^* > u_{i1} \text{ and } u_{i2}^* > u_{i3}$$

$$C_i^* = 3 \text{ if } u_{i3} > u_{i1} \text{ and } u_{i3} > u_{i2}^*$$

Using this methodology, any simulation scenario can be evaluated. This methodology can also be used to simulate the impact of means testing, that is, giving transfers only to poor households and not to non-poor ones.

Empirical illustration

The methodology outlined above is applied to the Philippines. For this purpose, we have used the latest Annual Poverty Indicators Survey (APIS) conducted in 2004, obtained from the National Statistical Office in Manila. The APIS is a nationwide survey designed to provide poverty indicators at the provincial level. This household survey is micro-unit recorded.

The APIS gathers information on various aspects of well-being for all of the Philippines' 78 provinces, including the cities and municipalities of Metro Manila. It provides detailed information on the following: demographic and economic characteristics; health status and education of family members; awareness and use of family planning methods; housing, water, and sanitation conditions of families; availability of credit to finance family business or enterprise; and family income and expenditures. The 2004 APIS collected these data from more than 38,000 households and 190,000 individuals across the country.

In defining the poor, we have used the official poverty lines of the Philippines at the provincial level.[3] If per-capita household expenditure/income is less (greater) than the poverty threshold, all members living in the household are classified as poor (non-poor).

A profile of the children

Children in elementary and secondary school age, that is, from 6 to 14 years old, make up almost 25% of the total population in the Philippines. Out of about 20 million children in this age group, 2 million—equivalent to 10%—fail to attend school. The pattern in the proportion of children not attending school by age exhibits a U-shaped curve, falling from age 6 to 8, holding steady from age 8 to 11, and then rising sharply afterward (Figure 7.1). While the same pattern emerges for poor children, the proportion of children outside school is greater than the average. More importantly, a greater proportion of children at the secondary school age group (i.e., 12–15 years old) stay out of school than their younger cohorts. This finding suggests that opportunity costs of sending children to school are higher at the secondary than the elementary level. This also implies that financial

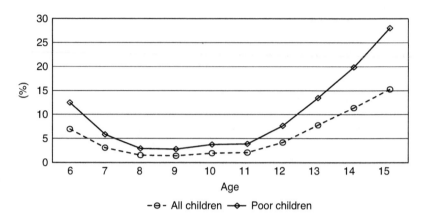

Figure 7.1 Percentage of children not attending school in the Philippines.
Source: Author's estimates.

incentives such as CCTs could be more effective for targeting older children if the main objective be to improve school enrollment.

Interestingly, the Philippines' elementary education system provides impressively wide access to children aged from 6 to 11 years. More than 94% of school-age children attended elementary school in 2004. However, the proportion of school attendance by children aged 12–15 years drops at the secondary level, that is, 84%. This stems from lack of personal interest (43%), affordability (27%), and employment (9%) as illustrated in Figure 7.2. At the elementary level, the main reason for not attending school is also lack of personal interest (30%). The lack of interest results, in turn, from a number of factors that discourage students from studying, including inadequate curriculum, unqualified teachers, lack of learning materials, parents' perception about schooling, and social and cultural barriers. Nevertheless, using household survey data and school data, there is little direct evidence in the Philippines of the impact of improved school quality on school enrollment.

We now look into poverty among children. Table 7.1 shows that the incidence of poverty among children aged below 15 years old is far higher than the national average (see also Figure 7.3). In particular, poverty is highest for the 6–11-year-old age group, almost 12 percentage points higher than the national average. Poverty among children aged 6–15 years accounts for more than 30% of aggregate poverty.

About 74% of children not attending school are found to be living below the national poverty threshold. This suggests that children are not attending school primarily due to their lack of resources to afford schooling, directly or indirectly, and/or due partly to supply-side factors such as unavailability of nearby schools. Therefore, assuming that supply-side concerns are properly dealt with, improving school attendance in the Philippines may require a good calibration of the amount

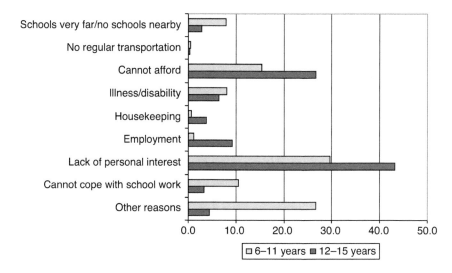

Figure 7.2 Reasons for not attending school among children aged 6–15 years in the
Philippines.

Source: Author's estimates.

Table 7.1 Percentage of poor by age group

Age group	Head-count ratio	Population share	% contribution to total poverty
Less than 5 years	45.4	13.8	17.8
6–11 years	46.9	15.1	20.2
12–15 years	41.6	9.8	11.6
16–24 years	29.6	16.2	13.7
25–59 years	29.4	38.3	32.1
More than 60 years	23.6	6.9	4.6
Total	35.1	100.0	100.0

Source: Author's estimates.

of resources transferred, and a well-crafted conditionality to effectively induce
children from low-income households to go to school.

Descriptive statistics and simulation results

Table 7.2 contains the basic description of the occupational structure of children
aged 6–15 years in the Philippines in 2004. In this age range, 90.6% of
children report that they dedicate themselves solely to studying. While 4%
both study and work, 5.5% do not attend school at all. This average pattern
hides considerable variation across ages: school attendance declines (and work

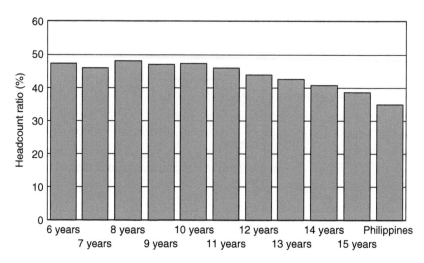

Figure 7.3 Poverty among children aged 6–15 years.
Source: Author's estimates.

increases) monotonically with age. Only 0.1% of 6-year-olds do not attend school because of working outside the home; the corresponding figure for 15-year-olds is 9.4%. In a similar context, 92.2% of 6-year-olds devote themselves only to studying, compared to 77.7% of 15-year-olds. These findings suggest greater opportunity costs incurred from attending school among older children.

Table 7.3 presents the mean individual and household characteristics of those children by different categories. Children not going to school are both older and less educated than those solely studying. Moreover, children not going to school are mostly male and also the eldest in a household than those currently enrolled. As expected, households with children not studying are on average poorer, less educated, male-headed, and larger than households with children currently attending school. Incidences of not studying and of engaging in child labor are relatively greater for households with older heads and located in the Visayas or Mindanao region.

Table 7.4 presents the results of the weighted least square estimation of the earnings function for the pooled sample.[4] In the model, an additional year of age increased earnings by about 18%. The coefficient for the dummy variable of studying and working reveals that if a child attends school and works at the same time, his/her average earnings are far less than earnings by a comparable child who is solely working outside the home. The results also reveal that education matters for higher earnings, and that if a child lives in the Visayas or Mindanao, his/her earnings are significantly less than the earnings of a comparable child living in Luzon.

Table 7.2 School attendance and occupation of children by age (%) in the Philippines

	Total	6 years	7 years	8 years	9 years	10 years	11 years	12 years	13 years	14 years	15 years
All children											
Not studying and working outside home	2.3	0.1	0.2	0.1	0.3	0.7	0.9	1.9	3.4	6.5	9.4
Not studying and working at home and others	3.2	6.9	3.0	1.4	1.2	1.3	1.3	2.4	4.4	5.0	6.0
Studying and working	4.0	0.8	1.1	1.7	2.5	3.7	4.6	5.7	5.8	7.5	7.0
Studying only	90.6	92.2	95.8	96.8	96.0	94.3	93.2	90.1	86.4	81.1	77.7
Total	100.0	100.0	100.0	100.0	100.0	100.0	100.0	100.0	100.0	100.0	100.0
Poor children											
Not studying and working outside home	3.9	0.2	0.3	0.3	0.6	1.3	1.6	3.5	6.3	8.6	17.7
Not studying and working at home and others	5.4	12.3	5.5	2.7	2.2	2.5	2.3	4.2	7.2	11.3	10.4
Studying and working	5.7	1.2	1.8	2.5	3.3	5.6	7.1	8.9	8.4	10.9	8.7
Studying only	85.0	86.3	92.4	94.5	93.9	90.6	89.0	83.4	78.1	69.2	63.2
Total	100.0	100.0	100.0	100.0	100.0	100.0	100.0	100.0	100.0	100.0	100.0

Source: Author's estimates.

Table 7.3 Sample means: characteristics of children and the household

	Total	Not studying	Working and studying	Studying
Child characteristics				
Age (years)	10.48	12.01	12.06	10.32
No formal education (%)	0.16	0.26	0.07	0.16
With elementary education (%)	0.66	0.64	0.65	0.66
With secondary education (%)	0.18	0.10	0.28	0.18
Male (%)	0.52	0.66	0.60	0.50
Oldest male (%)	0.25	0.42	0.35	0.24
Children's earnings (6 months)				
6–15 years old	3,853	5,297	2,159	–
12 years old	2,672	4,134	1,750	–
13 years old	2,912	3,606	2,121	–
14 years old	4,238	5,797	2,195	–
15 years old	5,183	6,073	3,294	–
Household characteristics				
Total income over 6 months (pesos)	69,835	36,321	42,746	72,770
Family size	5.66	6.24	5.99	5.61
Visayas (%)	0.20	0.23	0.30	0.20
Mindanao (%)	0.24	0.34	0.38	0.23
Luzon (%)	0.56	0.43	0.32	0.57
Age of head (years)	44.03	45.15	45.34	43.90
Gender of head (male) (%)	0.88	0.92	0.90	0.88
Head with no formal education (%)	0.03	0.09	0.03	0.02
Head with elementary education (%)	0.47	0.69	0.64	0.44
Head with secondary education (%)	0.37	0.19	0.27	0.38
Head with tertiary education (%)	0.13	0.03	0.06	0.16

Source: Author's estimates.

Table 7.4 Log earnings regression (children 6–15 years old reporting earnings)

	Coefficient	Robust std. error	P > |t|
Age	0.180*	0.026	0.0000
Studying and working	−0.957*	0.084	0.0000
Education at elementary	0.331	0.183	0.0710
Education at secondary	0.463*	0.209	0.0270
Male	0.115	0.080	0.1520
Visayas	−0.296*	0.092	0.0010
Mindanao	−0.531*	0.084	0.0000
Constant	5.395*	0.350	0.0000
R-squared = 0.309			

*statistically significant at 5%.

Source: Author's estimates.

The results from the estimation of the multinominal logit for occupational choice also appear eminently plausible, as reported in Table 7.5 for the pooled sample. The reference category is "not studying" ($j = 1$) throughout. As expected, household income (net of the child's earnings) has a positive effect on schooling, whereas the child's own predicted earnings have a negative effect. Household size reduces the probability of studying, compared to the reference category. Previous schooling at a given age has a positive effect. Gender has a significant effect on occupational choice, suggesting that a male child is more likely to choose the option of "studying and working" than the reference category, whereas a female child is more likely to opt for "solely studying" rather than "not studying". Parents' education has a positive effect on children's schooling, albeit decreasing at higher levels of education. Geographical location also has a significant effect on household decisions on children's schooling. Living in Mindanao reduces the probability of children solely studying, compared to the reference category.

The parameter M is estimated from taking an exponential of the estimated coefficient of the dummy variable "working and studying" in the earnings function among children. The results are presented in Table 7.4, where $M = \exp(m)$ and $m = -0.957$. The result suggests that the foregone income of children would be $1 - M$ or around 62% of their actual or potential market earnings if they attend school while working at the same time. This suggests that with transfer, we might expect no significant changes in the occupational choice from "not studying" to "working and studying" due to high opportunity costs involved in giving up working. Thus, the proportion of children choosing between "working and studying" to "studying only" would be small. In addition, the estimated parameters $\alpha_1 = 1.70$, $\alpha_2 = 1.71$, and $\alpha_3 = 1.72$ are marginal utilities of household income for three occupational categories. It is also of interest that the estimated marginal utilities from income at various categories are similar to each other. These estimates are used for the simulation to evaluate the impact of CCT on school attendance. The simulation results are discussed in the next section.

Ex ante *impact analysis of conditional cash transfer on school attendance and poverty*

Conditional cash transfers have dual objectives: (i) reducing poverty in the long run through the enhancement of capabilities obtained by the conditioning of the cash transfer, and (ii) reducing poverty in the short run through cash transfers. The main focus of this section is twofold. First, it develops a multi-logit model that explores the determinants of school attendance. Using this model, we simulate the impact of CCTs on school attendance. Second, it attempts to capture the impact of CCTs on poverty. The impact of different transfer amounts and different target populations on poverty reduction is evaluated. The cash transfers are given to families with school-age children. It must be recognized that all transfers given to families may not be spent solely on children. However, the household surveys do not provide any information on the distribution of resources within households.

Table 7.5 Multinomial logit coefficients

	Studying and working			Studying		
	Coefficient	Robust std. error	$P > \lvert z \rvert$	Coefficient	Robust std. error	$P > \lvert z \rvert$
Total household income net of children's ('000)	0.004	0.000	0.019	0.015	0.000	0.000
Potential children's earnings	−1.046	0.000	0.000	−0.973	0.000	0.000
Household size	−0.042	0.023	0.070	−0.111	0.016	0.000
Age of child	0.046	0.041	0.262	−0.268	0.028	0.000
Head with no formal education	−1.652	0.286	0.000	−1.822	0.181	0.000
Head with elementary	−0.593	0.203	0.004	−1.293	0.154	0.000
Head with secondary	−0.346	0.209	0.098	−0.628	0.158	0.000
Age of head	0.007	0.004	0.087	0.003	0.003	0.287
Gender of head (male)	−0.022	0.139	0.874	−0.124	0.095	0.191
Number of children below 6 years old	0.004	0.052	0.934	−0.066	0.034	0.051
Gender of child (male)	0.274	0.087	0.002	−0.170	0.062	0.006
Oldest and male child	−0.160	0.090	0.075	−0.150	0.068	0.027
Previous schooling at elementary	2.888	0.144	0.000	3.031	0.091	0.000
Previous schooling at secondary	5.416	0.207	0.000	5.722	0.150	0.000
Mindanao	−0.507	0.166	0.002	−1.183	0.105	0.000
Visayas	−0.052	0.133	0.696	−0.659	0.091	0.000
Constant	−0.639	0.377	0.090	6.975	0.261	0.000
Pseudo R-squared	0.195					

Estimates of parameters

M	0.384					
α_1	1.70					
α_2	1.71					
α_3	1.72					

Source: Author's estimates.

Table 7.6 Simulated effect of CCT on schooling and working status (when P300 is transferred to all children 6–15 years old)

	All households			
	Not studying	Work and study	Studying	Total
Not studying	26.81	36.03	37.16	5.81
Work and study		93.20	6.80	4.20
Studying			100	89.99
Total	1.56	6.01	92.44	100
	Poor households			
	Not Studying	Work and study	Studying	Total
Not studying	28.84	33.56	37.60	9.37
Work and study		92.31	7.69	5.72
Studying			100	84.92
Total	2.70	8.42	88.88	100

Source: Author's estimates.

In the simulation exercise, it is thus assumed that transfers given to children are pooled within families and distributed equally to members so that each member enjoys the same level of welfare.

Table 7.6 presents the transition matrix. It shows, with transfers, changes in the proportion of children moving from the reference choice to choices "studying and working" or "solely studying", and from "studying and working" to "solely studying". The results are a simulated counterfactual distribution of occupational choices based on the observed characteristics and the restrictions of residual terms for each child. The impact of the transfer will be evaluated by comparing the simulated results with the vector of occupational choices generated with the original before the transfer. The corresponding matrix is also shown in the table for all children 6–15 years old living in poor households. With the transfer of P300, Table 7.6 suggests that almost one in every three children aged 6–15 years who are currently not attending school would have enough incentive from the transfer to choose to go to school. Among them, about half would attend school, but also work outside the home. The other half would stop working to devote themselves to studying only. This would reduce the proportion of children not attending school from 5.81% to 1.56%. The impact on those currently studying and working is relatively small. About 6.8% of these children would choose to study only after abandoning their work outside the home.

As would be expected, the impacts are more pronounced when the targeted population for the program is children from poor households. The proportion of children aged 6–15 years in poor households is much higher than in non-poor households: 33% for the former and 22% for the latter. This is indeed consistent with an earlier finding that there are more children in poor households (Son 2008).

Table 7.6 also suggests that the proportion of children out of school is far higher among poor households: 9.37% instead of 5.81% for all households. More importantly, the results show that the CCT would be more effective in increasing school attendance among poor children. The simulation suggests that the program could increase school attendance among the poor by about 6.7 percentage points. Yet this improvement comes with a marginal increase in the proportion of children choosing the "working and studying" category.

A reduction of more than 60% in the proportion of poor children not attending school would be regarded as a substantial improvement. This is partly due to the fact that the current contributions of children attending school are quite significant in proportion to the potential earnings they would have earned in the labor market. This proportion is closely related to the estimated parameter M, which is equal to 0.384, as discussed earlier (see Table 7.5).

Our simulations suggest that the transfer of P300 per child per month, as currently formulated, would still leave more than 7.5% of children aged 6–15 years not solely studying in school. Thus, this motivates us to investigate alternative program parameters that can increase school attendance among children who are solely working instead of studying. This is, in fact, one of the main objectives of carrying out this type of *ex ante* evaluation exercise. Table 7.6 presents transition matrices with simulation results for alternative scenarios. The results are shown both for all children and separately for poor households only.

A few key findings emerge from Table 7.7. First, the results reveal that the impact of the program is responsive to the transfer amount in reducing the proportion of children outside school. Doubling the transfer from P100 to P200 reduces the percentage of unenrolled children from 44% to 37%. The proportion of children devoted only to studying rises steadily in response to increasing the transfers from P100 to P300. This does not come as a surprise because it is hard to improve school enrollment in a country like the Philippines, where the school enrollment rate is already high. Interestingly, the proportion of children in "work and study" increases (albeit falling slightly with the transfer amount) with the transfer. This is consistent with our earlier finding that the contribution of children's earnings to household welfare is quite large. As such, a significant proportion of children who are currently working only would enroll with the CCT program, but would choose to work at the same time. This suggests that the reasons for unenrollment are due not only to a lack of resources but also to household characteristics and the quality of schooling.

Second, it does matter to the reduction of unenrolled children whether a given transfer is uniform across ages or increases with the age of the child by 5%. Given the opportunity cost of attending school for older children, particularly at the secondary level, increasing the transfer amount progressively with the age of the child would seem a better option than uniform transfer. Similarly, targeting poor children is more sensitive to a reduction in the proportion of unenrolled children, compared with universal targeting with the same transfer amount. It should be noted, however, that there would be the administrative costs of identifying the poor, which would be part of the program costs. In the initial period of implementing

Table 7.7 Impact of conditional cash transfer (*T* in pesos) on school attendance

	Before transfer	After transfer					
	T = 0	*T = 100*	*T = 200*	*T = 300*			
				Universal	*Progressive transfer*	*Targeting poor*	*Targeting Mindanao*
All households							
Not studying	5.81	3.67	3.28	1.56	1.08	1.41	3.82
Work and study	4.20	6.21	6.12	6.01	5.99	5.26	4.79
Studying	89.99	90.11	90.60	92.44	92.93	93.33	91.39
Poor households							
Not studying	9.37	6.17	5.68	2.70	1.98	–	5.81
Work and study	5.72	8.76	8.61	8.42	8.39	7.98	6.69
Studying	84.92	85.07	85.71	88.88	89.63	92.02	87.50

Source: Author's estimates.

the program, the administrative costs could be substantial, but would decline over the period.

Third, conditionality plays a crucial role in inducing the change in household decisions on children's school enrollment. As can be seen in Table 7.8, there is a lack of correlation between the level of school attendance and the impact of the cash transfer. This suggests that a cash transfer program without conditionality is not enough to lead to a substantial increase in school attendance.

Using different simulation scenarios, we have attempted to quantify the impact of a transfer on poverty reduction at the national level. As for poverty simulation, it is assumed that transfers given to children are pooled within families and distributed to each member so that every member enjoys the same level of welfare. It is further assumed that all transfers received by families are spent on consumption goods. So the benefits received by the families are added to the family's total consumption expenditure which, on dividing by household size, gives per-capita family expenditure after the transfer. The new poverty estimates are derived using per-capita family expenditure after the transfer, which is then compared with the poverty estimates based on the family's per-capita expenditure before the transfer.

A few major findings emerge from Table 7.9. First, the transfer to school-age children has rather small impact on the head-count ratio, but its impact increases rapidly as we move to the poverty gap ratio and severity of poverty index. Since the severity of poverty gives greater weight to the poor who are living far below the poverty threshold, a larger reduction in this index suggests that the cash transfers have greater impact on poverty reduction among the ultra-poor than the poor. Thus, the impact of a CCT program should not be judged merely on the number of people that can be removed from conditions of poverty through the program. In fact, a CCT program provides greater financial relief to those who are still unable to escape poverty because the extra value of money is much greater for them. The head-count ratio is completely insensitive to any improvement in the standard of living of those who could not be removed from conditions of poverty by such CCT programs.

Second, targeting children from poor households leads to much greater poverty reduction at the national level as the per-capita benefits received by the poor recipients' families are likely to be higher under targeted programs than universal ones. Nevertheless, the total benefits of the transfer under the targeted programs will be partly offset by the administrative costs of identifying the poor. Another message emerging from the study is that the impact on poverty is generally greater if the transfer is given only to children living in Mindanao rather than to all children aged 6–15 years. This suggests that if targeting poor children is likely to create too much budgetary burden in terms of the administrative costs of identifying the targeted subjects, then targeting only Mindanao children is not an unfounded option in order to achieve a better outcome in poverty reduction relative to the universal program.

Third, our study suggests that the average pattern of outcomes of children not attending school exhibits a U-shaped curve, falling until 11 years old and then

Table 7.8 Impact of unconditional cash transfer (T in pesos) on school attendance

	Before transfer	After transfer						
	$T=0$	$T=100$	$T=200$	$T=300$				
				Universal	Progressive transfer	Targeting poor	Targeting Mindanao
All households							
Not studying	5.81	5.76	5.73	5.69	5.67	5.61	5.64
Work and study	4.20	4.13	4.07	4.00	4.00	3.96	4.10
Studying	89.99	90.10	90.20	90.31	90.33	90.43	90.26
Poor households							
Not studying	9.37	9.28	9.21	9.16	9.14	8.92	9.06
Work and study	5.72	5.65	5.57	5.43	5.41	5.22	5.53
Studying	84.92	85.07	85.22	85.41	85.44	85.86	85.42

Source: Author's estimates.

Table 7.9 Impact of conditional cash transfer on poverty reduction (%)

	Universal targeting			Targeting only poor children			Targeting children in Mindanao			Cost (% of GDP)
	Incidence	Gap	Severity	Incidence	Gap	Severity	Incidence	Gap	Severity	
Uniform transfer										
100	−3.8	−9.5	−14.4	−9.3	−20.6	−29.5	−4.6	−12.4	−18.3	0.5%
200	−8.1	−18.6	−26.9	−19.3	−38.2	−50.3	−11.3	−21.4	−27.8	1.0%
300	−12.4	−26.9	−37.6	−31.1	−52.5	−64.3	−17.5	−26.7	−32.3	1.5%
Progressive transfer										
100	−3.9	−9.8	−14.6	−9.5	−21.0	−30.2	−4.8	−12.7	−18.8	0.5%
300	−12.9	−27.6	−38.3	−32.3	−53.6	−65.2	−17.9	−27.0	−32.3	1.5%

GDP = gross domestic product.

Source: Author's estimates.

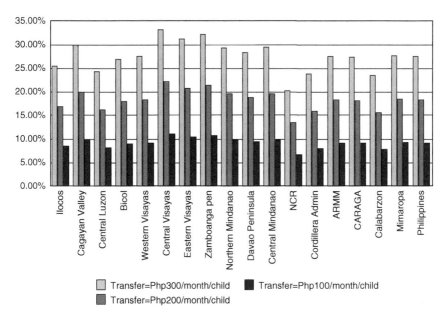

Figure 7.4 Costs of the CCT program as a percentage of official poverty lines across regions.

Source: Author's estimates.

rising sharply afterward. Based on this finding, we assess the impact of poverty reduction if 0.5% or 1.5% of gross domestic product (GDP) is transferred to children aged 6–15 years in a progressive manner. The transfer amount is increased by 5% for every extra year of a child's age from 11 years. This is because children at a higher level of education, particularly at the secondary level, are more likely to drop out of school or to encounter higher opportunity costs from attending school. The simulation results suggest that while the progressive transfer may not be as effective as uniform transfer, it is more effective if only poor children are targeted, than if the universal or geographical targeting method is used.

Fourth, although the transfer programs based on higher transfer amount do have much greater impacts on poverty reduction at the national level, they can be quite expensive and their affordability is questionable. With the transfer amount of P300 per child per month, the country has to bear a burden equivalent to 1.5% of its GDP that will be foregone. This is indeed not a small cost for any country. Nevertheless, the transfer levels considered are not sizable enough to have substantial impacts on poverty reduction at the national level. As can be seen from Figure 7.4, the proportion of the considered transfer amounts is quite small relative to the official poverty lines across regions. With the transfer level equal to P300 per month per child, the costs of the program would be merely 27% of the average official poverty line for the Philippines.

Conclusion

Poverty is high in the Philippines, with the proportion of poor people actually rising during 2003–06. Policies to reduce such poverty defy conventional wisdom. Single-focus solutions have proven ineffective. There is an urgent need to learn from both successful and failed efforts in other countries. This chapter has provided an *ex ante* assessment of the implementation of the Philippines' *PPP* program. In this study, we investigated the impact of the CCT program on current poverty, and the impact of this extra money on school attendance under alternative targeting criteria, namely universal targeting, geographical and poor targeting, and progressive targeting, and differing values of the transfers.

The key messages emerging from the study could also be regarded as recommendations for countries considering CCT interventions:

First, conditionality is imperative to CCT programs. Cash transfer, by itself, will not suffice to increase school attendance significantly; conditionality needs to be introduced. The quality of schooling would, possibly, also have to be improved when administering any cash transfer programs aimed at a sustained reduction in poverty.

Second, the emphasis on targeting helps maximize the program's impact and effectiveness. The results showed that the targeted CCT program led to greater school attendance and poverty reduction. Targeting and monitoring can increase the cost per beneficiary, which reduces the program's efficiency. However, designing a program with a weak or non-existent targeting strategy not only reduces the transfer cost per beneficiary, but also leads to leakage to the non-poor, driving down impact and effectiveness.

Third, to ensure success, complementing CCT programs with other components of social policy may prove meritorious. Complementary programs that can manage the supply side of services—such as high transportation costs and quality of teaching—and accommodate the heterogeneity of targeted household behavior will enhance the effectiveness of CCT programs, including the *PPP* program in the Philippines.

Fourth, good governance is an important component of a CCT program. As is the case for all effective social safety nets, a CCT program should be transparent in operation to encourage learning, minimize corruption, and ensure that beneficiaries and the wider population understand how the program functions. Corollary to this, political support at high levels for the program is among the main issues to consider in implementing a CCT program. It is critical to coordination across different sectors in the government, particularly education, health, and social welfare.

Finally, it is also imperative to ensure regular monitoring of operations and rigorous evaluation of the effectiveness of CCT programs, both *ex ante* and *ex post*. *Ex ante* impact evaluations, like the current study, would be useful in answering a number of policy-relevant counterfactual questions that *ex post* evaluations are unable to answer.

Notes

1 Other objectives are to improve preventive healthcare of pregnant women and young children, and to encourage parents' participation in the growth and development of young children, as well as involvement in the community.
2 A similar methodology is applied to evaluate the impact of *Bolsa Escola* in Brazil. See Bourguignon et al. (2002) for a detailed explanation of the methodology.
3 See NSCB (2000) for detailed explanations on the official poverty lines.
4 The estimated earnings function was not corrected for selection bias. One of major reasons for this is related to choosing an instrumental variable that would affect earnings but not the occupational choice. No such instrument is readily available (see Bourguignon et al. 2002).

8 A multi-country analysis of achievements and inequalities in economic growth and standards of living[1]

Introduction

It is commonly believed that economic growth ought to be broad-based enough to significantly improve the living standards of the poorer segments of society. The contemporary concept of human development encompasses a broader and richer process than mere economic growth and wealth accumulation (UNDP 2007). According to this concept, development means the creation of an environment in which all members of a society can take full advantage of their potential, live as they wish to, and have more choices. But in a number of countries, rapid growth has not led to strong improvements in human development. Countries with high per-capita incomes can have poor levels of achievement in human development, while those with low per-capita incomes or growth rates can nevertheless do well on this front.

Experience in economic development demonstrates that economic growth needs to be complemented by reform of public services if sustainable improvements in human development are to be achieved. Moreover, without such reform, rapid growth will likely be difficult to sustain. A key goal to achieve an equitable pattern of human development should be the equitable provision of basic public services such as education and health, which constitute the most important determinants of human development.

The main objective of this chapter is to assess inequalities and achievements in education and health outcomes across countries. This chapter uses an achievement function to assess how countries at different stages of economic development are performing on standards of living. It suggests that it is a greater achievement for a country already at a high level to make a further increase in its standard of living than for a country at a lower level to make an equal increase in its standard of living.

This chapter assesses the performance of 177 countries in different regions during 2000–07, making comparisons within and between regions with a particular focus on Asia. It also tests for the statistical relationship between indicators of the countries' standards of living and per-capita gross domestic product (GDP). The questions it addresses include: To what extent can aggregate income measures such as per-capita GDP explain standards of living? Can growth in per-capita GDP alone bring about significant improvements in standards of living in a reasonable period? How many years will it take for Asia to achieve the standards of living of the rich industrialized countries?

The first section discusses the concepts and indicators of standards of living. The next section is devoted to multi-country inequalities in living standards. Then the achievement index is introduced, followed by a section which looks into the relationship between income and standards of living. After this we explore the performance in standards of living in relation to a country's per-capita income, which is followed by an investigation into the possibility of the rest of the world catching up to the industrialized countries standards of living, and a discussion of the policies required to facilitate this convergence. The chapter concludes with a summary of the major findings.

Living standards: concepts and indicators

As stated in the United Nations' *Human Development Report 1990*, the primary objective of economic development is to improve well-being. Several approaches have been used to define well-being or standard of living, including social indicators, quality of life, and basic needs (see Sen 1973; Drewnowski 1974; Hicks 1979; Hicks and Streeten 1979; Morris 1979; Streeten 1979; Dasgupta 1990). While these approaches are evidently related to the concept of standard of living, they lack a unifying conceptual framework for defining and measuring it. Sen (1985, 1987) has developed such a framework, defining standard of living in terms of functionings and capabilities. According to Sen (1985), standard of living must be seen in terms of an indivdiual's achievements (functionings) and ability to achieve (capabilities), and not merely in terms of that individual's means.

Ideally, the measurement of standard of living should incorporate all the capabilities that enhance human well-being, but this is not feasible from an empirical standpoint. First, many capabilities cannot easily be quantified. For instance, democracy can be regarded as an important component of standard of living, but it can be a problem to quantify. Second, for many capabilities, consistent data are not available across countries and over time. This chapter focuses on six selected indicators based on the availability of data and their ability to reflect quality of life: namely, life expectancy at birth, adult literacy rate, primary school enrollment rate, under-five survival rate, births attended by skilled health personnel, and per-capita GDP. Together, it is reasonable to believe that these indicators adequately reflect overall standard of living.

Reiterating Sen's conceptualization of standard of living, the primary concern should be with individual achievements and not with means. While input indicators are important because they enhance capabilities and extend functionings, they are not indicators of achievements. Hicks and Streeten (1979) argue that output indicators are, in general, better measures of the level of welfare and basic needs achievement.

The six indicators selected are a mixture of results and inputs. Note that the distribution between input and output indicators may not always be precise.

For instance, primary and secondary school enrollments are input indicators because they provide the means to achieve higher literacy in the population. However, can literacy itself be considered an ultimate achievement of a society, or is it only a means to some other end? It is clear that a literate person has access to many capabilities—he or she can read and write and may be able to communicate more effectively with other members of a society. An illiterate person may face many disadvantages because he or she cannot perform these basic functions. Thus, literacy is classified as an output indicator.

The under-five survival rate and life expectancy at birth are the two most important indicators of achievement. The under-five survival rate shows the number of children per 1,000 live births who survive until their fifth birthday. This is a good indicator of the availability of sanitation and clean water facilities, which can protect children from diseases and infections caused by unsanitary household conditions. Moreover, the survival rate of children under five years old is largely determined by their nutritional status; thus, a child who is seriously malnourished because of dietary inadequacies or deficiencies in the mother's diet during pregnancy and lactation has a lower chance of survival. The infant mortality (or survival) rate, similarly, points to the fulfillment of several basic needs—such as health, sanitation, clean water supply, and good nutrition—making it a good indicator of achievement. Both are classified as output indicators.

Life expectancy at birth indicates the number of years a newborn infant would live if patterns of mortality prevailing in the country at the time of birth were to stay the same throughout his or her life. It is the outcome of several input variables such as nutrition, water supply, sanitation, and medical facilities. As most people would prefer to live longer irrespective of the quality of life, life expectancy can be regarded as an indicator of achievement and, therefore, can be considered an important component of standard of living.

Births attended by skilled health personnel measures the proportion of births at which a skilled health personnel is present. According to the World Health Organization (2008), complications arising from pregnancy and childbirth kill more than half a million women every year and leave many others with serious and lifelong health problems. This input indicator is related to the accessibility of appropriate healthcare services throughout pregnancy and childbirth. Evidence suggests that having a skilled health worker present during delivery is highly associated with reduced maternal mortality (Graham, Bell, and Bullough 2001). In this regard, the indicator can be regarded as an input measure because it is a means to achieve lower maternal mortality.

Per-capita GDP is considered an input variable because it provides a measure of the degree of command people have over commodities. It is an indicator of affluence, which is not the same thing as standard of living.

By confining itself to the five measures of well-being, in addition to per-capital GDP, this study excludes many other social and psychological aspects that affect quality of life, such as security, justice, freedom of choice, human rights, employment, and satisfaction (see Morris 1979). This analysis is rather restricted, mainly due to the unavailability of appropriate data, and may appear to be too narrow in its scope. Nevertheless, the selected indicators, apart from per-capita GDP, are proxies to a large number of important capabilities that influence human well-being.

The five indicators described above are highly aggregated measures of well-being. Ideal measures would reflect the well-being of individuals or groups. In this context, Dasgupta (1990) correctly argues that focus should be on the distribution of well-being across class, caste, gender, or religion. It should be pointed out that the methodology used in this chapter can be applied to analyze the standards of living at individual or socioeconomic group levels. However, it may not be feasible to carry out the same analysis for a large number of countries because of the demanding data requirements.

This chapter does not attempt to construct a single index of living standards. Several such attempts have been made, including the widely known human development index (UNRISD 1972, Morris 1979, United Nations 1990). It is convenient and appealing to have a single overall index of well-being by which to rank countries. But the construction of such an index has many drawbacks. One of the main difficulties is the aggregation of several components of well-being into a single measure, which requires the assigning of appropriate weights to each component. In 1979, Morris constructed a single index derived by the simple averaging of three components: life expectancy at birth, the infant mortality rate, and the literacy rate. While this index has the merit of being simple, it is obviously arbitrary. There exists no rational economic justification for assigning equal weights to the different components. An alternative approach suggested in the literature assigns weights to indicators in proportion to a principal component of the correlation matrix. The rationale behind this approach is that the data determine the optimal weights that capture the largest variation in the selected indicators.

Rather than attempting to combine the five indicators into one single index, this chapter analyzes each country's achievements in terms of the five separate indicators of living standards. According to Sen (1987), measurements of living standards or well-being that have inherent plurality, such as weight or height, should not be seen as one-dimensional; therefore, a partial-ordering approach is adopted in which comparisons of living standards are made by ranking countries in accordance with each of the capabilities considered.

Multi-country inequalities in standards of living

The analysis is based on data from 177 countries, divided into eight regions. As discussed earlier, standard of living is measured by five indicators: life expectancy at birth, adult literacy rate, primary school enrollment rate, under-five survival rate, and births attended by skilled health personnel. Per-capita GDP is used as an additional measure of a country's affluence or the command people have over

Table 8.1 Average standard of living by region, 2000–07

Region	GDP per capita at 2005 PPP (US$)	Life expectancy at birth (years)	Adult literacy rate (%)	Net primary enrollment rate (%)	Under-5 survival rate (per 1,000 births)	Births attended by skilled personnel (%)
East Asia and Pacific	4,217	70.4	98.2	94.7	969	89.8
South Asia	1,959	63.8	74.0	85.6	918	39.5
Central Asia	3,547	68.0	99.7	92.0	948	95.3
Eastern Europe	10,204	69.3	98.6	91.2	981	96.6
Latin America and Caribbean	8,256	72.2	96.1	95.2	972	89.2
Middle East and North Africa	8,330	70.5	88.9	89.9	961	78.4
Sub-Saharan Africa	1,686	49.7	69.7	64.2	844	46.2
Industrialized countries	33,641	78.9	99.7	97.5	994	99.4
World	8,469	68	87	88	947	74

GDP = gross domestic product; PPP = purchasing power parity.

Source: Author's calculations based on World Development Indicators 2008.

goods and services: the higher this measure, the richer the country. Since per-capita GDP is measured in terms of 2005 purchasing power parity (PPP), values are comparable across countries. The six indicators are selected from the World Bank's World Development Indicators.

Table 8.1 presents, on a regional basis[2], the weighted average of per-capita GDP (at 2005 PPP) and the five standard of living indicators, using the countries' relative populations as weights. It is appropriate that larger countries are assigned a heavier weight when aggregating standard of living across regions.

It is evident that inequality in per-capita GDP is extremely high between regions. Sub-Saharan Africa is the poorest region with per-capita GDP only 19.9% of the world average, and South Asia the second poorest (at 23.1%). The gap in per-capita GDP between industrialized countries (excluding Japan) and the rest of the world is extremely large, with the former having a per-capita GDP almost four times the world average.

To assess the regions' relative performance, the average standard of living shown in Table 8.1 is normalized by making the average world standard of living equal to 100. The normalized results are presented in Table 8.2.

In addition, the disparity between countries can be assessed through the Theil index, a well-known measure of inequality, with each country as an observation. The estimated index for per-capita GDP is 66.51, which could be considered extremely high. The Theil (1967) index has an interesting property: it can be decomposed into between- and within-group inequalities. The groups in this case correspond to the eight regions shown in Table 8.2. The between-region inequality is calculated to be 54. This means that the disparity in per-capita GDP

Table 8.2 Relative standard of living index by region, 2000–07

Region	GDP per capita at 2005 PPP	Life expectancy at birth	Adult literacy rate	Net primary enrollment rate	Under-5 survival rate	Births attended by skilled personnel
East Asia and Pacific	49.8	103.9	112.6	107.7	102.3	121.9
South Asia	23.1	94.1	84.9	97.3	97.0	53.7
Central Asia	41.9	100.3	114.2	104.6	100.1	129.4
Eastern Europe	120.5	102.2	113.1	103.7	103.6	131.2
Latin America and Caribbean	97.5	106.5	110.1	108.3	102.6	121.1
Middle East and North Africa	98.4	104.0	101.9	102.2	101.5	106.5
Sub-Saharan Africa	19.9	73.4	79.9	73.0	89.2	62.8
Industrialized countries	397.2	116.5	114.2	110.9	105.0	135.0
World	100.0	100.0	100.0	100.0	100.0	100.0
Between-region inequality	54.00 (81.26%)	0.80 (87.44%)	1.00 (67.78%)	0.80 (55.61%)	0.10 (81.01%)	6.60 (58.09%)
Within-region inequality	12.51 (18.74%)	0.07 (12.56%)	0.50 (32.22%)	0.55 (44.39%)	0.04 (18.99%)	4.76 (41.91%)
Theil index	66.51	0.87	1.50	1.35	0.14	11.36

GDP = gross domestic product; PPP = purchasing power parity.

Note: Figures in parentheses indicate the percentage contribution to the total inequality.

Source: Author's calculations.

between regions explains 81.26% of the total inequality in GDP per capita between countries.

By comparison, the between-country inequality for the five indicators of standard of living is much lower than that for per-capita GDP. For instance, inequality in life expectancy at birth between countries is just 0.87, compared with 66.51 for per-capita GDP. For births attended by skilled health personnel, the corresponding measure of inequality is 11.36, which is much higher relative to the other four non-income indicators but substantially lower compared to per-capita GDP.

It should be noted, though, that a lower between-country inequality in standard of living does not suggest that poorer countries with a lower standard of living perform relatively better in achieving a higher standard of living. The issue of standard of living should be distinguished from that of raw value before assessing individual country achievements. This issue will be dealt with in the next section.

Achievements in standards of living

Unlike per-capita GDP, the indicators of standard of living have asymptotic limits, reflecting physical and biological maximums—they cannot go on increasing infinitely. For example, life expectancy at birth has an upper limit of around 85 years and the adult literacy rate cannot exceed 100%. Another important characteristic is that as the standard of living reaches progressively higher limits, any incremental improvement represents a higher level of achievement than does a similar incremental improvement from a lower base. For instance, an increase in life expectancy at birth from 70 to 75 years would imply a greater achievement than an increase from 45 to 50 years. In this regard, the relationship between achievement and the value of the indicator is not linear; thus, the observed differences in the levels of indicators of living standards do not reflect their true achievement.

A hypothetical example will help to explain the idea of non-linearity. Suppose there are two countries: country A in Africa and country B in Europe. Country A is relatively poorer than country B. Further assume that both countries have life expectancy at birth of 50 years. It would be much easier for country B to increase its life expectancy to 60 years. Similarly, it would be much harder for country A to achieve the same increase because the country may not have the resources to invest in a good healthcare system. Equivalently, if country B has already achieved the life expectancy of 80 years, the increase from 80 to 90 years (or even to 85 years) would be infinitely harder than that from 50 to 60 years. In this hypothetical example, the performance of country B in increasing its life expectancy from 80 to 85 years could be considered more impressive than its counterpart's increase from 50 to 60 years.

Is this argument of non-linearity also pertinent to the literacy rate? For instance, it may be argued that closing a literacy rate gap between 90% and 100% would be easier than closing the gap between 40% and 50%. This argument may be valid on the grounds that the latter requires more fundamental steps, such as moving people out of agriculture to attend school, building new schools, and training teachers, among other difficulties and inefficiencies that the country is facing. On the contrary, any incremental improvement would be more difficult to achieve at a higher level than from a lower base. Experience suggests that even rich countries have not been able to achieve 100% literacy.[3]

Using this idea of non-linearity, Kakwani (1993) derived an achievement index that lies between 0 and 100. The achievement index considers a further increase in the standard of living of a country, which is already at a higher level, as an achievement which is greater than that of another country with an equal increase in standard of living but from a lower base. While Kakwani (1993) derived a class of achievement functions, the current study uses only the following member of the class:[4]

$$f(y, M_0, M) = \frac{100 \times [\ln(M - M_0) - \ln(M - y)]}{\ln(M - M_0)} \qquad (8.1)$$

where y is a value of an indicator of living standard that has a minimum value of M_0 and a maximum value of M. The achievement function becomes 0 when $y = M_0$ and becomes equal to 100 when y approaches M.

To compute the achievement index, the minimum and maximum values need to be specified. Based on the data for 177 countries, the following minimum and maximum values were calculated:

- Life expectancy at birth: 35–86 years
- Adult literacy rate: 0–100%
- Net primary enrolment rate: 0–100%
- Under-five survival rate: 0–1,000
- Births attended by skilled health personnel: 0–100

Table 8.3 presents the weighted average of the achievement index by region. Table 8.4 presents the relative achievement index, which is the normalized index of achievement relative to the average achievement of the world; that is, the world index is set to 100. Recall from Table 8.2 that the average life expectancy at birth for industrialized countries was about 16.5% higher than the world average. According to Table 8.4, however, the average achievement in this indicator for industrialized countries is 76.3% higher than the average of achievement in the world. This suggests that the disparity in achievement in life expectancy at birth between countries is far greater than that in actual terms. The Theil inequality measure also shows that between countries, the inequality of achievement in this indicator is much greater than the inequality in actual life expectancy at birth. Similar results hold for the other four indicators of living standards considered in this chapter.

Figure 8.1 shows that countries in South Asia have lower achievement in standards of living than countries in East Asia and the Pacific and Central Asia. This result holds uniformly for all six indicators of standard of living. The gap

Table 8.3 Achievements in standards of living by region, 2000–07

Region	Life expectancy at birth	Adult literacy rate	Net primary enrollment rate	Under-5 survival rate	Births attended by skilled personnel
East Asia and Pacific	30.6	92.8	69.7	51.7	65.1
South Asia	21.2	29.9	44.5	36.4	11.7
Central Asia	26.6	100.0	63.0	43.7	77.4
Eastern Europe	29.0	91.3	55.0	58.6	88.6
Latin America and Caribbean	33.7	74.4	72.9	52.5	60.4
Middle East and North Africa	30.8	56.2	57.3	48.6	42.2
Sub-Saharan Africa	8.9	28.7	25.7	27.7	16.3
Industrialized countries	51.0	99.8	84.5	74.8	99.8
World	28.9	63.3	57.2	48.9	50.6

Source: Author's calculations.

Table 8.4 Relative achievements in standards of living by region, 2000–07

Region	Life expectancy at birth	Adult literacy rate	Net primary enrollment rate	Under-5 survival rate	Births attended by skilled personnel
East Asia and Pacific	105.6	146.6	121.9	105.5	128.5
South Asia	73.3	47.2	77.8	74.4	23.2
Central Asia	92.0	157.9	110.2	89.3	152.9
Eastern Europe	100.2	144.3	96.2	119.8	175.0
Latin America and Caribbean	116.4	117.5	127.4	107.3	119.4
Middle East and North Africa	106.5	88.7	100.2	99.3	83.3
Sub-Saharan Africa	30.8	45.4	45.0	56.7	32.2
Industrialized countries	176.3	157.7	147.7	152.7	197.2
World	100.0	100.0	100.0	100.0	100.0
Between-region inequality	9.50 (84.22%)	13.10 (83.92%)	6.20 (59.50%)	4.10 (85.95%)	27.80 (68.78%)
Within-region inequality	1.78 (15.78%)	2.51 (16.08%)	4.22 (40.50%)	0.67 (14.05%)	12.62 (31.22%)
Theil index	11.28	15.61	10.42	4.77	40.42

Note: Figures in parentheses indicate the percentage contribution to the total inequality.

Source: Author's calculations.

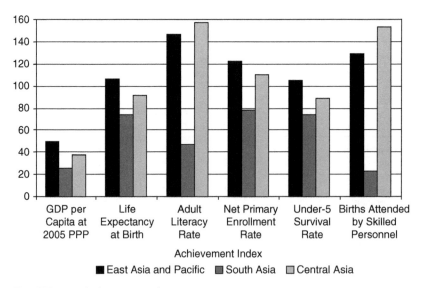

Note: PPP = purchasing power parity.

Figure 8.1 Relative achievements in standards of living in Asia.

between South Asia and the rest of Asia is narrowest in per-capita GDP, but is much wider in the adult literacy rate and births attended by skilled health personnel, suggesting that the South Asian region needs to pay greater attention to improving its education and health sectors. Yet, individual country experiences may differ between countries in South Asia.

Table 8.5 provides the relative achievements of five major countries in South Asia along with six other Asian countries and the group of industrialized countries for comparison. Sri Lanka has the most outstanding achievements in standards of living in South Asia, with a higher per-capita GDP than its four neighbors and a growth rate lower only than India. Furthermore, achievements in standards of living in Sri Lanka are far superior to other countries in the region. Two indicators in particular stand out: life expectancy at birth and net primary enrollment rate, which are the highest among the selected countries in Asia.

In East Asia and the Pacific, the People's Republic of China (PRC) is the fastest growing economy and its overall performance in virtually all available indicators of living standards surpasses world averages by wide margins, particularly in adult literacy rate and births attended by skilled health personnel. On the other hand, while Thailand has higher per-capita GDP than the PRC, its standards of living achievements are not as consistent. Note that although achievements in life expectancy at birth and adult literacy rate are better for the PRC, Thailand

Table 8.5 Relative achievements in standards of living in selected countries in Asia

Economy	*Growth rate*	*GDP per capita at 2005 PPP*	*Life expectancy at birth*	*Adult literacy rate*	*Net primary enrollment rate*	*Under-5 survival rate*	*Births attended by skilled personnel*
Bangladesh	3.8	12.0	68.0	34.7	85.6	75.0	6.6
India	6.1	24.4	72.9	49.6	81.6	74.0	25.3
Nepal	1.1	11.1	23.4	41.4	56.4	79.0	6.8
Pakistan	3.1	24.7	75.8	36.1	36.6	68.0	12.7
Sri Lanka	4.5	39.9	129.3	107.1	152.3	123.0	138.1
China, People's Rep. of	9.5	43.5	109.0	153.5	–	105.0	150.4
Indonesia	3.7	36.2	87.1	149.2	148.0	96.0	48.0
Lao PDR	4.8	20.1	68.1	52.7	60.7	73.0	9.3
Philippines	2.9	33.7	105.2	103.4	102.2	99.0	38.1
Thailand	4.3	78.2	98.0	134.2	82.8	137.0	174.8
Viet Nam	6.3	23.4	102.2	–	95.1	113.0	75.4
Industrialized countries	1.5	397.2	176.3	157.7	147.7	152.7	197.2
World	5.0	100.0	100.0	100.0	100.0	100.0	100.0

– indicates data not available.
GDP = gross domestic product; PPP = purchasing power parity.

Source: Author's calculations.

has superior achievements in the two other health indicators. Gaps—urban-rural gaps, regional disparities, gender gaps, and gaps among different social groups— in access to basic public services in education and health remain among the challenges facing the PRC in its current phase of development (UNDP 2007).

Relationship between per-capita GDP and standards of living

Per-capita GDP measures the total output per person produced in an economy; the higher the output, the greater the access that people have to goods and services. Therefore, there should be a strong association between national income and standards of living, with higher national income being strongly associated with lower child mortality and higher primary school completion (World Bank 2004).

As noted earlier, however, the relationship between per-capita GDP and standards of living is non-linear. As per-capita GDP increases, the standard of living increases less and less steeply until it reaches an asymptotic limit (Hicks and Streeten 1979). Many attempts have been made to estimate the non-linear relationship, which captures the asymptotic behavior of indicators of standard of living (Morris 1979; Sheehan and Hopkins 1979; Grosse and Perry 1983; Goldstein 1985). All these models are generally flawed because of their inherent misspecification of the nature of non-linearity.

The achievement index discussed in the previous section captures the nature of non-linearity of indicators of standards of living. To calculate this non-linearity, Kakwani (1993) argues that it is more natural to relate the achievement index to per-capita GDP. Following this argument, the adopted model is:

$$f_i(y_i, M_0, M) = \alpha + \beta \log(x_i) + u_i \tag{8.2}$$

where $f_i(y_i, M_0, M)$ defined in equation (8.1) is the achievement index of the ith country with a social indicator y_i, x_i is the per-capita GDP of the ith country, and u_i is the error term. The use of the achievement function captures the non-linear characteristics of standards of living.

Equation (8.2) is estimated for each of the five indicators of living standards using the least squares method. The coefficient estimates along with the t-values are presented in Table 8.6. One of the assumptions of the least squares method is that the residual variance is constant over the observations. This assumption is unlikely to hold using multi-country data. Even if this assumption is violated, the least squares estimates are still unbiased, but the estimates of t-values are biased. To remedy this situation, the robust t-values were calculated using a heteroskedasticity-consistent covariance matrix estimator proposed by White (1980).

The coefficient of determination, the R-squared, is estimated to assess the accuracy of regression models. Table 8.6 shows that the estimated values of the coefficient of determination for the regression equations vary from 0.4 to 0.8, which could be regarded as quite high given that the sample observations range

Table 8.6 Regression coefficients of achievement in standards of living on per-capita gross domestic product (GDP)

Achievements in standards of living	Log (GDP per capita)	Robust t-values	R-squared	Number of observations
Life expectancy at birth	9.5	21.2	0.7	177
Adult literacy rate	18.1	11.3	0.6	108
Net primary enrollment rate	13.6	11.1	0.4	159
Under-5 survival rate	11.7	12.4	0.8	175
Births attended by skilled health personnel	23.2	22.7	0.6	162

Source: Author's calculations.

from 108 to 177. This suggests that the model is reasonably well specified and that per-capita GDP at 2005 PPP is an important determinant of achievements in standards of living.

Differentiating equation (8.2) and using equation (8.1), the elasticity of standard of living y_i with respect to x_i is obtained as

$$\eta_i = \beta \log(M - M_0)\left(\frac{M}{y_i} - 1\right)\bigg/100 \tag{8.3}$$

which shows that the higher the standard of living of a country is, the smaller the elasticity. When the standard of living (y_i) approaches its maximum value M, the elasticity approaches 0. The implication is that economic growth will have a greater impact on standards of living in poorer countries than in richer ones. This is explained by the fact that standard of living becomes more difficult to raise as it reaches a higher level. A study by Bruns, Mingat, and Rakotomalala (2003) finds that in lower-income countries, 10% more income per capita is associated with, on average, a 6.6% lower child mortality rate and a 4.8% higher primary school completion rate. In middle-income countries, however, 10% more income per capita is associated with 7.7% less child mortality but little improvement in primary completion.[5]

The growth elasticity of standards of living defined in equation (8.3) is a useful indicator because it shows the responsiveness of changes in standards of living to economic growth. This elasticity was calculated for each of the 177 countries, and Table 8.7 presents the weighted average of elasticities for the eight regions using the population of each country as the corresponding weight.

A 1% increase in GDP per capita in the world increases the world's life expectancy at birth by 0.11%. The impact of economic growth on life expectancy at birth in sub-Saharan Africa is much greater, as indicated by an elasticity of 0.27. This is expected, because given the current shortness of life expectancy at birth in Africa, the indicator would be easily improved with small increases in per-capita income. In industrialized countries, on the other hand, the growth elasticity of life expectancy at birth is extremely low, at 0.03, since these countries

Table 8.7 Average elasticity of standards of living by region, 2000–07

Region	Life expectancy at birth	Adult literacy rate	Net primary enrollment rate	Under-5 survival rate	Births attended by skilled personnel
East Asia and Pacific	0.08	0.02	0.04	0.03	0.17
South Asia	0.13	0.30	0.11	0.07	2.12
Central Asia	0.10	0.00	0.06	0.04	0.06
Eastern Europe	0.09	0.01	0.06	0.02	0.04
Latin America and Caribbean	0.07	0.03	0.03	0.02	0.20
Middle East and North Africa	0.08	0.11	0.08	0.03	0.45
Sub-Saharan Africa	0.27	0.44	0.41	0.15	2.99
Industrialized countries	0.03	0.00	0.02	0.00	0.01
World	0.11	0.15	0.11	0.05	0.96

Source: Author's calculations.

have already achieved high levels for this indicator and further improvements will require substantially larger resources.

Moreover, results reveal that life expectancy at birth is more responsive to per-capita GDP than the under-five survival rate, and this result holds uniformly across regions. This finding suggests that more progress has been made thus far in improving child mortality than improving life expectancy and, thus, higher growth rates would be required to achieve the same level of improvement in life expectancy in the future. The magnitude of elasticity for sub-Saharan Africa, 0.15, can be considered high; as such, economic growth will play a significant role in improving the under-five survival rate in Africa.

Compared with the other indicators, the number of births attended by skilled health personnel was found to be the most responsive to economic growth. A 1% increase in GDP per capita in the world would improve this health indicator by 0.96%. In sub-Saharan Africa, the same growth rate would lead to an almost 3% higher proportion of births with skilled health staff. In South Asia, an extra 1% growth in income per capita would improve this indicator by 2.12%.

The education indicators—adult literacy rate and net primary school enrollment rate—are much more responsive to per-capita income in South Asia and in sub-Saharan Africa. In both, higher income per capita would result in more school-age children attending primary school and, thus, in a higher adult literacy rate.

This section has shown that income and standards of living are strongly associated, particularly in low-income countries. However, the low elasticities shown in Table 8.7 suggest that improving living standards will require significantly high growth rates if this is the only channel used for achieving such goals.

Performance in standards of living

Methodological framework

Per-capita GDP in PPP dollars measures how rich a country is in terms of material consumption. The regression model estimated in the previous section demonstrates that per-capita GDP is an important determinant of a country's standard of living. The positive and highly statistically significant values of β imply that the richer a country is, the higher the expected standards of living are. However, a one-to-one relationship between the country's material prosperity and the standards of living does not exist because the model only explains around 60%–80% of variations in standards of living. There is still a considerable unexplained variation, which implies that factors other than income impact a country's standard of living. These factors may include the scope and quality of basic services in education and health provided by governments.

The unexplained variation in the model suggests that the level and distribution of education and health services vary widely between countries, even if they have the same level of per-capita income. A country may be assessed as having superior (inferior) performance in standards of living if it enjoys higher (lower) living standards than what is expected on the basis of its per-capita income. The residual term in the model (the difference between actual and expected values of the achievement index) includes the effect of factors other than income that affect living standards. If the residual is positive (negative), it can be said that the country has higher (lower) standards of living relative to its per-capita income. This methodology allows the identification of countries that have superior (inferior) performance in standards of living.

The residual term in equation (8.2) is given by

$$\hat{u}_i = [f_i - \beta \log(x_i)] \tag{8.4}$$

For large samples, it is expected that $\hat{u}_i$ is normally distributed with zero mean and variance s^2, where s is the estimated standard of error of the regression. This gives the studentized residual as

$$\hat{u}_i^* = \frac{[f_i - \hat{\beta} \log(x_i)]}{s} \tag{8.5}$$

which, for large samples, is normally distributed with zero mean and unit variance. In this chapter, the value of $\hat{u}_i$ was calculated for each country. The performance of a country on standards of living can be assessed by the magnitude of $\hat{u}_i$: the larger this value, the better the performance of the ith country. The average value of $\hat{u}_i^*$ for all countries is equal to zero as some countries will register a positive value and others will record a negative value, with positive (negative) values implying superior (inferior) performance. Thus, $\hat{u}_i^*$ can be used as an indicator of a country's relative performance in living standards.

If $\hat{u}_i^*$ is greater than 1.96, the ith country can be regarded as an outlier or a country with exceptionally superior performance. This is because the probability of achieving such an outcome is less than 0.05; that is, the estimate is statistically significant at the 5% level. Similarly, if $\hat{u}_i^*$ is less than negative 1.96, the ith country can be regarded as a country with exceptionally inferior performance in standards of living. Such outliers deserve special attention from the standpoint of policy making.

Identifying countries with exceptional performance

Using the proposed indicator of a country's relative performance, this section identifies the countries that have exceptionally superior or inferior performance in standards of living. Table A.8.2 in the Appendix to this chapter presents the values of relative performance for individual countries.

The results show that Japan is the only country with exceptionally superior performance in life expectancy at birth. Other higher achievers in this indicator include Costa Rica; Hong Kong, China; and Sri Lanka. On the other hand, countries that have exceptionally inferior performance in life expectancy at birth are Equatorial Guinea, Botswana, South Africa, Gabon, Swaziland, Angola, and Namibia. None of the Asian countries is included in the list of these negative outliers. In fact, all the exceptionally inferior-performing countries are in sub-Saharan Africa.

The high incidence of HIV/AIDS in Africa could be a cause of such short life expectancy relative to per-capita income level. Combating the pandemic there has been particularly challenging. The disease has reversed gains in life expectancy made over decades and is undermining economic growth, reducing the productivity of the workforce, and diverting scarce public resources away from other health issues and education. Moreover, the pandemic is now threatening countries with huge populations such as the PRC and India. Effective policies, backed by adequate resources, are required to check its spread and to provide healthcare for the millions who are, or will be, affected.

The under-five survival rate is an indicator that reflects the health status of a country's population. The results show that no country can be categorized as an exceptionally high achiever by this indicator. But three countries—Sri Lanka, Viet Nam, and Moldova—are close to being exceptional and could be regarded as having relatively better performance in the under-five survival rate compared with the other 174 countries. The value of this performance indicator for these three countries is higher than 1.70 but less than 1.96. In contrast, the performance of six countries—Angola, Botswana, Equatorial Guinea, Gabon, Qatar, and Swaziland—has been exceptionally inferior on this indicator. This could largely be explained by the barriers to quality basic health services such as lack of information and knowledge, inaccessibility and poor quality of service, unresponsive service providers, and the high costs of seeking healthcare.

Access to safe water and adequate sanitation has a direct impact on health status and mortality, particularly on children. The World Bank's (2004) study of eight countries found that the prevalence of diarrhea in children under three years of age from households with no sanitation declined by six percentage points as conditions shifted from no improved water to "optimal" water. Moreover, the same study found that moving from no sanitation to "optimal" sanitation resulted in a ten-percentage-point drop in diarrhea in households with no improved water source. As with education, there are spillover effects associated with sanitation at the community level. In Peru, for example, sanitation investments by a family's neighbors were associated with better nutritional status for that family's children (Alderman, Hoddinott, and Kinsey 2006).

Another indicator related to the delivery of health services is the number of births attended by skilled personnel. The results suggest that the performance of seven countries—Fiji, Jordan, Kyrgyz Republic, Moldova, Mongolia, Samoa, and Uzbekistan—was exceptionally superior on the basis of this indicator. In contrast, Equatorial Guinea is the only negative outlier, suggesting an exceptionally low achievement by this indicator.

Regarding the net primary school enrollment rate, results suggest that Oman is an exceptionally inferior performer in relation to its per-capita GDP, while another rich country in the Middle East and North African region, Qatar, was found to have exceptionally low achievement in adult literacy rate. These findings suggest that an overriding focus on economic growth without similar attention to public service systems and institutions will not produce a strong human development outcome. The absence of complementary actions to establish effective social services can be detrimental to long-term growth.

Relative performance of Asian countries

This section introduces a relative performance index to analyze the performance of Asian countries with respect to the world average. The average value of the relative performance index for all countries included in the present study is equal to zero and is regarded as a benchmark for assessing a country's relative performance in standards of living. If an individual country has a value for the index greater (less) than zero, then the performance of that country is judged as better (worse) than the average performance of the world. The average values of the relative performance index are presented in Table 8.8 for eight different regions of the world; the corresponding values for individual countries are shown in Table A.8.3.

The relative performance indexes for sub-Saharan Africa and the Middle East and North Africa are negative for all aspects of living standards considered in the current study, suggesting lower standards of living relative to what is expected from their per-capita income levels. As noted earlier, the per-capita GDP of sub-Saharan Africa is, on average, only 19% of world GDP per capita. While sustainable and rapid economic growth is a prerequisite for improving living standards, most people have higher expectations of governments; they are expected to provide basic health services that reduce infant and maternal mortality rates, as well as primary school and higher education that enable people to compete in the labor market.

Table 8.8 Performance in standard of living by region, 2000–07

Region	Life expectancy at birth	Adult literacy rate	Net primary enrollment rate	Under-5 survival rate	Births attended by skilled personnel
East Asia and Pacific	0.37	0.50	0.38	0.51	0.18
South Asia	0.36	−0.31	0.23	0.12	−0.84
Central Asia	0.56	2.46	0.30	0.07	1.18
Eastern Europe	−0.10	0.92	−0.16	0.73	0.96
Latin America and Caribbean	0.26	0.04	0.39	−0.02	−0.07
Middle East and North Africa	−0.12	−0.64	−0.51	−0.50	−0.46
Sub-Saharan Africa	−0.75	−0.46	−0.50	−0.68	−0.35
Industrialized countries	0.61	0.22	0.44	0.51	−0.18
World	0.00	0.00	0.00	0.00	0.00

Source: Author's calculations.

It is surprising that the relative performance of countries in Central Asia is impressive in all aspects of living standards. On adult literacy rate, in particular, two countries—Tajikistan and Armenia—perform exceptionally highly. While statistics indicate very high adult literacy rates in Central Asia, there is a clear need to continue expanding access to adult literacy programs and provide an enabling literacy environment for all (World Bank 2004). Equally important are concerns over gender disparity, as these remain a challenge in some countries in the region. In Tajikistan, for instance, boys are favored, such that only 95 girls are enrolled in primary education per 100 boys. By contrast, primary education appears to favor girls in Armenia, where 104 are enrolled for every 100 boys.

Countries in East Asia and the Pacific surpass the world average performance in all aspects of living standards, although Papua New Guinea and Brunei Darussalam have the worst outcomes in the region. In contrast, South Asia as a whole has performed worse than the world average in adult literacy rate and births attended by skilled health personnel, but better than the world average in life expectancy at birth, under-five survival rate, and net primary enrollment rate.

South Asia faces many challenges in health services and outcomes. The indicator for births attended by skilled health staff is extremely poor compared with other regions. The region accounts for one-third of maternal deaths worldwide (ADB 2007), and the chances of dying during pregnancy are 1 in 43 compared to 1 in 30,000 in Sweden. Maternal death rates vary widely within the region, however, ranging from 58 per 100,000 live births in Sri Lanka to 450 in India in 2005 (World Bank 2005). Maternal mortality can be prevented with appropriate medical care and management, and thus depends mainly on health services. It is worth noting that midwifery services are linked to dramatic declines in maternal mortality in Sri Lanka (World Bank 2004). On the other hand, nutrition and child mortality depend on many other factors such as education, water, food security, communication, electrification, and transportation.

In South Asia, the worst performing countries in all dimensions of standards of living are Bhutan and Pakistan. In Pakistan, poor performance in the social sector is attributed to the effects of elite dominance (Hussain 1999), as well as to the division into linguistic, religious, and regional factions that challenge its ability to provide social services (Easterly 2001). In India, performance is particularly poor in births attended by skilled personnel and adult literacy rate. All countries in South Asia except Sri Lanka perform particularly poorly in births attended by skilled personnel, suggesting a strong need for the provision of government health services. It should be noted that Sri Lanka is a superior performer in every dimension of standards of living considered in the current study, exceptionally so in the net primary enrollment rate and the under-five survival rate (see Figure 8.2).

The factors contributing to observed achievements were the center of debate in the 1980s (Isenman 1980; Sen 1981; Bhalla and Glewwe 1986; Pyatt 1987; Dreze and Sen 1989). The countries with the best achievements identified in the current study are also known for excellent public welfare programs that include direct public provision of education, health, and other vital services. Sri Lanka has long been known as a unique example of a developing country with impressive achievement in terms of basic needs relative to its income level. Sen (1981) and Isenman (1980) have concluded that government action made Sri Lanka an extraordinary country in promoting extensive social opportunities and providing widespread and equitable schooling, health, and other basic services.

The Sri Lankan government in 1977 diverged from the country's earlier welfare-oriented development strategy and introduced new economic policies

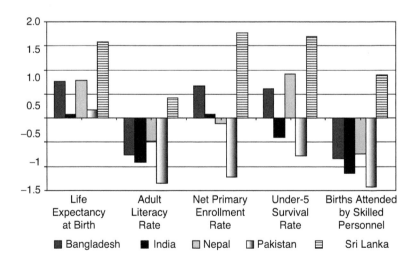

Figure 8.2 Relative performance in standards of living in selected countries in South Asia.
Source: Author's calculations.

that focused more on growth and investment. One of the many policy changes was the substitution of food subsidies by a means-tested food stamps program. The enormous savings that were realized as a result of the policy changes were directed to production and employment activities. In addition, the trade sector was liberalized and foreign exchange control was virtually withdrawn. The results of the current study suggest that cuts in welfare expenditures in the late 1970s did not make Sri Lanka an inferior performer in the 1980s and onward.

Government expenditures on education and health can influence human development outcomes; public spending must therefore concentrate on areas where market failure is pervasive and positive spillover is largest. Given limited public resources, the balance needs to shift more toward investments in primary education and health services. Additionally, the private sector and public–private partnerships should be encouraged to provide tertiary education and health services where market failure is minimal.

Convergence in standards of living

So far, it has been noted that disparity in standards of living between industrialized countries and the rest of the world is extremely large. As pointed out in the section above on comparative living standards among countries, the average GDP per capita of industrialized countries is almost four times the world average. This section explores the likelihood of the rest of the world catching up. Assuming that is feasible, the number of years it will take for the different regions to catch up with the average standard of living in industrialized countries is calculated.

Suppose x_k is the per-capita GDP of the kth region, which is growing at an annual rate of γ_k percent on average. Over the period of n years, the per-capita GDP of the kth region will be given by

$$x_{kn} = x_k(1+\gamma_k)^n \tag{8.6}$$

Following this, a similar expression can be derived for the reference group, that is the industrialized countries. Consider that the per-capita GDP of the reference group is denoted as x_0 and it grows at an annual rate of γ_0 percent on average. In n years, the average per-capita GDP of the reference group will be

$$x_{0n} = x_0(1+\gamma_0)^n \tag{8.7}$$

Suppose that after n years, the per-capita GDP of the kth region approaches that of the reference group. This scenario results in $x_{kn} = x_{0n}$ and also

$$n = \frac{\log(x_0) - \log(x_k)}{\log(1+\gamma_k) - \log(1+\gamma_0)} \tag{8.8}$$

which is obtained from equations (8.6) and (8.7). Since $x_0 > x_k$ for all k regions, n will be positive if $\gamma_k > \gamma_0$. Estimating the number of years (n) in equation (8.8) requires the growth rate γ_k for the kth region.

Based on per-capita GDP at 2005 PPP, the annual growth rate was calculated for each of the 177 countries for 2000–07. The growth rate was then averaged over the period for each country. The aggregate growth rates for each region were calculated by averaging the countries' growth rates using their respective populations as weights. The regional growth rates are presented in the first numerical column of Table 8.9.[6] The regions that exhibited the highest growth were Central Asia and East Asia and the Pacific. Although Central Asia went through a severe economic crisis in the first half of the 1990s, it performed well in 2000–07, when its average growth rate was 8.13% per annum. East Asia and the Pacific includes rapidly-growing economies such as the PRC and slow-growing ones such as the Pacific island countries, putting the region's average growth rate at 7.82% over the first seven years of the 21st century.

As seen in the second column of Table 8.9, it will take 40 years for the different regions to achieve the average per-capita GDP of industrialized countries. Sub-Saharan Africa will take 188 years and South Asia 74 years. In Latin America, although countries enjoyed high growth rates in the 1960s and 1970s, growth was extremely slow in the 2000s, suggesting it will take 184 years to catch up. Note that these results are based on the assumption that countries in the different regions will maintain the same average growth rates over time. Calculating the number of years to catch up with the reference group in the five living standard indicators requires a different approach. The growth elasticity of living standards presented in Table 8.7 cannot be used to project future standards of living. This is because elasticity does not remain constant over time, but declines with rising standards of living. To tackle this problem, the following methodology was adopted.

The regression model presented in equation (8.2) provides the estimated achievement for the kth region as

$$\hat{f}_k = \hat{\alpha} + \hat{\beta} \log(x_k) \tag{8.9}$$

which, on taking first differences, gives the change in achievement as

$$\Delta \hat{f}_k = \hat{\beta} \Delta \log(x_k) = \hat{\beta} \gamma_k \tag{8.10}$$

where $\gamma_k = \Delta \log(x_k)$ is the growth rate of the kth region and $\Delta \hat{f}_k$ is the annual absolute change in achievement of the kth region, of which the per-capita GDP increases at an annual rate of γ_k percent.

In n years, the achievement of the kth region will be given by

$$f_{kn} = f_k + n \hat{\beta} \gamma_k \tag{8.11}$$

Similarly, the achievement of the reference group over n years will be given by

$$f_{0n} = f_0 + n \hat{\beta} \gamma_0 \tag{8.12}$$

Table 8.9 Years to catch up with industrialized countries' living standards by region[7]

Region	Average annual growth rate	Number of years for convergence					
		GDP per capita at 2005 PPP	Life expectancy at birth	Adult literacy rate	Net primary enrollment rate	Under-5 survival rate	Births attended by skilled personnel
East Asia and Pacific	7.82	34	34	6	17	31	24
South Asia	5.43	74	79	97	74	82	96
Central Asia	8.13	35	39	0	24	40	15
Eastern Europe	6.11	27	50	10	47	30	10
Latin America and Caribbean	2.24	184	235	181	110	243	219
Middle East and North Africa	2.91	98	147	166	138	153	172
Sub-Saharan Africa	3.09	188	273	241	265	246	222
Industrialized countries	1.46	0	0	0	0	0	0
World	5.01	40	66	57	57	62	60

GDP = gross domestic product; PPP = purchasing power parity.

Source: Author's calculations.

Suppose that after n years, the achievement of the kth region approaches the achievement of the reference group. This will lead to $f_{kn} = f_{0n}$ as well as

$$n = \frac{(f_0 - f_k)}{\hat{\beta}(\gamma_k - \gamma_0)} \tag{8.13}$$

which is obtained equations (8.11) and (8.12). The n in equation (8.13) is the number of years it will take for the standard of living in the kth region to approach that of the reference group, that is, the industrialized countries. Note that n should always be positive: since $f_0 > f_k$ for all k regions, n will be positive if $\gamma_k > \gamma_0$.

The results in Table 8.9 suggest that convergence in standards of living will take longer than convergence in per-capita GDP. Sub-Saharan Africa will take 273 years to catch up with the reference group in life expectancy at birth while South Asia will take only 79 years.

This regional picture, however, hides the challenges faced by individual countries. Table 8.10 shows a more detailed picture through the results for selected Asian countries. For instance, Pakistan and Bangladesh would take 187 and 141 years, respectively, to catch up with industrialized countries' achievement on life expectancy at birth. The results also show that Nepal would not be able to catch up because its average growth rate of 1.1% during 2000–07 falls short of the 1.5% achieved by industrialized countries during the same period. This suggests

Table 8.10 Years required for selected Asian countries to catch up with industrialized countries

Economy	GDP per capita at 2005 PPP	Life expectancy at birth	Adult literacy rate	Net primary enrollment rate	Under-5 survival rate	Births attended by skilled personnel
Bangladesh	153	141	184	112	138	178
India	62	68	81	60	71	81
Nepal	*	*	*	*	*	*
Pakistan	173	187	259	285	216	246
Sri Lanka	78	47	58	−6	40	43
China, People's Rep. of	29	26	2	–	25	13
Indonesia	110	121	13	0	106	146
Lao PDR	92	99	110	110	100	123
Philippines	175	151	132	133	155	241
Thailand	59	84	29	96	23	17
Viet Nam	61	47	–	46	34	55
Industrialized countries	0	0	0	0	0	0
World	40	66	57	57	62	60

– indicates data not available; * indicates unable to catch up.

Source: Author's calculations.

that for Nepal to catch up would require a substantially higher growth rate in per-capita income and/or public policies that can promote greater efficiencies and effective delivery mechanisms, with a focus on improved education and health outcomes.

In calculating n, it was assumed that while per-capita GDP changes over time, other factors that may influence standards of living remain constant. This means that income is assumed to be a major contributor to improving standards of living. Yet results suggest that if growth is the only channel, it will take an exceptionally long time—perhaps unrealistically so—to improve living standards. Policies other than those aimed at increasing growth alone are required to achieve this objective.

Public spending and standards of living

This chapter has demonstrated that per-capita GDP is an important determinant of a country's living standards; the richer a country, the higher the expected standard of living. An implication of this observation is that a country can enhance its living standards by promoting economic growth. This chapter, however, finds that countries' relative performance in standards of living varies widely in relation to their per-capita GDP.

This finding suggests that a one-to-one relationship between a country's material prosperity and its living standards does not exist. There are factors other than income that have an impact on a country's standard of living, including the basic services provided by governments in education and health, and access to these services, which determines education and health outcomes. Countries whose performance on standards of living is inferior in relation to their per-capita GDP do not have systems that promote the efficient delivery of services in education and health. While economic growth is essential, it is not enough to improve citizens' well-being.

If growth is not enough, then, what else can governments do to improve standards of living?[8] One approach would be to increase public spending. This can be crucial in promoting improvements in education and health outcomes. For instance, policy interventions to reduce mortality may require increased public spending or, similarly, it may be necessary to spend more on educational programs that aim to increase primary completion rates. However, what matters is not only how much was spent, but also how effectively this money was spent.

A handful of countries suggest an inconsistent relationship between changes in public spending and outcomes. For example, Thailand has increased public spending on primary schooling more than Peru, yet primary school completion fell in Thailand and increased in Peru. Likewise, an analysis of Malaysia covering the late 1980s found little association between public spending on doctors and infant or maternal mortality, while the construction of more public schools in Indonesia in the 1970s did not have a significant positive impact on school enrollment. The multi-country association between public spending and outcomes, after controlling for national income, is found to be statistically and substantially weak. The message is not that public funding cannot be successful; rather, it is commitment and appropriate policies, backed by effective public spending that can achieve these goals.

Most poor people do not get their fair share of government spending on public services in education and health. Benefit incidence analysis on public expenditure provides a clearer picture of who benefits from government spending. Evidence largely suggests that the poorest fifth of the population receives less than a fifth of education and health expenditures, while the richest fifth gets more: 46% of education spending in Nepal goes to the richest fifth, and the poorest fifth receives only 1% (Filmer 2003). Similarly, in India the richest fifth receives three times the curative healthcare subsidy of the poorest fifth. One reason for this imbalance is that spending is biased toward services that are used mainly by richer people; another reason is that while channeling public spending toward services used by the poor helps, such services may not be reaching the targeted beneficiaries.

Indeed, public spending is not always effective in providing quality services and reaching the intended beneficiaries, who are often the poor; this partly explains why spending has a weak relationship with outcomes. Another reason is the interaction between the private and public sectors. Increasing public provision may simply crowd out, in part or in whole, equally effective services offered by non-government providers. Unless resources support services that work for poor people, the public resources spent on these services will not produce the optimal outcome.

If more public money is spent on services and more of that money is spent on services used by the poor, the spending pattern will determine the efficacy of spending. For instance, wages and salaries of teachers on average account for 75% of recurrent public expenditure on education. There is no doubt that teachers play a critical role in the schooling process, and giving them adequate incentives is important; however, spending on other vital inputs (such as textbooks) is also important. Too much spending on one input will have a negative impact on the quality of learning. To address this issue, governments must tackle not only the technical or managerial questions of how much to spend on one input relative to another, but also the institutional and political contexts that generate these decisions.

Conclusion

There are numerous cases in which a country's rapid economic growth has not generated strong improvements on human development. Countries with high per-capita incomes can have poor records on human development, while those with low per-capita incomes or growth rates can nevertheless do well on this front. The lack of a systematic relationship between progress in human development and economic growth suggests that in order to achieve social progress, patterns of investment in human development matter more than economic growth *per se*. Empirical evidence suggests that growth in per-capita GDP does not necessarily translate into progress in human development, and similar results were found in this chapter on multi-country variations in standards of living. However, more work on causality is required to explain the major findings here.

Several important implications have emerged. First, bridging the gap in indicators of living standards between low-income and industrialized economies appears to be a more feasible goal than closing the gap in per-capita incomes. Second, bridging the gap in per-capita incomes is not a necessary condition for bridging the gap in standards of living reflected by life expectancy, child mortality, births attended by skilled health personnel, and education. Third, adequate resources must flow into human development in education and health to bridge the gap in standards of living between developing and developed economies. While increased public spending is essential, it is not enough to improve standards of living. Rather, governments' planning, delivery, and management of public services are major factors that determine progress in human development.

It should be noted that this study does not call for de-emphasizing economic growth. On the contrary, it finds that per-capita income is an important explanatory variable for standard of living, and that standard of living is more responsive to growth in per-capita income in lower-income countries than in higher-income countries. Yet, it also finds that there are countries that have comparable per-capita incomes but are poles apart with respect to standards of living. For the countries with inferior achievement, public policies and institutions that enable better delivery of quality basic services can play a more important role than growth in per-capita GDP alone in improving life expectancy and education, as well as in reducing child and maternal mortality.

Notes

1 This chapter has been published in the *Asian Development Review* Vol. 27, No. 1, pp. 1–42.
2 The composition of each region is defined in Table A.8.1.
3 The idea of non-linearity may also apply to democracy, but no empirical evidence of this exists because it is difficult to quantify the degree of democracy.
4 This study focuses only on one member of a class of achievement functions because (i) it is the most relevant to the current analysis and (ii) using other members of the class does not add new insight into the analysis.
5 The elasticity can change if richer countries put greater resources into the health sector.
6 In the calculation, we assume that the industrialized countries' living standards are also improving.
7 In the calculation, we assume that the industrialized countries' living standards are also improving.
8 Governments often see improving health and education outcomes as a public responsibility. There are two economic rationales for this. The first is market failure; more specifically, if there is no government intervention, the amount of services produced and consumed would be less than optimal from society's point of view. As there is no market incentive to produce public goods, government intervention is required. The other rationale is related to equity concerns. Issues such as improving outcomes in health and education for poor people or reducing the gaps in outcomes between the poor and the better-off are often considered a government responsibility.

Appendix

Table A.8.1 Standards of living by country, 2000–07

Economy	GDP per capita at 2005 PPP ($)	Life expectancy at birth (years)	Adult literacy rate (%)	Net primary enrollment rate (%)	Under-5 survival rate (per 1,000 births)	Births attended by skilled personnel (%)
East Asia and the Pacific						
Brunei Darussalam	47,938	76.7	98.9	96.9	991	99.8
Cambodia	1,299	57.6	83.4	91.1	909	37.8
China, People's Rep. of	3,683	71.2	98.9	–[a]	971	97.0
Fiji	4,152	68.1	–	97.6	982	99.0
Hong Kong, China	33,450	81.4	–	97.0	–	100.0
Indonesia	3,064	67.1	98.7	98.0	961	67.3
Kiribati	1,374	62.3	–	99.7	934	88.9
Korea, Rep. of	20,228	77.3	–	97.1	995	100.0
Lao People's Dem. Rep.	1,706	62.5	78.5	79.8	915	19.4
Macau, China	33,196	80.0	99.6	88.5	–	100.0
Malaysia	11,201	73.4	97.2	96.8	987	97.3
Micronesia, Federated States of	2,899	67.8	–	92.3	957	87.7
Mongolia	2,428	66.1	97.7	91.1	950	98.3
Myanmar	735	60.7	94.5	97.7	894	62.3
Papua New Guinea	1,899	57.1	66.7	74.9	924	41.5
Philippines	2,852	70.6	95.1	93.2	965	58.9
Samoa	3,477	70.5	99.3	97.1	970	100.0
Singapore	40,965	79.1	99.5	–	996	99.9
Solomon Islands	1,464	62.6	–	63.3	921	–
Thailand	6,623	69.3	98.0	88.7	990	98.3
Timor-Leste	746	55.8	–	68.1	926	21.0
Tonga	3,391	72.5	–	96.6	975	96.7
Vanuatu	3,254	68.9	–	95.2	959	88.0
Viet Nam	1,979	70.1	–	91.8	978	82.8
South Asia						
Bangladesh	1,019	62.5	63.6	89.5	922	14.2
Bhutan	3,498	63.8	–	65.3	918	43.6
India	2070	63.7	76.4	88.4	919	44.6
Maldives	4,071	66.4	98.2	98.6	961	77.2
Nepal	940	61.9	70.1	77.3	930	14.7
Pakistan	2,089	64.5	65.1	61.9	899	25.7
Sri Lanka	3,378	74.3	95.6	98.2	985	96.0
Central Asia						
Armenia	3,612	71.3	99.8	86.4	971	97.3
Azerbaijan	4,076	72.1	–	83.7	910	90.6
Georgia	3,180	70.5	–	82.5	966	95.7

(*Continued*)

Table A.8.1 Cont'd

Economy	GDP per capita at 2005 PPP ($)	Life expectancy at birth (years)	Adult literacy rate (%)	Net primary enrollment rate (%)	Under-5 survival rate (per 1,000 births)	Births attended by skilled personnel (%)
Kazakhstan	7,763	65.9	–	97.9	966	99.6
Kyrgyz Rep.	1,672	68.2	–	93.7	955	98.6
Tajikistan	1,331	66.0	99.9	96.9	923	77.3
Uzbekistan	1,890	67.4	–	–	949	97.8
Eastern Europe						
Albania	5,120	75.7	99.4	92.8	980	99.0
Belarus	7,660	68.4	–	91.6	985	99.9
Bosnia and Herzegovina	5,880	74.2	99.8	–	984	99.6
Bulgaria	8,607	72.1	98.2	96.6	985	99.3
Croatia	12,430	74.7	99.7	92.7	993	99.9
Cyprus	24,157	78.9	99.8	98.5	995	99.0
Czech Rep.	19,158	75.6	–	92.5	995	99.9
Estonia	15,007	71.5	99.8	98.1	992	99.7
Hungary	15,896	72.4	–	96.4	992	99.6
Latvia	11,945	70.7	99.8	92.2	989	100.0
Lithuania	12,674	71.6	99.7	95.1	991	100.0
Macedonia	7,174	73.6	98.7	97.6	984	98.0
Moldova	1,940	68.0	99.7	90.3	979	99.5
Montenegro	7,721	74.4	–	–	989	98.8
Poland	13,026	74.5	–	97.6	992	99.9
Romania	8,686	71.4	97.8	94.3	980	98.5
Russia	10,901	65.3	99.7	89.4	981	99.4
Serbia	8,010	72.4	–	–	990	99.0
Slovak Rep.	15,157	73.7	–	92.1	991	99.5
Slovenia	22,014	76.8	99.9	96.4	995	99.8
Turkey	9,615	70.9	95.6	90.2	967	83.0
Ukraine	5,050	68.1	99.8	88.0	977	99.9
Latin America and the Caribbean						
Antigua and Barbuda	15,372	75.2	–	–	987	99.9
Argentina	10,353	74.5	98.9	99.3	983	98.8
Belize	6,101	71.9	–	98.0	981	89.3
Bolivia	3,691	64.2	97.3	96.4	930	66.9
Brazil	8,302	71.3	95.5	93.5	976	96.6
Chile	11,578	77.8	99.0	94.1	990	99.9
Colombia	5,737	71.9	98.0	91.5	977	91.4
Costa Rica	8,747	78.3	97.6	–	987	98.0
Dominica	6,526	76.5	–	93.2	984	100.0
Dominican Rep.	5,360	71.3	94.2	85.9	967	97.0
Ecuador	6,271	74.3	96.4	99.4	973	74.7

(Continued)

Table A.8.1 Cont'd

Economy	GDP per capita at 2005 PPP ($)	Life expectancy at birth (years)	Adult literacy rate (%)	Net primary enrollment rate (%)	Under-5 survival rate (per 1,000 births)	Births attended by skilled personnel (%)
El Salvador	5,131	70.9	88.5	94.1	971	92.4
Grenada	6,743	72.7	–	90.9	978	100.0
Guatemala	4,069	69.1	82.2	90.5	954	41.4
Guyana	2,607	64.6	–	–	935	89.8
Haiti	1,113	58.9	–	–	909	25.0
Honduras	3,168	69.1	88.9	92.5	968	63.2
Jamaica	6,012	70.9	–	90.9	969	97.0
Mexico	11,240	74.3	97.4	99.6	963	89.2
Nicaragua	2,238	71.3	86.2	89.6	961	66.9
Panama	8,882	74.9	96.1	99.0	976	91.9
Paraguay	3,798	71.1	95.9	94.5	976	77.1
Peru	6,200	70.3	96.9	99.6	969	73.2
St. Kitts and Nevis	12,592	71.1	–	97.0	979	99.8
St. Lucia	8,599	73.5	–	98.5	985	99.7
St. Vincent and the Grenadines	6,232	70.9	–	93.3	979	100.0
Suriname	6,226	69.5	94.9	94.3	960	84.5
Trinidad and Tobago	16,949	69.3	99.5	91.3	964	96.8
Uruguay	8,905	75.1	–	97.3	986	99.4
Venezuela	9,646	73.8	97.2	92.3	978	94.5
Middle East and North Africa						
Algeria	6,736	71.2	90.1	97.0	960	94.4
Bahrain	30,186	75.2	97.0	98.9	989	99.0
Djibouti	1,824	53.8	–	31.0	863	76.8
Egypt	4,497	70.1	84.9	96.8	959	68.2
Iran	8,861	69.8	97.4	86.5	962	89.6
Israel	22,494	79.5	–	97.9	994	–
Jordan	4,095	71.5	99.1	96.4	973	99.5
Kuwait	38,632	77.3	99.7	88.5	989	100.0
Lebanon	9,107	71.3	–	86.5	970	95.5
Libya	12,397	73.3	98.0	–	980	–
Malta	20,280	78.6	–	94.8	994	100.0
Morocco	3,423	69.8	70.5	84.0	956	62.6
Oman	18,631	74.7	97.3	81.1	987	96.4
Qatar	64,681	74.7	95.9	97.3	979	100.0
Saudi Arabia	20,371	72.0	95.9	86.5	973	94.5
Syria	3,940	73.3	93.8	96.9	984	84.2
Tunisia	6,157	73.1	94.3	97.1	974	89.9
United Arab Emirates	43,316	78.7	97.0	85.9	991	100.0
Yemen	2,139	60.9	75.2	67.8	896	26.8

(Continued)

Table A.8.1 Cont'd

Economy	GDP per capita at 2005 PPP ($)	Life expectancy at birth (years)	Adult literacy rate (%)	Net primary enrollment rate (%)	Under-5 survival rate (per 1,000 births)	Births attended by skilled personnel (%)
Sub-Saharan Africa						
Angola	3,442	41.6	72.2	–	740	45.9
Benin	1,212	55.2	45.3	73.8	847	73.1
Botswana	11,299	48.6	94.0	86.1	885	94.2
Burkina Faso	985	51.1	32.1	38.6	800	45.7
Burundi	329	47.8	73.3	52.1	819	29.4
Cameroon	1,929	50.3	–	–	850	61.6
Cape Verde	2,530	70.2	96.3	94.8	963	–
Central African Rep.	678	44.0	58.5	–	821	48.8
Chad	1,199	50.6	37.6	56.7	793	15.4
Comoros	1,111	62.2	–	55.5	926	61.8
Congo, Dem. Rep.	259	45.2	70.4	–	795	67.4
Congo, Rep.	3,190	53.7	97.4	54.4	877	86.2
Côte d'Ivoire	1,647	47.5	60.7	56.2	869	62.5
Equatorial Guinea	22,248	50.0	94.9	91.6	796	64.6
Eritrea	535	55.9	–	44.4	917	28.3
Ethiopia	596	51.3	49.9	48.4	867	5.7
Gabon	13,816	57.1	96.2	89.5	909	85.5
Gambia, The	1,070	58.3	–	70.2	879	55.8
Ghana	1,116	59.0	70.7	60.7	883	48.4
Guinea	1,058	54.2	46.6	60.4	830	46.8
Guinea-Bissau	479	45.7	–	45.4	793	36.8
Kenya	1,328	52.4	80.3	71.3	881	41.6
Lesotho	1,289	44.9	–	77.4	876	57.6
Liberia	364	44.3	67.4	66.2	765	50.9
Madagascar	835	57.8	70.2	76.4	876	48.8
Malawi	661	46.4	–	94.0	866	56.5
Mali	968	52.4	–	55.2	780	40.6
Mauritania	1,668	62.7	61.3	71.5	875	56.9
Mauritius	9,532	72.3	94.5	94.1	984	99.0
Mozambique	629	43.5	–	64.3	846	47.7
Namibia	4,353	52.6	92.3	77.1	936	75.5
Niger	582	55.0	36.6	35.9	740	16.7
Nigeria	1,625	46.8	84.2	63.3	803	36.3
Rwanda	732	43.6	77.6	72.1	831	35.0
Sao Tome and Principe	1,359	64.6	95.4	99.1	904	78.6
Senegal	1,482	62.0	49.1	62.2	878	56.5
Seychelles	14,916	72.2	99.1	95.6	986	–
Sierra Leone	536	41.4	47.9	–	727	42.5
South Africa	8,156	47.2	–	95.0	933	92.0

(Continued)

Table A.8.1 Cont'd

Economy	GDP per capita at 2005 PPP ($)	Life expectancy at birth (years)	Adult literacy rate (%)	Net primary enrollment rate (%)	Under-5 survival rate (per 1,000 births)	Births attended by skilled personnel (%)
Sudan	1,622	57.0	77.2	44.0	908	68.1
Swaziland	4,448	42.8	88.4	75.9	845	72.0
Tanzania	993	50.5	78.4	78.3	873	43.4
Togo	767	57.9	74.4	80.0	886	57.3
Uganda	816	48.7	76.6	–	862	40.6
Zambia	1,138	40.4	–	76.7	818	43.4
Industrialized countries						
Australia	30,773	80.2	–	95.8	994	99.7
Austria	33,729	78.9	–	96.9	995	–
Belgium	31,328	78.6	–	98.9	995	–
Canada	34,114	79.8	–	99.5	994	99.2
Denmark	33,032	77.4	–	98.8	995	–
Finland	29,696	78.4	–	99.5	996	99.9
France	30,167	79.6	–	99.6	995	–
Germany	30,396	78.5	–	–	995	100.0
Greece	27,716	78.7	98.9	98.6	995	–
Iceland	33,087	80.1	–	98.9	997	–
Ireland	36,276	78.0	–	94.3	994	100.0
Italy	27,966	80.1	99.8	99.6	995	99.0
Japan	29,665	81.7	–	99.9	996	99.8
Luxembourg	67,689	78.4	–	97.8	995	99.9
Netherlands	34,342	78.7	–	98.9	994	100.0
New Zealand	23,928	79.2	–	99.1	993	96.6
Norway	46,361	79.4	–	99.3	996	–
Portugal	20,044	77.4	99.6	99.2	994	99.8
Spain	26,595	79.7	–	99.8	995	–
Sweden	31,025	80.2	–	99.1	996	–
Switzerland	35,095	80.6	–	97.0	995	100.0
United Kingdom	30,518	78.4	–	99.9	994	–
United States	40,665	77.3	–	94.4	992	–

[a] – Indicates data not available. GDP = gross domestic product; PPP = purchasing power parity.

Source: Author's calculations based on World Development Indicators 2008.

Table A.8.2 Relative achievement in standards of living, 2000–07

Economy	GDP per capita at 2005 PPP	Life expectancy at birth	Adult literacy rate	Net primary enrollment rate	Under-5 survival rate	Births attended by skilled personnel
East Asia and the Pacific						
Brunei Darussalam	566	149.5	154.4	131.9	140	197.5
Cambodia	15	51.4	61.5	91.7	71	20.4
China, People's Rep. of	43	109.0	153.5	–[a]	105	150.4
Fiji	49	91.9	–	141.0	119	197.5
Hong Kong, China	395	212.3	–	132.8		197.5
Indonesia	36	87.1	149.2	148.0	96	48.0
Kiribati	16	67.5	–	174.9	80	94.3
Korea, Rep. of	239	155.4	–	134.2	156	197.5
Lao People's Dem. Rep.	20	68.1	52.7	60.7	73	9.3
Macau, China	392	188.1	157.9	82.1		197.5
Malaysia	132	122.9	123.1	130.7	130	154.9
Micronesia, Federated States of	34	90.7	–	97.4	93	89.9
Mongolia	29	82.9	129.5	91.7	89	175.8
Myanmar	9	61.7	99.6	143.9	66	41.8
Papua New Guinea	22	49.8	37.7	52.5	76	23.0
Philippines	34	105.2	103.4	102.2	99	38.1
Samoa	41	104.9	157.9	134.6	103	197.5
Singapore	484	175.2	157.9	–	167	197.5
Solomon Islands	17	68.5	–	38.0	75	–
Thailand	78	98.0	134.2	82.8	137	174.8
Timor-Leste	9	46.1	–	43.4	77	10.1
Tonga	40	116.7	–	127.9	110	145.7
Vanuatu	38	96.0	–	114.9	95	90.9
Viet Nam	23	102.2	–	95.1	113	75.4
South Asia						
Bangladesh	12	68.0	34.7	85.6	75	6.6
Bhutan	41	73.2	–	40.2	74	24.5
India	24	72.9	49.6	81.6	74	25.3
Maldives	48	84.1	137.2	161.0	96	63.3
Nepal	11	66.0	41.4	56.4	79	6.8
Pakistan	25	75.8	36.1	36.6	68	12.7
Sri Lanka	40	129.3	107.1	152.3	123	138.1
Central Asia						
Armenia	43	109.2	157.9	75.6	105	154.9
Azerbaijan	48	114.5	–	68.8	71	101.4
Georgia	38	104.7	–	66.2	100	135.0
Kazakhstan	92	81.8	–	145.8	100	197.5
Kyrgyz Rep.	20	92.6	–	105.1	92	182.6
Tajikistan	16	82.3	157.9	131.9	76	63.5
Uzbekistan	22	88.8	–	–	88	162.7

(Continued)

Table A.8.2 Cont'd

Economy	GDP per capita at 2005 PPP	Life expectancy at birth	Adult literacy rate	Net primary enrollment rate	Under-5 survival rate	Births attended by skilled personnel
Eastern Europe						
Albania	60	140.7	157.9	99.9	116	196.1
Belarus	90	93.6	–	94.0	125	197.5
Bosnia and Herzegovina	69	128.3	157.9	–	123	197.5
Bulgaria	102	114.5	138.0	128.4	123	197.5
Croatia	147	132.9	157.9	99.3	147	197.5
Cyprus	285	172.9	157.9	160.2	156	197.5
Czech Rep.	226	139.4	–	98.4	159	197.5
Estonia	177	110.8	157.9	150.1	141	197.5
Hungary	188	116.0	–	126.4	144	197.5
Latvia	141	105.9	157.9	96.9	134	197.5
Lithuania	150	111.4	157.9	114.1	138	197.5
Macedonia	85	124.2	150.0	141.0	122	167.8
Moldova	23	91.5	157.9	88.5	114	197.5
Montenegro	91	129.9	–	–	133	189.7
Poland	154	131.1	–	141.5	143	197.5
Romania	103	110.1	130.3	108.5	116	180.1
Russia	129	79.4	157.9	85.1	117	197.5
Serbia	95	116.4	–	–	136	197.5
Slovak Rep.	179	125.4	–	96.4	140	197.5
Slovenia	260	150.9	157.9	126.0	159	197.5
Turkey	114	107.2	107.1	88.3	101	76.0
Ukraine	60	92.1	157.9	80.6	111	197.5
Latin American and the Caribbean						
Antigua and Barbuda	182	136.2	–	–	129	197.5
Argentina	122	130.9	155.3	174.9	120	190.9
Belize	72	112.9	–	148.3	118	95.9
Bolivia	44	74.9	124.1	126.2	79	47.4
Brazil	98	109.4	106.4	103.7	111	144.8
Chile	137	160.4	157.6	107.7	137	197.5
Colombia	68	113.1	133.7	93.6	112	105.2
Costa Rica	103	165.9	128.1	–	129	167.8
Dominica	77	147.4	–	101.9	123	197.5
Dominican Rep.	63	109.5	97.8	74.5	101	149.9
Ecuador	74	129.3	114.4	174.9	107	59.0
El Salvador	61	107.0	74.1	107.5	105	110.5
Grenada	80	118.4	–	91.0	112	197.5
Guatemala	48	97.1	59.2	89.5	91	22.9
Guyana	31	76.2	–	–	81	97.9
Haiti	13	55.7	–	–	71	12.3

(Continued)

Table A.8.2 Cont'd

Economy	GDP per capita at 2005 PPP	Life expectancy at birth	Adult literacy rate	Net primary enrollment rate	Under-5 survival rate	Births attended by skilled personnel
Honduras	37	97.0	75.5	98.6	102	42.8
Jamaica	71	107.2	–	91.0	102	150.4
Mexico	133	129.6	124.5	174.9	98	95.3
Nicaragua	26	109.4	68.0	86.0	96	47.4
Panama	105	134.3	111.1	173.7	110	107.8
Paraguay	45	108.0	109.6	110.2	110	63.2
Peru	73	103.5	119.6	174.9	102	56.5
St. Kitts and Nevis	149	108.0	–	132.6	114	197.5
St. Lucia	102	123.4	–	159.7	124	197.5
St. Vincent and the Grenadines	74	106.9	–	102.7	114	197.5
Suriname	74	99.2	101.9	108.8	96	80.0
Trinidad and Tobago	200	97.9	157.9	92.6	98	147.6
Uruguay	105	136.0	–	137.6	127	197.5
Venezuela	114	125.9	122.6	97.5	113	124.4
Middle East and North Africa						
Algeria	80	108.8	79.5	133.1	95	123.4
Bahrain	356	136.3	120.5	169.5	133	197.5
Djibouti	22	40.5	–	14.1	59	62.6
Egypt	53	102.3	64.9	130.2	94	49.1
Iran	105	101.0	125.6	76.1	97	97.1
Israel	266	181.2	–	147.2	152	–
Jordan	48	110.8	157.9	126.4	107	197.5
Kuwait	456	155.7	157.9	82.1	132	197.5
Lebanon	108	109.2	–	75.9	103	133.0
Libya	146	122.3	134.9	–	116	–
Malta	239	170.0	–	111.9	149	197.5
Morocco	40	101.0	41.8	69.5	93	42.2
Oman	220	132.3	123.6	63.2	129	142.0
Qatar	764	132.5	109.7	137.4	114	197.5
Saudi Arabia	241	113.9	109.4	75.9	107	124.4
Syria	47	121.9	95.5	132.1	122	79.2
Tunisia	73	121.0	98.5	134.6	108	98.3
United Arab Emirates	511	170.4	119.9	74.4	139	197.5
Yemen	25	62.4	47.8	43.0	67	13.4
Sub-Saharan Africa						
Angola	41	12.1	43.9	–	40	26.4
Benin	14	44.3	20.7	50.8	56	56.3
Botswana	133	27.2	96.3	74.9	64	122.1
Burkina Faso	12	33.3	13.3	18.5	48	26.2

(Continued)

Table A.8.2 Cont'd

Economy	GDP per capita at 2005 PPP	Life expectancy at birth	Adult literacy rate	Net primary enrollment rate	Under-5 survival rate	Births attended by skilled personnel
Burundi	4	25.5	45.3	27.9	51	14.9
Cameroon	23	31.3	–	–	56	41.0
Cape Verde	30	103.0	112.6	112.0	98	–
Central African Rep.	8	17.1	30.2	–	51	28.7
Chad	14	32.2	16.2	31.7	47	7.1
Comoros	13	66.9	–	30.7	77	41.3
Congo, Dem. Rep.	3	19.6	41.8	–	47	48.0
Congo, Rep.	38	40.3	125.7	29.8	62	84.9
Cote d'Ivoire	19	24.8	32.0	31.3	60	42.1
Equatorial Guinea	263	30.6	101.8	93.8	47	44.5
Eritrea	6	46.3	–	22.3	74	14.3
Ethiopia	7	34.0	23.7	25.1	60	2.5
Gabon	163	50.0	112.5	85.5	71	82.8
Gambia, The	13	53.6	–	46.0	63	35.0
Ghana	13	55.9	42.1	35.4	63	28.4
Guinea	12	41.7	21.5	35.1	52	27.1
Guinea-Bissau	6	20.8	–	22.9	47	19.6
Kenya	16	36.7	55.8	47.4	63	23.1
Lesotho	15	18.9	–	56.5	62	36.8
Liberia	4	17.6	38.4	41.2	43	30.5
Madagascar	10	52.0	41.6	54.8	62	28.7
Malawi	8	22.3	–	106.8	60	35.7
Mali	11	36.7	–	30.5	45	22.3
Mauritania	20	68.8	32.6	47.6	61	36.1
Mauritius	113	115.6	99.7	107.4	123	197.5
Mozambique	7	16.1	–	39.1	55	27.8
Namibia	51	37.3	88.1	56.0	81	60.3
Niger	7	43.9	15.6	16.9	40	7.8
Nigeria	19	23.0	63.3	38.0	48	19.3
Rwanda	9	16.2	51.4	48.4	53	18.4
Sao Tome and Principe	16	76.2	105.8	174.9	69	66.1
Senegal	17	66.1	23.2	37.0	62	35.7
Seychelles	176	115.0	157.9	118.3	127	–
Sierra Leone	6	11.8	22.4	–	38	23.7
South Africa	96	24.1	–	113.4	80	108.3
Sudan	19	49.7	50.7	22.0	71	49.0
Swaziland	53	14.5	73.9	54.0	55	54.6
Tanzania	12	31.8	52.6	58.0	61	24.4

(*Continued*)

Table A.8.2 Cont'd

Economy	GDP per capita at 2005 PPP	Life expectancy at birth	Adult literacy rate	Net primary enrollment rate	Under-5 survival rate	Births attended by skilled personnel
Togo	9	52.4	46.7	61.1	64	36.5
Uganda	10	27.6	49.9	–	58	22.3
Zambia	13	9.8	–	55.4	50	24.4
Industrialized countries						
Australia	363	191.0	–	120.3	152	197.5
Austria	398	173.5	–	131.7	154	–
Belgium	370	170.0	–	172.6	156	–
Canada	403	184.7	–	174.9	152	197.5
Denmark	390	156.3	–	168.2	155	–
Finland	351	167.2	–	174.9	164	197.5
France	356	183.1	–	174.9	157	–
Germany	359	168.5	–	–	159	197.5
Greece	327	170.8	155.9	163.2	155	–
Iceland	391	189.5	–	172.6	173	–
Ireland	428	163.3	–	108.6	153	197.5
Italy	330	189.6	157.9	174.9	158	197.5
Japan	350	218.4	–	174.9	163	197.5
Luxembourg	799	166.9	–	145.4	157	197.5
Netherlands	406	170.5	–	170.9	153	197.5
New Zealand	283	177.4	–	174.9	148	145.0
Norway	547	180.2	–	174.9	161	–
Portugal	237	156.0	157.9	174.9	153	197.5
Spain	314	184.4	–	174.9	158	–
Sweden	366	190.6	–	174.9	166	–
Switzerland	414	197.8	–	133.4	154	197.5
United Kingdom	360	167.6	–	174.9	151	–
United States	480	155.9	–	109.4	143	–

[a]– Indicates data not available. GDP = gross domestic product; PPP = purchasing power parity.

Source: Author's calculations based on World Development Indicators 2008.

Table A.8.3 Individual country performance, 2000–07

Economy	Life expectancy at birth	Adult literacy rate	Net primary enrollment rate	Under-5 survival rate	Births attended by skilled personnel
East Asia and the Pacific					
Brunei Darussalam	−0.91	−0.46	−0.63	−0.95	−0.49
Cambodia	−0.15	−0.13	0.67	0.04	−0.76
China, People's Rep. of	0.72	1.81	−ᵃ	0.55	1.09
Fiji	−0.06	–	1.29	1.16	2.04
Hong Kong, China	1.89	–	−0.36	–	−0.12
Indonesia	0.13	1.85	1.71	0.28	−1.02
Kiribati	0.38	–	3.09	0.48	0.84
Korea, Rep. of	0.37	–	0.02	1.12	0.40
Lao People's Dem. Rep.	0.14	−0.65	−0.39	−0.22	−1.30
Macau, China	0.99	−0.02	−1.82	–	−0.11
Malaysia	−0.12	−0.13	0.32	0.43	0.05
Micronesia, Federated States of	0.33	–	0.29	0.20	−0.03
Mongolia	0.26	1.43	0.25	0.20	2.11
Myanmar	0.93	1.58	2.61	0.54	0.30
Papua New Guinea	−0.67	−1.21	−0.70	−0.18	−1.10
Philippines	0.89	0.47	0.44	0.57	−1.17
Samoa	0.64	2.00*	1.23	0.53	2.23*
Singapore	0.25	−0.20	–	0.77	0.33
Solomon Islands	0.34	–	−0.94	0.12	–
Thailand	−0.40	0.67	−0.68	1.57	1.03
Timor-Leste	0.33	–	−0.33	1.12	−0.42
Tonga	1.11	–	1.06	0.91	1.06
Vanuatu	0.39	–	0.71	0.14	−0.12
Viet Nam	1.23	–	0.49	1.84*	0.04
South Asia					
Bangladesh	0.76	−0.75	0.67	0.62	−0.83
Bhutan	−0.55	–	−1.47	−1.12	−1.69*
India	0.08	−0.91	0.07	−0.40	−1.13
Maldives	−0.33	1.20	1.89*	−0.11	−0.97
Nepal	0.79	−0.47	−0.11	0.92	−0.74
Pakistan	0.18	−1.35	−1.22	−0.78	−1.43
Sri Lanka	1.59	0.43	1.77*	1.70*	0.90
Central Asia					
Armenia	0.75	1.98	−0.47	0.58	1.21
Azerbaijan	0.80	–	−0.75	−1.49	−0.12
Georgia	0.74	–	−0.66	0.47	0.89
Kazakhstan	−1.20	–	1.00	−0.75	1.38
Kyrgyz Rep.	1.07	–	0.89	0.87	2.67
Tajikistan	0.97	2.95*	1.82*	0.27	0.18
Uzbekistan	0.78	–	–	0.51	2.07*

(*Continued*)

Table A.8.3 Cont'd

Economy	Life expectancy at birth	Adult literacy rate	Net primary enrollment rate	Under-5 survival rate	Births attended by skilled personnel
Eastern Europe					
Albania	1.50	1.65*	−0.02	0.71	1.78*
Belarus	−0.74	–	−0.46	0.66	1.40
Bosnia and Herzegovina	0.87	1.53	–	0.94	1.67*
Bulgaria	−0.11	0.56	0.44	0.44	1.28
Croatia	0.12	0.86	−0.64	1.28	0.90
Cyprus	0.80	0.27	0.65	0.87	0.21
Czech Rep.	−0.16	–	−0.96	1.38	0.45
Estonia	−0.93	0.69	0.68	0.68	0.70
Hungary	−0.80	–	−0.03	0.74	0.64
Latvia	−0.83	0.89	−0.68	0.61	0.94
Lithuania	−0.70	0.84	−0.23	0.76	0.88
Macedonia	0.47	1.10	0.92	0.58	0.79
Moldova	0.85	2.57*	0.31	1.94*	2.87
Montenegro	0.59	–	–	1.13	1.21
Poland	0.00	–	0.53	0.99	0.85
Romania	−0.28	0.31	−0.13	0.01	0.87
Russia	−1.71*	0.97	−0.95	−0.22	1.03
Serbia	0.05	–	–	1.24	1.35
Slovak Rep.	−0.40	–	−0.86	0.59	0.69
Slovenia	0.10	0.35	−0.27	1.18	0.31
Turkey	−0.52	−0.49	−0.78	−0.97	−1.58
Ukraine	−0.29	1.67*	−0.56	0.46	1.83*
Latin America and the Caribbean					
Antigua and Barbuda	−0.01	–	–	−0.03	0.68
Argentina	0.27	0.94	1.65*	−0.01	0.93
Belize	0.25	–	1.24	0.57	−0.65
Bolivia	−0.55	0.88	0.95	−0.93	−1.23
Brazil	−0.25	−0.38	−0.24	−0.22	0.13
Chile	1.24	0.91	−0.35	0.79	0.97
Colombia	0.33	0.79	−0.28	0.34	−0.38
Costa Rica	1.79	0.24	–	0.74	0.59
Dominica	1.46	–	−0.13	0.78	1.56
Dominican Rep.	0.28	−0.26	−0.77	−0.21	0.69
Ecuador	0.82	0.11	1.99	−0.06	−1.52
El Salvador	0.24	−0.96	0.19	0.08	−0.15
Grenada	0.33	–	−0.46	0.15	1.53
Guatemala	0.15	−1.22	−0.16	−0.36	−1.89*
Guyana	−0.08	–	–	−0.34	0.26
Haiti	0.20	–	–	0.24	−0.79
Honduras	0.46	−0.48	0.26	0.58	−1.17
Jamaica	0.06	–	−0.38	−0.26	0.58

(Continued)

Table A.8.3 Cont'd

Economy	Life expectancy at birth	Adult literacy rate	Net primary enrollment rate	Under-5 survival rate	Births attended by skilled personnel
Mexico	0.12	−0.09	1.59	−1.36	−1.30
Nicaragua	1.35	−0.41	0.14	0.73	−0.71
Panama	0.59	−0.30	1.72	−0.34	−0.77
Paraguay	0.64	0.40	0.47	0.80	−0.90
Peru	−0.12	0.28	2.00	−0.29	−1.56
St. Kitts and Nevis	−0.81	–	0.30	−0.61	0.88
St. Lucia	0.22	–	1.33	0.49	1.28
St. Vincent and Grenadines	0.00	–	−0.07	0.34	1.61
Suriname	−0.28	−0.27	0.10	−0.69	−1.03
Trinidad and Tobago	−1.56	0.58	−1.04	−1.91*	−0.54
Uruguay	0.65	–	0.68	0.58	1.24
Venezuela	0.18	−0.01	−0.52	−0.32	−0.48
Middle East and North Africa					
Algeria	−0.02	−1.03	0.74	−0.83	−0.14
Bahrain	−0.83	−1.11	0.76	−0.70	−0.02
Djibouti	−0.97	–	−1.78*	−1.10	−0.16
Egypt	0.23	−1.13	0.93	−0.31	−1.40
Iran	−0.64	0.15	−1.07	−1.10	−1.01
Israel	1.20	–	0.32	0.76	–
Jordan	0.65	1.86	0.88	0.50	2.05
Kuwait	−0.41	−0.15	−1.92*	−1.09	−0.27
Lebanon	−0.37	–	−1.09	−0.76	−0.23
Libya	−0.26	0.14	–	−0.47	–
Malta	0.91	–	−0.61	0.74	0.39
Morocco	0.51	−1.61	−0.61	−0.05	−1.27
Oman	−0.39	−0.57	−1.96*	−0.28	−0.77
Qatar	−1.93*	−2.19*	−0.68	−2.90*	−0.81
Saudi Arabia	−1.19	−1.10	−1.65	−1.65	−1.26
Syria	1.12	−0.06	1.07	1.43	−0.58
Tunisia	0.54	−0.36	0.84	0.03	−0.61
United Arab Emirates	−0.00	−1.46	−2.24*	−0.85	−0.39
Yemen	−0.35	−1.00	−1.05	−0.86	−1.44
Sub-Saharan Africa					
Angola	−2.85*	−1.55	–	−3.09*	−1.64
Benin	−0.33	−1.34	−0.44	−0.73	0.11
Botswana	−3.83*	−0.97	−1.27	−3.36*	−0.70
Burkina Faso	−0.49	−1.39	−1.23	−0.90	−0.35
Burundi	0.56	0.60	−0.22	0.75	0.53
Cameroon	−1.39	–	–	−1.32	−0.70
Cape Verde	0.95	0.86	0.80	0.64	–
Central African Rep.	−0.64	−0.53	–	−0.21	0.09

(Continued)

Table A.8.3 Cont'd

Economy	Life expectancy at birth	Adult literacy rate	Net primary enrollment rate	Under-5 survival rate	Births attended by skilled personnel
Chad	−0.77	−1.48	−0.98	−1.23	−0.98
Comoros	0.62	–	−0.96	0.58	−0.13
Congo, Dem. Rep.	0.64	0.70	–	0.87	1.54
Congo, Rep.	−1.67*	1.06	−1.71*	−1.68*	−0.23
Cote d'Ivoire	−1.44	−1.26	−1.21	−0.88	−0.52
Equatorial Guinea	−4.65*	−1.42	−1.19	−5.56*	−3.24*
Eritrea	0.75	–	−0.71	1.39	0.01
Ethiopia	0.15	−0.62	−0.70	0.45	−0.37
Gabon	−3.17*	−0.65	−1.11	−3.23*	−1.80*
Gambia, The	0.17	–	−0.50	−0.17	−0.24
Ghana	0.20	−0.60	−0.83	−0.18	−0.43
Guinea	−0.26	−1.20	−0.80	−0.73	−0.40
Guinea-Bissau	−0.07	–	−0.61	0.02	0.25
Kenya	−0.73	−0.33	−0.60	−0.44	−0.73
Lesotho	−1.36	–	−0.32	−0.47	−0.39
Liberia	0.14	0.29	0.10	0.17	0.78
Madagascar	0.41	−0.36	−0.08	0.12	−0.12
Malawi	−0.41	–	1.58	0.31	0.27
Mali	−0.34	–	−0.87	−1.03	−0.42
Mauritania	0.19	−1.25	−0.75	−0.83	−0.67
Mauritius	−0.19	−0.71	−0.23	0.26	1.17
Mozambique	−0.58	–	−0.33	0.14	0.15
Namibia	−2.17*	−0.38	−1.16	−1.00	−1.11
Niger	0.55	−0.85	−0.92	−0.63	−0.22
Nigeria	−1.49	−0.27	−1.01	−1.56	−1.02
Rwanda	−0.76	0.06	−0.17	−0.22	−0.22
Sao Tome and Principe	0.72	1.21	3.10*	−0.12	0.22
Senegal	0.24	−1.45	−0.98	−0.63	−0.55
Seychelles	−0.76	0.69	−0.22	−0.10	–
Sierra Leone	−0.55	−0.56	–	−0.60	0.22
South Africa	−3.51*	–	0.05	−1.93*	−0.67
Sudan	−0.49	−0.66	−1.47	−0.28	−0.35
Swaziland	−3.09*	−0.83	−1.23	−2.54*	−1.26
Tanzania	−0.55	−0.17	−0.10	−0.16	−0.40
Togo	0.53	−0.12	0.16	0.37	0.14
Uganda	−0.47	−0.08	–	−0.03	−0.24
Zambia	−1.55	–	−0.27	−0.94	−0.54
Industrialized countries					
Australia	1.19	–	−0.66	0.34	−0.04
Austria	0.42	–	−0.39	0.33	–
Belgium	0.38	–	0.83	0.55	–

(Continued)

Table A.8.3 Cont'd

Economy	Life expectancy at birth	Adult literacy rate	Net primary enrollment rate	Under-5 survival rate	Births attended by skilled personnel
Canada	0.83	–	0.83	0.16	−0.14
Denmark	−0.20	–	0.67	0.39	–
Finland	0.34	–	0.93	1.05	0.00
France	0.92	–	0.92	0.62	–
Germany	0.36	–	–	0.71	−0.02
Greece	0.56	0.08	0.64	0.66	–
Iceland	1.04	–	0.79	1.42	–
Ireland	−0.05	–	−1.11	0.16	−0.20
Italy	1.25	0.14	0.97	0.78	0.06
Japan	2.28*	–	0.93	0.99	0.00
Luxembourg	−0.68	–	−0.48	−0.43	−0.85
Netherlands	0.29	–	0.72	0.22	−0.15
New Zealand	0.98	–	1.07	0.44	−0.96
Norway	0.28	–	0.63	0.27	–
Portugal	0.40	0.43	1.19	0.95	0.41
Spain	1.12	–	1.00	0.84	–
Sweden	1.16	–	0.90	1.12	–
Switzerland	1.28	–	−0.37	0.29	−0.17
United Kingdom	0.32	–	0.91	0.31	–
United States	−0.46	–	−1.16	−0.53	−0.32
World	0	0	0	0	0

[a] – Indicates data not available; * – indicates statistically significant at the 5% level.

Source: Author's calculations.

9 Equity in education and health services in the Philippines[1]

Joseph J. Capuno and Aleli D. Kraft

Introduction

The Philippine government remains committed to providing universal access to basic healthcare and education, as mandated in the 1987 Constitution and evidenced in its support of the Millennium Development Goals (MDGs). In health, the government specifically aims to reduce the child and maternal mortality rates, the prevalence of underweight children, and the incidence of malaria and other major diseases. Through its "Fourmula One for Health," the Department of Health (DOH) adopts key reform strategies in health financing, regulation, service delivery, and governance to provide secure, quality and equitable health services to all, particularly the poor (DOH 2008a). A major component of the strategy is to secure public funds to provide health insurance coverage to five million poor and near-poor households, aiming to reach the target of universal insurance coverage by 2013.

Through its Basic Education Sector Reform Agenda (BESRA), the Department of Education (DepEd) endeavors to make all adults functionally literate and all school-age children enroll in and stay in school, and to satisfactorily complete basic education (DepEd 2006). To improve student performance, the BESRA's main thrust is to improve the capacity and responsiveness of schools to student needs, with inputs from students, parents, local governments, and the larger community. Thus, much like the DOH's own strategy, the DepEd adopts a decentralized approach in delegating additional functions to local education officials, and makes them more accountable to service clients.

The government faces considerable challenges in achieving its policy aims. In the health sector, infant and child mortality rates[2] have declined only gradually, from about 38 and 64 deaths per 1,000 in 1993, respectively, to about 25 and 34 deaths per 1,000 in 2008. The decline in maternal mortality rates has also been slow, from 209 to about 162 deaths per 100,000 live births from 1998 to 2006. This is insufficient to meet the Philippines' 2015 MDG targets for reducing child and maternal mortality (NEDA 2005). Infant mortality is also declining more slowly than in comparable countries in the Association of Southeast Asian Nations, and the overall rate masks provincial variation.

Greater use of selected health services such as skilled birth attendance and treatment of pneumonia can help. Yet, while we see that the use of skilled birth attendance increased from 56% to 60% from 1998 to 2003, use by those belonging to the lowest quintiles—at 20.8% and 24.6% of live births for 1998 and 2003, respectively—are way below the national average.

If children with fever are brought to see health providers, they can be diagnosed and treated for pneumonia. Yet rates of seeking treatment for fever are also lower for the lowest wealth quintile relative to the rest of the population. Health system factors at the local level partly contribute to patterns of inequitable utilization of services and health outcomes. This includes the absence of doctors in several municipalities and variations in provider quality, as measured on structural or process dimensions (Capuno and Kraft 2010). Financing constraints also contribute to the challenges: a low percentage share of social health insurance in healthcare financing implies that the poor are not yet protected from impoverishing catastrophic health payments (NSCB 2010). Out-of-pocket payment costs and susceptibility to poverty from catastrophic costs vary across regions (Ico 2008).

In the education sector, access to or completion of primary education remains less than universal, with significant regional and socioeconomic dimensions (Manasan 2000; Mesa 2008; Maligalig and Albert 2008). According to the DepEd, during the academic year 2007–08, about one in five children 6–11 years old still had not enrolled, and only about three in five of those who started elementary schooling finished the required 6 years. Moreover, most of those who stay on until Grade 6, especially in public schools, do not perform passably well enough in mathematics, science, English and other core subjects included in the National Achievement Test. Figures for the previous academic years are not particularly better.

Despite free primary education in public schools, a disproportionate number of children from poor households still drop out or do not enroll in school. Based on the results of the Annual Poverty Indicators Survey in 2007, for every child of 6–11 years old in the richest decile not in school, there were about 20 children in the poorest income decile not attending school. The most commonly cited reasons for staying out of school are lack of personal interest (18%), employment/looking for work (13%), and the high cost of education (15%). Interestingly, 34% cited "too young to go to school" despite the fact that 6 years old is the official age of entry to primary school. These reasons suggest that both choice and circumstance factors influence household schooling decisions, including household income, quality of public schools, and local government support to education. Thus, an assessment of the possible effects of school improvement under the BESRA on enrollment could help refine policy.

To inform policy discussions, we seek to answer three questions in this chapter. First, how equitable is access to basic health and education services? Second, what determines access of households to such services? Third, what policy reforms may be undertaken to improve the equity of access to such services? The equity of access to both services is important, since health and education are critical and related aspects of human development. Indeed, in developing countries, households with low health status—often in areas with low levels and poor quality of public services—also have inferior educational achievement, and both are more prevalent among low-income households. In characterizing the equity of access to health and education services, we use the equity index of opportunity (EIO), the opportunity index (OI), and the opportunity curves discussed in Son (2009) and in Ali and Son (2007).

Inequality of health or education outcomes can be the result of household choices, of the circumstances that define a household's opportunities, or of both. As such, increasingly, policies that reduce inequity of opportunity are advocated over policies that reduce overall inequality of outcome (Williams and Cookson 2000; World Bank 2006). As argued in Sen (1985a, b), Dworkin (1981), Rawls (1971) and especially Roemer (1998), this policy shift has occurred because inequality arising from differences in household or individual choices (or effort) is not as unfair as inequality arising from differences in opportunity (or circumstance), over which households and individuals have no control.

Government should therefore pursue policies that offset the social or economic disadvantages associated with gender, ethnicity, location of birth, or family background. Evidence of the adverse effects of some of these circumstance variables on economic outcomes are found in Latin America, Africa and Europe (e.g., Checchi and Peragine 2005; Bourguignon, Ferreira, and Menendez 2007; Cogneau and Mesple-Somps 2008; Paes de Barros et al. 2009). This paper adopts a similar approach to investigate the consequences of choice and circumstance factors on access to and equity of healthcare and education services in the Philippines. To tease out the effects, we apply logit regression analysis on official household survey data for 2003 and 2007. In the analysis, we further emphasize the relative importance of choice and circumstance factors.

Among circumstance variables, we focus on Philippine Health Insurance Corporation (PhilHealth) coverage and location. PhilHealth provides a social health insurance program for all Filipinos that the government also extends for free to the indigent population. Household location is supposed to capture all area-specific characteristics, such as the accessibility or quality of public health and education services in the community, that the government can control. We assume location to be exogenous to health-seeking or schooling decisions because employment prospects and the costs of migration are more likely to influence household migration decisions, and because households are not easily excluded from local public services in places where they choose to reside. Our findings confirm the importance to health-seeking and schooling decisions of household factors such as income, mother's education, family composition, and child characteristics. Moreover, we also find that PhilHealth improves decisions in both areas, while location has variable effects on the equity of access to health and education services. The implication is that supply-side interventions alone may not reduce inequities in access, while targeted demand-side interventions will.

Equity in access to health and education services

Health services

The financing and delivery of services have a bearing on the supply and demand sides of the health sector and are reflected in the utilization of services. In turn, the utilization pattern largely explains the extent of equity or inequity of health outcomes. Table 9.1 reprises the estimates of equity of opportunity of utilization of any health facility in Son (2009). The estimates show that the EIO for utilization of any health facility has declined from 0.88 in 1998 to 0.81 in 2007, indicating that overall utilization has become more inequitable. The EIO for utilization of government hospitals also remains inequitable. Thus, the objective of improving equity in health outcomes has not been accomplished.

There are several possible explanations for these trends. First, the utilization of healthcare services by the poor may have declined more than that of the rich, which would show a decline in the use of facilities that are more often patronized by the poor. Financial difficulties may have forced the poor to postpone seeking care until their conditions worsen to more severe stages of the illness, thus necessitating them to bypass lower level facilities (Kraft et al. 2009). Another explanation is that the lower level facilities may lack supplies, materials, staff, or equipment, which may have forced the poor to go to public hospitals that are better equipped and staffed, even for basic and primary care needs. These explanations are plausible given the persistent inequities in healthcare inputs, especially in lower level facilities, and the lack of financial protection of the poor.

These trends have implications for the recipients of government subsidies. Public facilities, being largely tax financed, offer care at zero or reduced fees to those who use them. About two-thirds of the DOH budget is spent for personal care services and these are largely spent on its retained hospitals and medical centers that are located in the National Capital Region (NCR) and other main urban areas outside the NCR. The benefits of these subsidies would therefore accrue to those using these healthcare facilities. However, the utilization rates of these facilities indicate that the recipients of subsidies may well be the middle-income households rather than the poorest.

Table 9.1 Equity index of opportunity for utilization of health services

	1998	*2002*	*2004*	*2007*	*Growth rate*
Government hospitals	0.85	0.81	0.82	0.81	−0.8
Private hospitals	0.45	0.41	0.42	0.39	−1.6
Private clinics	0.57	0.53	0.50	0.46	−2.3
Rural health units	1.26	1.18	1.13	1.14	−1.5
Barangay health station	1.33	1.28	1.25	1.29	−0.7
Other services	1.21	1.03	1.20	1.28	−0.6
Any health facility	0.88	0.85	0.84	0.81	−1.0

Source: Son (2009).

Table 9.2 Equity index of opportunity for utilization of a health facility by region

Region	1998	2002	2004	2007	Growth rate
Ilocos	0.95	0.94	0.84	0.77	−1.8
Cagayan Valley	0.82	0.83	0.75	0.78	−0.7
Central Luzon	0.95	0.87	0.87	0.76	−2.1
Southern Luzon	0.93	0.94	0.82	0.91	−0.7
Bicol	0.94	0.85	0.80	0.79	−2.2
Western Visayas	0.87	0.78	0.84	0.79	−1.3
Central Visayas	0.98	0.82	0.81	0.78	−3.2
Eastern Visayas	0.83	0.75	0.85	0.86	−0.1
Western Mindanao	0.96	0.87	0.98	0.88	−0.8
Northern Mindanao	0.95	0.79	0.89	0.81	−2.1
Southern Mindanao	0.87	0.81	0.76	0.64	−2.6
Central Mindanao	0.91	0.98	0.90	0.84	−0.1
Caraga	0.86	0.91	0.92	0.86	0.6
National Capital Region	0.93	0.95	0.99	0.92	0.3
Cordillera Administrative Region	0.91	0.99	0.88	0.84	−0.2
Autonomous Region of Muslim Mindanao	1.02	1.00	0.71	0.83	−3.1
Philippines	0.88	0.85	0.84	0.81	−1.0
Between-region	0.96	0.96	0.98	0.97	0.2
Within-region	0.92	0.88	0.86	0.83	−1.2

Source: Son (2009).

Table 9.2, which is derived from Son (2009), addresses whether the health services available across regions are used more by the poor than by the non-poor. As shown in the table, the use of health services is inequitable across all regions in the country, with the most equitable utilization registered in the NCR and the most inequitable in Southern Mindanao. Most disturbing is that the rising inequality is accompanied by lower levels of overall utilization in regions over time. Particularly alarming are the inequities in the Autonomous Region of Muslim Mindanao (ARMM) and Southern Mindanao, because they are coupled with very low overall utilization. These indicate that the poorest in these regions must have very low utilization levels.

What would contribute more to equity—reducing inequalities between or within regions? The results in Table 9.2 reveal that the within-region inequity is greater than the between-region inequity, and inequity within regions has been increasing at a faster rate than that between regions. Thus, after controlling for the inequities within regions, use of a health facility between regions becomes almost equitable, as suggested by the value of the between-region EIO being close to 1. This finding suggests that interventions aimed at reducing inequities should be addressed or tailored toward subregional groupings; that is, toward particular provinces. This would make sense, since the provinces are more financially capable of providing services and they are the immediate local government units below the national government. While regional coordination can be performed by national agencies—the DOH's Centers for Development, for instance—these regional coordination units still have to engage the provincial governments, since the latter have the executive and the political power to implement health projects. The provincial governments can then engage the municipalities under them.

Maternal and newborn health outcomes are partly determined by the use of critical services during pregnancy, the place of delivery, and who assists in the delivery. When mothers opt not to deliver in facilities and opt not to be assisted by health professionals, they are distanced from life-saving interventions (DOH 2008b). Likewise, they are unable to maximize the use of health facility-based services like tetanus toxoid injections, iron supplementation, and assistance during breastfeeding given during the antenatal and postnatal periods. Thus, their utilization of selected maternal care services is a crucial component in reducing maternal and child mortality, specifically neonatal mortality.

The proportions of women of reproductive age utilizing such services in their pregnancies are presented in Table 9.3. It can be seen that the proportions of those using antenatal care services are lower for the lowest income decile: in 2003 less than half of pregnancies among women from the poorest decile had antenatal care from a skilled health provider—that is, a physician, nurse, or midwife. By contrast, the proportion is close to 100% among women from the highest income quintile for the same year. However, we see increases in the proportions of women having antenatal care services from a skilled provider from 1998 to 2003, with greater increases in the proportions among the bottom half of the population. This resulted

Table 9.3 Selected maternal health service utilization indicators, 1998 and 2003

Decile	Antenatal care from a skilled provider		Skilled birth attendance		Facility-based delivery		Delivery in a public facility	
	1998	2003	1998	2003	1998	2003	1998	2003
1	37.01	47.27	15.14	17.89	5.08	7.01	4.30	6.25
2	40.79	55.27	23.50	31.55	9.77	13.56	8.10	12.14
3	46.68	66.12	31.08	45.01	13.63	20.99	10.55	16.50
4	51.77	64.56	45.35	53.32	19.12	25.73	14.83	21.01
5	59.16	66.56	56.13	66.45	27.27	35.49	21.61	28.25
6	68.82	71.74	70.64	72.33	35.04	46.04	24.21	34.41
7	73.27	79.60	79.38	80.49	47.91	53.89	34.47	37.67
8	78.08	86.44	83.03	86.72	52.09	61.42	29.59	38.12
9	82.26	86.30	88.27	88.75	66.69	67.66	30.80	34.23
10	89.24	91.61	93.12	94.89	82.81	84.06	23.17	27.59
Total	61.45	70.60	56.54	60.15	34.31	38.11	19.46	24.22
Opportunity index	49.26	60.75	37.07	43.48	18.26	23.38	12.87	17.53
Equity index of opportunity	0.7856	0.8490	0.6330	0.6822	0.5082	0.56	0.6384	0.6842

Source: Authors' calculation based on National Demographic and Health Survey 1998 and 2003.

in higher OIs and an improvement in the EIO. However, the distribution remains inequitable.

Inequity in skilled birth attendance and facility-based delivery is also apparent, in that their EIOs are very far from 1. Less than 10% of women from the lowest income deciles deliver in health facilities, while about 84% of their richest counterparts do. Less than one-fifth of deliveries of the poorest pregnant women are assisted by skilled birth attendants—midwives or doctors—the rest being assisted by traditional birth attendants ("*hilots*") or by families and friends. Over the two years, we observe an increase in the amount of and the equity of opportunities from these indicators, albeit very slight.

Major precursors of childhood mortality are pneumonia, diarrhea, and measles (DOH 2008). Utilization of a set of critical health services influence the prevalence of and recovery from these diseases. Table 9.4 shows that less than half of children in the poorest quintiles obtained DPT (diphtheria, pertussis, tetanus), OPV (oral polio vaccine), BCG (Bacille Calmette-Guerin) and measles vaccinations. A more disturbing trend is the relative decline in the average proportion of children being fully immunized, with a trend toward greater inequity. Nearly half of children experiencing fever sought treatment, with less than half of children from the poorest groups seeking care. There was a slight increase in the average proportion of children seeking care across the income groups, resulting in an improvement of the EIO between 1998 and 2003. As for treatment for diarrhea, there were reductions across the two years for most wealth deciles in the proportions of those seeking care among those who experienced symptoms. The OI decreased by a significant amount accompanied by a move toward more inequity.

Table 9.4 Selected child health service utilization indicators, 1998 and 2003

Decile	Fully immunized children		Treatment sought for fever		Treatment sought for diarrhea	
	1998	2003	1998	2003	1998	2003
1	58.34	46.54	40.80	44.48	48.42	26.90
2	60.67	62.41	37.31	49.40	36.63	32.02
3	65.66	72.51	48.25	45.61	43.09	34.09
4	71.34	67.98	47.68	50.94	42.22	31.24
5	74.59	74.18	43.86	54.09	41.26	36.87
6	72.56	76.92	56.62	53.10	45.22	32.64
7	82.29	69.22	57.18	52.13	54.28	45.16
8	82.91	74.96	60.60	56.05	62.29	31.58
9	73.24	82.05	67.67	48.57	46.71	34.83
10	90.19	84.36	62.21	64.35	36.29	51.91
Total	72.81	69.91	51.21	50.82	45.19	34.16
Opportunity index	66.16	63.13	45.46	48.71	44.48	32.05
Equity index of opportunity	0.9041	0.8877	0.8705	0.9390	0.9746	0.8973

Source: Authors' calculations based on National Demographic and Health Survey 1998 and 2003.

Education services

For the country as a whole, the EIO of elementary school attendance improved modestly from 0.941 in 1998 to 0.954 in 2007, although it dropped between 2002 and 2004 from 0.953 to 0.949 (Table 9.5). From 2004 to 2007, the distribution of opportunities for school attendance became less inequitable in only 7 of the 16 regions in the country and remained the same in 2 of them. The regions with the lowest EIOs in 2007 included Davao Region (0.93) and Zamboanga Peninsula (0.94). In the ARMM, the EIO in 1998 was 1.01, which suggests that school attendance favored the poor children, but it subsequently deteriorated to 0.95 in 2007.

There are also significant inequities in school attendance between and within regions in 1998, 2002, 2004, and 2007 (Table 9.5). While the inequities between regions improved from 0.987 in 1998 to 0.991 in 2007, the inequities within regions are more significant. The EIO for within-regions is 0.962 in 2007, only 0.03 percentage points higher than that in 2004. As suggested in Son (2009), the inequities within regions call for more targeted or perhaps province-specific interventions. Consistent with this suggestion, the School-Based Management

Table 9.5 Incidence and equity index of opportunity for primary school attendance (among population 6–11 years old) by region in 2002, 2004, and 2007

Region	Incidence (%)				Equity index of opportunity			
	1998	2002	2004	2007	1998	2002	2004	2007
National Capital Region	96.7	97.5	96.7	97.3	0.97	0.97	0.96	0.98
Cordillera Administrative Region	92.2	96.7	97.0	97.1	0.96	0.99	0.97	0.98
Ilocos	94.8	94.7	96.5	97.7	0.97	0.96	0.98	0.98
Cagayan Valley	92.1	97.6	96.1	95.6	0.94	0.98	0.97	0.96
Central Luzon	94.7	95.8	97.1	96.9	0.97	0.97	0.97	0.96
Southern Tagalog	93.5	96.7	96.0	95.3	0.96	0.97	0.97	0.95
Bicol	88.8	94.0	93.6	95.0	0.92	0.97	0.96	0.97
Western Visayas	90.2	95.0	94.2	95.6	0.97	0.97	0.96	0.97
Central Visayas	88.9	91.3	93.4	93.5	0.94	0.93	0.94	0.96
Eastern Visayas	88.6	92.9	94.2	94.3	0.95	0.96	0.98	0.97
Zamboanga Pen.	83.8	90.4	90.2	89.2	0.94	0.96	0.92	0.94
Northern Mindanao	90.5	93.7	94.1	94.3	0.93	0.95	0.97	0.95
Davao	89.4	92.2	92.4	93.5	0.93	0.91	0.93	0.93
SOCCSKSARGEN	92.6	93.1	87.9	93.3	0.93	0.97	0.88	0.95
Caraga	88.8	95.5	95.8	94.6	0.92	0.97	0.98	0.96
Autonomous Region of Muslim Mindanao	70.3	70.7	77.5	77.3	1.01	0.99	0.95	0.95
Philippines	90.9	93.9	94.0	94.4	0.941	0.953	0.949	0.954
Between-region					0.987	0.990	0.989	0.991
Within-region					0.953	0.963	0.959	0.962

SOCCSKSARGEN = South Cotabato, Cotabato City, Sultan Kudarat, Sarangani and General Santos City.
Source: Son (2009).

Table 9.6 Incidence and equity index of opportunity for secondary school attendance (among population 12–15 years old and over) by region in 2002, 2004, and 2007

Region	Incidence (%)				Equity index of opportunity			
	1998	2002	2004	2007	1998	2002	2004	2007
National Capital Region	93.6	95.1	94.4	94.7	0.96	0.96	0.94	0.97
Cordillera Administrative Region	93.5	94.3	92.0	92.7	0.97	0.95	0.95	0.94
Ilocos	90.8	93.6	91.2	91.0	0.95	0.95	0.95	0.94
Cagayan Valley	83.2	89.2	88.2	88.1	0.87	0.93	0.87	0.89
Central Luzon	89.1	91.0	89.1	88.7	0.92	0.94	0.93	0.90
Southern Tagalog	90.6	91.6	90.3	89.5	0.92	0.94	0.91	0.91
Bicol	85.2	87.7	88.6	87.4	0.92	0.93	0.92	0.92
Western Visayas	89.9	90.6	89.8	88.9	0.98	0.95	0.92	0.95
Central Visayas	82.8	86.4	86.4	87.4	0.91	0.90	0.91	0.93
Eastern Visayas	80.5	85.4	83.8	85.7	0.95	0.94	0.93	0.91
Zamboanga Pen.	82.7	87.9	81.4	84.5	0.91	0.95	0.88	0.89
Northern Mindanao	86.6	91.4	87.8	86.6	0.90	0.93	0.92	0.92
Davao	84.0	88.3	88.2	85.2	0.89	0.90	0.91	0.89
SOCCSKSARGEN	86.5	91.0	85.5	87.6	0.90	0.95	0.89	0.93
Caraga	85.6	90.0	89.5	87.1	0.91	0.94	0.92	0.91
Autonomous Region of Muslim Mindanao	82.6	86.8	82.3	81.7	0.99	0.92	0.92	0.98
Philippines	87.4	90.3	88.6	88.5	0.921	0.932	0.914	0.920
Between-region					0.985	0.990	0.988	0.990
Within-region					0.934	0.941	0.925	0.929

SOCCSKSARGEN = South Cotabato, Cotabato City, Sultan Kudarat, Sarangani and General Santos City.

Source: Son (2009).

approach adopted under BESRA may thus help even out average school attendance across provinces.

The School-Based Management approach finds additional support from the analysis of the incidence rates and EIO of school attendance among children 12–15 years old (Table 9.6). In 2007, the incidence rates are at least 91 only in the NCR, Cordillera Administrative Region (CAR) and Ilocos region. The rates are lower and vary widely in the rest of the regions, ranging from 81.7 in ARMM to 89.5 in the Southern Tagalog region (i.e., combined CALABARZON and MIMAROPA regions). The overall EIO in 2007 (0.920) is worse than that in 1998 (0.921) and 2002 (0.932), although better than that in 2004 (0.914). While the inequities between regions have narrowed from 1998 to 2007, as indicated by the rise in EIO from 0.985 to 0.990, the inequities within region have widened, from an EIO of 0.934 to 0.929. Again, this finding indicates that a more location-specific education intervention may yield greater impact on overall equity in high school attendance. Such focused intervention may be appropriate where inequities have worsened in recent years, such as the Eastern Visayas and Davao regions.

Methodological framework

This section presents the two-step procedure used to identify the choice and circumstance variables that determine household decisions to seek healthcare or attend schools, and to simulate the equity impact of policies that influence the circumstance factors that households face. The circumstance variables of interest are the public services available to households, including social health insurance coverage. However, only community-level data on public services are available. To get around the data and estimation problems, we adapt here a two-step procedure suggested in O'Donnell et al. (2008). In the first step we estimate a logit model of household decision-making with community fixed effects. We then regress the community fixed effects against community-level variables, including those directly affected by policies. We then plug in the partial effects of the policy variables obtained in the second step into the logit model estimated in the first step to simulate the policy impact on household decisions and on equity of access.

The baseline estimates of EIO and OI shown in the succeeding sections are based on the predicted outcomes (e.g., the use of health facility or school attendance) obtained from the first step. In the second step, predicted outcomes corresponding to a policy scenario are obtained and then used to calculate the new EIOs and OIs. The difference between the old and new EIOs and OIs indicate the policy's effect on overall equity.

To fix ideas, consider the following logit regression model (Greene 2003) adopted to identify the factors that influence household decision-making:

$$\text{Prob}(Y_i = 1 | \mathbf{X}_i, \mathbf{P}_i) = \frac{e^{(\alpha + \mathbf{X}_i'\beta + \mathbf{P}_i'\delta)}}{1 + e^{(\alpha + \mathbf{X}_i'\beta + \mathbf{P}_i'\delta)}} \tag{9.1}$$

where i refers to the ith individual, Y is the outcome (say, school attendance), $\mathbf{X}$ is a vector of child and household characteristics, including household income per capita, $\mathbf{P}$ is a vector of provincial dummy variables, α is the intercept, and and are vectors of regression coefficients. From equation (9.1), each child would then have a predicted probability of schooling. They can also be arranged in terms of increasing income, that is,

$$\hat{Y}_1 \leq \hat{Y}_2 \leq \hat{Y}_3 \leq \ldots \leq \hat{Y}_N \tag{9.2}$$

where $\hat{Y}_1$ is the predicted probability of schooling of the child with the lowest household income per capita, $\hat{Y}_2$ is the predicted probability of schooling of the child with the second to the lowest household income per capita, and so forth. These predicted probabilities are then used to compute the baseline EIO and OI.

From equation (9.1), the marginal effect on Y of a particular provincial dummy variable, say P_j, is estimated as follows:

$$\hat{\delta}_j = \text{Prob}(Y = 1 | \overline{\mathbf{X}}, P_j = 1) - \text{Prob}(Y = 1 | \overline{\mathbf{X}}, P_j = 0) \tag{9.3}$$

where $\bar{\mathbf{x}}$ is a vector of the mean values of the child and household characteristics. Note that because the marginal effect would be the same for all children that lived in the same province, the total number of marginal effects would be equal to the number of provinces, say j. The marginal effect on Y of a particular child-level or household-level characteristic $X_j \in \bar{\mathbf{X}}$ is defined analogously. We use the estimated marginal probabilities to identify the critical household-level and community-level factors that promote or deter access to health or education services.

We then use the provincial marginal effects to simulate the effect of a policy on the equity of access, for example, the impact of local government's education expenditures per pupil on the marginal probability of school attendance. Let I be a policy variable and $\mathbf{Z}$ be a vector of other variables, both at the provincial level. Suppose that such a relationship between these variables and the estimated provincial marginal effects exists and is linear, as given below:

$$\hat{\delta}_j = \alpha_0 + \alpha_1 I_j + \mathbf{Z}'_j \alpha_{\mathbf{z}} + \varepsilon_j \tag{9.4}$$

where the α values are regression coefficients and ε is the error term. Suppose further that the government sets the desired policy to I^* in province j. Then its adoption would induce a change in the marginal effects equal to $\Delta\hat{\delta}_j = \hat{\alpha}_1(I^* - I_j)$.

Given the parameter estimates in equation (9.1), plugging in $\Delta\hat{\delta}_j$ yields the new predicted probability of schooling for the ith child in province j, $\hat{Y}^*_{ij}$,

$$\text{Prob}(Y_{ij} = 1 | \mathbf{X}_{ij}, \mathbf{P}_{ij}) = \frac{e^{(\alpha + \mathbf{X}_{ij}\hat{\beta} + \mathbf{P}'_j(\hat{\delta}_j + \Delta\hat{\delta}_j))}}{1 + e^{(\alpha + \mathbf{X}_{ij}\hat{\beta} + \mathbf{P}'_j(\hat{\delta}_j + \Delta\hat{\delta}_j))}} = \hat{Y}^*_{ij} \tag{9.5}$$

If the same policy I^* is adopted in all provinces, then equation (9.5) yields a new estimate of the probability of, say, schooling for each child, that is, $\hat{Y}^*_{ij}$, $\forall_i$ and $\forall_j$. Together with their corresponding new estimates of probabilities induced by the new policy (I^*), these children can then be arrayed as well in ascending order of per-capita income as in equation (9.2):

$$\hat{Y}^*_1 \leq \hat{Y}^*_2 \leq \hat{Y}^*_3 \leq \dots \hat{Y}^*_N \tag{9.6}$$

where $\hat{Y}^*_1$ is the new predicted probability of schooling of the ith child. These new predicted probabilities can then be used to calculate the EIO corresponding to I^*. The difference in the EIOs obtained using equations (9.2) and (9.6) yields a measure of the equity impact of the policy change.

Data

The two main survey data sets used in the analysis of household decisions concerning health and schooling are the 2003 National Demographic and Health Survey (NDHS) and the 2007 Annual Poverty Indicators Survey (APIS). Both are undertaken by the National Statistic Office, and have regionally representative samples of 14,000 and 52,000 households, respectively. The NDHS contains information obtained from women of reproductive age concerning maternal and child health, reproductive health practices, healthcare use, and others. The APIS provides information on different indicators related to poverty, including demographic and economic characteristics of the family, health status and education of family members, housing, water and sanitation facilities of the household, and income and expenditures. Additional administrative data are culled from the health and education departments and other national government agencies.

To assess the role of various factors in the use of healthcare services, we use the women's and children's samples from the 2003 NDHS. We linked these individual samples with the household characteristics obtained from the household module and the characteristics of pertinent household members—that is, the parents and spouses—where available. We limit our analysis to two main variables representing utilization of maternal and child healthcare. The first one takes on a value of 1 when a woman's last delivery was attended by a doctor, nurse, or midwife, and the other also takes on a value of 1 when treatment was sought for children 0–5 years old with fever. We regressed both binary variables against individual, household, and area variables that represent the need, costs and benefits of utilization, as well as indicators of household efficiency in health production.

Among the individual variables included are the age and sex of the mother and/or child as a proxy for their health stock. The employment characteristics of those who may influence use of health services—parents in the case of child healthcare utilization and spouse in the case of women's utilization—are included to represent the ability to earn income and as indicators of the opportunity costs of time of household members.

The educational characteristics of decision-makers, as well as their knowledge of treatment alternatives are also included to represent their preferences toward health and how efficiently they can access healthcare. We also included variables on household composition that represent the opportunity costs of time that could serve as barriers or support to utilization. Dummy variables for wealth deciles are included to represent households' capacity to pay for care. A binary variable, which takes on a value of 1 when any member of the household is a PhilHealth member (either as a regular or indigent member), is included to gauge whether insurance serves to alleviate the out-of-pocket costs of health services.

Ideally, other aspects of supply and demand that the household faces should be included among the determinants of use. These include, among others, the prices of the services, the distance to the healthcare facility, and the availability and quality of both public and private providers. To represent these circumstances, we use dummy variables that take on a value of 1 when the individual belongs to a particular province. The estimated coefficients of these province variables represent the collective effect of area characteristics on use aside from the individual and household characteristics included in the regression.

These represent the impacts of the circumstances of the families' location on their healthcare use.

To decompose the effects of these circumstance variables, we regress the estimated marginal effects on variables such as municipal and provincial spending on health, nutrition and population to represent the salaries and wages of personnel, the materials, and the commodities purchased by the local government unit for its facilities.

Alternatively, we include either the ratio or number of government health personnel (doctor, *barangay* health workers, or midwives) to represent the availability of public providers. The number of *barangay* health stations, government and private hospitals—in both number and ratio to population—are included to represent the availability of facilities close to the household.

Private sector hospitals and beds also serve as indicators of the presence of private providers. Moreover, we include the availability of accredited facilities, both rural health units and hospitals, to represent not just the availability of providers of certain minimum quality, but also the assurance that PhilHealth benefits can be accessed by the population. These variables are represented as either numbers of municipalities with accredited facilities or ratios relative to the number of municipalities.[3]

In the analysis of household schooling decisions, we limited the sample to households with children 6–11 years old. In the Philippines, 6-year-olds are expected to commence elementary education at Grade I and then complete it by finishing Grade VI. There were 32,765 sample children in this age group. The main dependent variable is in-school, which is equal to 1 if the child is currently attending school and 0 if not. About 94% of the sample children were in-school. There are three sets of regressors. The first set is categorical variables that pertain to the child's characteristics, namely gender (1 if male and 0 otherwise), age (in years), illness or disability (1 if ill or disabled and 0 otherwise), and relation to the household head (1 if child or grandchild of head and 0 otherwise). About half of the samples are male. The mean age is 8.5 years. About 22.7% were ill or injured. About 84% were children of the household heads, and 13.6% were grandchildren.

The second set of variables pertains to the socioeconomic and demographic characteristics of the household, including that of the head. Of the household heads, about 88% were male, approximately 90% were married or had work during the last 6 months, and nearly 41% had finished at least high school. The households are further classified into income per capita deciles, homeownership status, status of insurance coverage with PhilHealth, and the proportion of household members 15 years old and younger in total family size. The decile that is left out is the richest (10th). Of the total sample, roughly 39% had PhilHealth coverage. The average share of minors (15 years old and below) was roughly half of the total family size, and about 67% of households owned the house and lot they lived in.

The last set of regressors comprises area dummy variables, one each for the 80 "provinces"[4] and two cities (Isabela and Cotabato) included in the APIS data set.

The base "province" is the NCR (Metro Manila), which comprises the 17 cities and municipalities of the Metropolitan Manila area, although in reality, these 17 local government units are independent and belong to no province. Nevertheless, Metro Manila accounts for 10% of the country's population and excluding it from the sample would bias the result.

The definitions and summary statistics of the variables used in the province-level regressions are given in Table 9.7. The dependent variable (i.e., province effects), with a mean of -0.0109, is the marginal effect of the area dummy variables obtained from the logit analysis of household decisions concerning the school attendance of 6–11-year-old members in 2007. The explanatory variables are school characteristics, local government expenditures, and measures of household poverty. Due to a lack of more recent data, the school-level data used here are for 2004.

For the 71 provinces in the sample, the mean proportion of principal-led public elementary schools in the province was 18.84. The average number of pupils was 34.80 per room, 1.18 per seat, 32.33 per chair, 4.05 per desk and 34.14 per teacher for all public elementary schools in the sample provinces. The average expenditure of the local governments in the province (provincial, municipal and city governments) was 2,052 pesos per person. However, their combined average education expenditures, based on their School Education Fund (SEF) distributed to local public schools, was only 32.42 pesos per pupil. The average poverty incidence rate and poverty severity were about 32% and 3.18%, respectively.

Empirical results on access to healthcare

Determinants

Table 9.8 shows the marginal effects from logit estimates of the likelihood of having a skilled birth attendant at delivery. The role of knowledge and information is underscored by our results, which show that the mother's years of education are significant in explaining the likelihood of a doctor, nurse, or midwife attending the delivery. At 10 years of education (equivalent to about high-school level), skilled birth attendance increases by 30 percentage points. These imply that information on the risks of childbearing should be targeted toward those who have less years of schooling.

The number of antenatal visits is significant in explaining the likelihood of having skilled birth attendance. This is consistent with the finding that antenatal care visits are crucial to checking the progress of pregnancy, ensuring that needed immunizations, such as tetanus toxoid, are done and determining whether the pregnancy is of high risk and therefore requires skilled birth attendants and complicated delivery services (e.g., cesarean delivery). These imply that information campaigns about pregnancy should include not just an emphasis on delivery, but also on the prenatal phases.

The demands of household management and child care are significant con-straints on maternal use of prenatal services. If a woman is the wife of the household

Table 9.7 Variable definition and descriptive statistics, 2007 (marginal effects of provincial dummy variables)

Variable	Definition	No	Mean	Standard deviation	Minimum	Maximum
Province effects	Marginal effects of provincial dummies	71	−0.109	0.04	−0.18	0.02
Principal	Proportion of principal-led public elementary schools in the province	71	18.84	10.55	0.00	50.94
Pupils per room	Average number of pupils per room	71	34.80	7.96	22.09	69.64
Pupils per chair	Average number of pupils per chair	71	32.33	24.89	11.23	188.08
Pupils per seat	Average number of pupils per seat	71	1.18	0.31	0.78	2.65
Pupils per desk	Average number of pupils per desk	71	4.05	1.54	2.06	12.03
Pupils per teacher	Average number of pupils per teacher	71	34.14	5.98	22.59	52.36
LGU expenditure per capita	Total expenditures per capita of all local governments in the province	71	2,052.30	819.00	1,189.67	6,456.86
LGU education expenditure per pupil	Total School Education Fund per pupil of all local governments in the province	71	401.64	481.25	2.87	2,880.81
Poverty incidence	Proportion of households who are poor in the province	71	32.42	17.68	1.20	88.8
Poverty severity	Severity of poverty among poor households in the province	71	3.18	3.05	0.00	17.8

LGU = local government unit.
Note: All variables are province-level estimates.

Source: Authors' calculations based on data from Department of Education, National Statistical Coordination Board and Bureau of Local Government Finance.

Table 9.8 Determinants of skilled birth attendance (marginal effects after logit)

Variable	Skilled birth attendance	
	Marginal effects	*z*
Rural	−0.1239**	−3.21
Age	0.0008	0.37
Years of education	0.0291**	6.64
Female is wife of household head	−0.0718**	−2.77
At least 4 antenatal care visits	0.1468**	6.02
Years of education of partner	0.0111**	2.2
Partner is a professional	0.0471	0.83
Age of partner	0.001	0.42
Woman is employed in agriculture	−0.0864	−1.63
Number of children under 5 years old	−0.0389**	−2.21
Number of household members	−0.0209**	−4.24
Any household member is PhilHealth member	0.0617**	2.52
Wealth decile 1	−0.5201**	−10.15
Wealth decile 2	−0.3957**	−6.19
Wealth decile 3	−0.3816**	−5.78
Wealth decile 4	−0.392**	−6.11
Wealth decile 5	−0.3358**	−4.72
Wealth decile 6	−0.3416**	−4.39
Wealth decile 7	−0.2539**	−3.45
Wealth decile 8	−0.1661**	−2.19
Wealth decile 9	−0.1845**	−2.28
Number of observations	4,610	
Pseudo *R*-squared	0.3418	

Note: The list of regressors includes provincial dummy variables. Detailed results available upon request.
** Significant at the 5% level; * Significant at the 10% level.
Source: Authors' calculations based on the National Demographic and Health Survey 2003.

head, or there is a child under five years old in the household, she is less likely to use a skilled birth attendant. Additionally, mothers with young children may not want to be away from the house for a long time after delivery if there is no one to care for them. This is consistent with observations that women prefer traditional birth attendants because of the extra services they provide, such as cleaning, cooking, and taking care of children after delivery. The inclusion of traditional birth attendants as part of women's health teams, designating them to provide the household care services to the mother in efforts to encourage skilled-birth delivery, may thus work. Alternatively, programs may be initiated in which mothers can plan ahead for birth, including arrangements for child care.

That the greater the number of children under five years old in the household leads to less likelihood of seeking maternal care services partially supports the contention that birth spacing can have significant maternal health implications. Aside from letting the mother recover from childbirth, birth spacing, by alleviating the burden of care for children under five years old, can increase the use of needed health services.

Financial constraints are likewise significant in explaining the likelihood of using skilled birth attendants, with households belonging to lower income deciles less likely to have skilled birth attendance. Indeed, financial factors seem to be the most significant constraints, accounting for reductions of about 18 to 50 percentage points in the likelihood of skilled birth attendance relative to the highest income decile. Indeed, the presence of a family member with PhilHealth coverage partially mitigates this constraint, as it contributes to an increase of about a six percentage points in the likelihood of seeking care. Expansion of insurance coverage, especially under PhilHealth's Sponsored Program for those in the lower income deciles, could therefore increase the probability of those groups using maternal healthcare services.

The marginal effects of the province dummy variables are significantly different from zero, implying that location-specific barriers are important in explaining outcomes. For skilled birth attendance, only about nine provinces have a higher likelihood of use than Metro Manila, as well as areas such as Rizal, Cavite, Bulacan that are near the NCR. Most of these provinces are in Luzon. Thus, efforts to increase skilled birth attendance can focus on the Visayas (central Philippines) and Mindanao (southern Philippines), where use is lower.

Table 9.9 shows the ordinary least-squares estimates of the impacts of community characteristics on the province-level fixed effects for use of maternal healthcare services. The higher the ratio of physicians to population or the higher the number of municipalities in the province with accredited hospitals, the higher is the likelihood of skilled birth attendance. A higher density of doctors suggests a greater availability of government providers who may be called upon to deliver babies, implying shorter waiting time. These are intuitively understood in that a higher density of doctors and accredited hospitals in the respective municipalities

Table 9.9 Effects of area characteristics on skilled birth attendance

Variable	Skilled birth attendance	
	Coefficients	*t*
Doctors to population	717.8619**	2.05
Midwives to population	151.8361	0.67
Government hospital bed to population	100.0149	1.21
Private hospital bed to population	−27.2324	−0.79
Number of municipalities with accredited RHU	0.0042	0.46
Number of municipalities with accredited hospitals	0.0133**	2.63
Constant	−0.4031	−5.78
Number of observations	77	
R-squared	0.1850	

RHU = rural health unit.
** Significant at the 5% level; * Significant at the 10% level.

Source: Authors' calculations based on the National Demographic and Health Survey 2003.

may imply shorter travel time to providers and the facilities where benefits can be accessed. This is imperative for complicated deliveries in which emergency facilities with the requisite manpower should be within 30 minutes to two hours of the mother's home (DOH 2008b). This underlines the importance not only of increasing coverage by PhilHealth but also of having accessible facilities (i.e., within the municipality) where pregnant women can use their PhilHealth benefits. This implies that to increase the use of services, increasing PhilHealth coverage should be coupled with steps to ensure that facilities are accredited.

In seeking care for fever, the age of the child is a more significant consideration (Table 9.10), in that older children are less likely to be brought in for care. On the other hand, children of mothers who are allowed to make decisions about seeking treatment are more likely to be brought to healthcare providers. This implies that household decision-making relationships matter, especially in the care of children. PhilHealth membership of any household member is a significant factor explaining the decision to seek care for fever, which may be because insurance coverage reduces out-of-pocket expenses. Only those from deciles 1 and 3 are significantly

Table 9.10 Marginal effects, seeking care for fever in children

Variable	Seek care for fever	
	Marginal effects	z
Rural	−0.0377	−1.27
Female child	0.0101	0.49
Age of mother	−0.0013	−0.58
Years of education of mother	−0.0004	−0.13
Years of education of partner	0.0058*	1.81
Partner is a professional	0.0188	0.47
Number of household members	−0.0058	−1.04
Number of children under 5 years old	−0.0041	−0.26
Any household member is PhilHealth member	0.0565*	1.78
Mother can decide about seeking treatment	0.0919**	2.12
Wealth decile 1	−0.1177**	−1.75
Wealth decile 2	−0.0981	−1.39
Wealth decile 3	−0.1427**	−2.16
Wealth decile 4	−0.0738	−1.01
Wealth decile 5	−0.0809	−1.17
Wealth decile 6	−0.0514	−0.65
Wealth decile 7	−0.0909	−1.61
Wealth decile 8	−0.0305	−0.43
Wealth decile 9	−0.1073*	−1.74
Number of observations	2,493	
Pseudo *R*-squared	0.0687	

Note: The list of regressors includes provincial dummy variables. Detailed results available upon request.

** Significant at the 5% level; * Significant at the 10% level.

Source: Authors' calculations based on the National Demographic and Health Survey 2003.

less likely to seek care; however, PhilHealth membership can partly mitigate the financial constraints these households face.

Provincial variables also significantly explain the likelihood of using child healthcare services. However, it seems that children living in most provinces are more likely to seek care for fever than those living in Metro Manila, while children residing in about 14 provinces show lower rates of utilization than those in Metro Manila. There seems to be no pattern of likelihood of care increasing with provincial income, suggesting that other factors may account for the discrepancy. For instance, those showing the least and greatest likelihood of seeking care relative to Metro Manila both belong to the Cordillera Administrative Region. This indicates that even between regions, provincial variations in utilization exist.

Seeking of care for children with fever is higher in provinces with more government hospitals relative to the population and with more municipalities with accredited hospitals (Table 9.11). However, the more private hospitals there are relative to the population, the lower the likelihood of seeking care for fever, which suggests the importance of financial considerations. Fees in government hospitals are usually cheaper than private hospitals; thus, the more government hospitals there are, the higher the likelihood that sick children can be admitted to less expensive facilities. The presence of government hospitals can also be a countervailing factor to the higher prices of private hospitals, hence the positive effect on care-seeking. On the other hand, the more municipalities there are with accredited hospitals, the higher the likelihood of seeking care. This has implications on the access to benefits of PhilHealth: not only should the population be covered, the facilities where they can access these services are also needed. Thus, the encouragement of PhilHealth membership should be coupled with efforts to ensure there are accredited facilities available for members.

Table 9.11 Effects of area characteristics on seeking care for fever

Variable	Seek care for children with fever	
	Coefficients	t
Government hospital to population	5986.188*	1.71
Private hospital to population	−3119.812*	−1.98
Number of municipalities with accredited hospital	0.0059399*	1.82
Province and municipalities per-capita health expenditures	−0.0002317	−1.14
Constant	0.0397579	0.76
Number of observations	75	
R-squared	0.1179	

** Significant at the 5% level; * Significant at the 10% level.

Source: Authors' calculations based on the National Demographic and Health Survey 2003.

Equity of policy options for healthcare

Four policy options were considered to improve coverage of skilled birth attendance: (i) full coverage of the bottom 40% in PhilHealth; (ii) ensuring that all pregnant women have at least four antenatal care visits; (iii) increasing the doctor-to-population ratio to reach mean levels (i.e., one doctor per about 27,000 people); and (iv) increasing the number of hospitals such that two-thirds of the municipalities in the province have an accredited hospital. The results for skilled birth attendance reveal that ensuring all pregnant women have at least four antenatal care visits and increasing the number of municipalities with accredited hospitals increases the OI and generates larger upward shifts in the opportunity curves (Figure 9.1). These two interventions also generate a larger increase in the EIO, signifying movements toward a more equitable distribution, albeit the EIOs are still below 1 (Table 9.12). These results imply that information on the risks of complicated pregnancies and the consequences of unsafe deliveries that could be given during antenatal care visits may convince mothers of the need to have skilled birth attendance in health facilities.

The simulation results for seeking care for fever in children are shown in Table 9.13. The estimated opportunity curves for accredited hospitals and PhilHealth coverage result in nearly equal opportunity indices (Figure 9.2). However, the opportunities associated with increasing the count of accredited

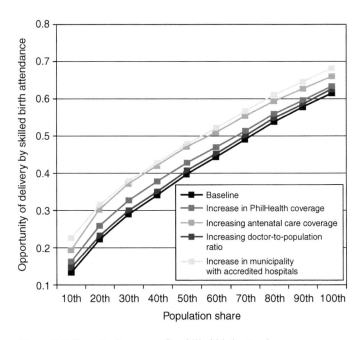

Figure 9.1 Opportunity curves for skilled birth attendance.

Source: Authors' calculations based on the National Demographic and Health Survey 2003.

Table 9.12 Equity impacts of policies on skilled birth attendance

Policy	Skilled birth attendance	
	OI	*EOI*
Baseline	0.4061	0.6586
Increase in PhilHealth coverage of bottom 40%	0.4327	0.6847
Increasing antenatal care coverage to 100%	0.4708	0.7123
Increasing doctor to population ratio to mean levels	0.4135	0.6633
Increase to two-thirds municipalities with accredited hospitals	0.4853	0.7103

Source: Authors' calculations based on the National Demographic and Health Survey 2003.

Table 9.13 Equity impacts of policies on seeking care for children with fever

Policy variables	Seek care for fever	
	OI	*EOI*
Baseline	0.4094	0.9111
Increase in PhilHealth coverage of bottom 40%	0.4412	0.9463
Increase to two-thirds municipalities with accredited hospitals	0.4433	0.9259
Increasing government-hospital to population ratio to mean levels	0.4272	0.9137

Source: Authors' calculations based on the National Demographic and Health Survey 2003.

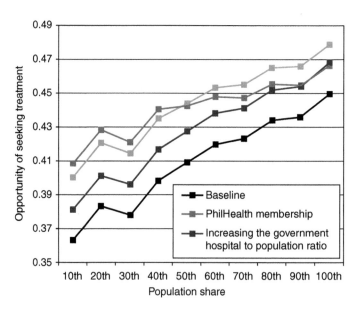

Figure 9.2 Opportunity curves for seeking treatment for children with fever.
Source: Authors' calculations based on the National Demographic and Health Survey 2003.

hospitals are higher for the higher income deciles such that the opportunity curve is steeper than that of PhilHealth coverage. As far as seeking care for children is concerned, increasing the government hospital-to-population ratio results in greater opportunity for everybody and does not favor the poor in particular. This confirms the earlier finding that recipients of subsidies from government hospitals may not always be the poor.

Empirical results on access to education

Determinants

Arguably, the best proof of the government's resolve to provide basic education to all, without exception, is the absence of any systematic exclusion based on gender, socioeconomic status, location, or ethnic background. However, the regression results presented in Table 9.14 suggest otherwise. Estimated using logit models,[5] the figures are the estimated marginal effects (or marginal probabilities) of the relevant variables on school attendance of children 6–11 years old and 12–15 years old in 2007.

Among the child-level characteristics, gender, age, and relationship to household head are found to be statistically significant factors. Relative to female children, male children are about 0.9% and 4.5% less likely to attend primary and secondary schools, respectively. As the child grows older, he or she is about 1.2% more likely to be in primary school, but about 3.4% less likely to be in secondary school. Illness or physical disability does not appear to be a critical deterrent to school attendance. In addition, both the children and grandchildren of the household head are about one to four percentage points more likely to be in elementary or secondary schools than other children in the household.

Among the characteristics of the household head, only educational attainment and marital status seem to matter. Specifically, those whose household heads completed at least high school are about 2.7% and 6.9% more likely to attend primary and secondary schools, respectively. The likelihood of high school attendance is greater in households whose heads are married; however, the head's marital status and work status do not appear to be significant determinants for primary school attendance.

Household income or wealth does not appear to be a significant barrier to access to elementary education, but is so for high-school education. In general, attendance at the elementary level among children from the lowest income per capita decile (decile 1) to the second highest (decile 9) does not appear to be statistically different from those in the richest households (decile 10). In contrast, the children of lower income households are generally more likely to drop out of high school than those in the richest income decile. Household wealth, as indicated by ownership of the house and lot in which the household currently resides, improves the probability of high-school attendance by around 1%, but not of primary schooling. These results

Table 9.14 Determinants of school attendance, 2007 (marginal effects of logit estimates)

Explanatory variables	6–11 years old		12–15 years old	
	Marginal probability	z	Marginal probability	z
Household member is male	−0.008767***	−4.79	−0.04501***	−11.57
Age of household member	0.0115061***	12.6	−0.03421***	−20.44
Household member is ill or disabled	−0.000069	−0.03	0.006508	1.55
Household member is child of household head	0.023554**	2.37	0.041066***	3.81
Household member is grandchild of household head	0.0124163***	3	0.04659***	7.81
Household head is male	−0.0056	−1.22	−0.00496	−0.65
Household head is married	0.0038012	0.7	0.030251***	3.41
Household head finished at least high school	0.0267419***	10.7	0.068519***	14.98
Household head is employed	0.0040486	0.96	0.002092	0.36
Income Decile 1	−0.041477	−1.62	−0.22859***	−5.24
Income Decile 2	−0.038264	−1.61	−0.20537***	−5.05
Income Decile 3	−0.046459*	−1.80	−0.20607***	−5.09
Income Decile 4	−0.034632	−1.58	−0.17985***	−5.11
Income Decile 5	−0.028344	−1.40	−0.14162***	−4.23
Income Decile 6	−0.015346	−0.86	−0.1089***	−3.20
Income Decile 7	−0.007383	−0.47	−0.10617***	−3.19
Income Decile 8	−0.000278	−0.02	−0.0566**	−2.25
Income Decile 9	0.0031138	0.29	−0.01593	−0.74
Household owns house and lot	0.0030195	1.35	0.009978**	2.33
PhilHealth covered	0.0189722***	7.65	0.031522***	7.35
Proportion of household members ≤ 15 years old	−0.019508***	−3.26	−0.04561***	−4.65
Number of observations	32,765		19,261	
Pseudo *R*-squared	0.2414		0.1471	

Note: The list of regressors includes provincial dummy variables. Detailed results are available upon request. Due to multicollinearity, the provinces of Camiguin, Siquijor and Guimaras are excluded in 2004, and Batanes province in 2004 and 2007.

*** Significant at the 1% level; ** Significant at the 5% level; * Significant at the 10% level.

Source: Authors' calculations based on Annual Poverty Indicator Survey 2007.

indicate that the government has been successful only in overcoming income barriers to elementary education, but not to secondary schooling.

Households with a large proportion of members 15 years or younger tend to have children not attending school, by about 2% among 6–11 years old and 5% among 12–15 years old. This could indicate the inability of working-age members to support the cost of education of so many school-age members. Interestingly, households with social health insurance coverage have a greater likelihood of children attending either primary school (by 1.9%) or high school (by 3.2%), even after controlling for household income and wealth or work status of the head.

While Philhealth coverage *per se* does not increase the household's disposable income, perhaps by providing financial protection to the household it frees up resources for education and other expenses.

The provincial dummy variables introduced in the logit regressions are meant to capture the effects of community-level factors, such as geography (terrain, climate), proximity to or quality of schools, local government support to schools or students, availability of transportation facilities, and peace and order problems. The probabilities of school attendance at either the primary or secondary level are generally lower in provinces and cities outside the NCR, the base region. When compared to the 6–11 year olds in the NCR, children in 39 provinces and cities are less likely to be attending school, while those in 25 provinces are more likely to be in school. Those residing in the rest of the 13 provinces and cities are just as likely to be attending.

However, the high-school age children (12–15 years) in 68 areas outside the NCR are less likely to be attending school when compared to their cohorts in the NCR. In particular, residence in some of the ARMM provinces—Sulu, Lanao del Sur, Maguindanao, and Tawi-Tawi—reduces the probability of school attendance at both levels of education, despite the fact that a special curriculum for Muslim children has been introduced in local schools. Perhaps this is to be expected, since many of the country's conflict areas are found in these places, which makes the hiring and deployment of qualified teachers difficult and costly for ARMM's own Department of Education. Further, wide seas divide the ARMM provinces, and some of them are more accessible via Zamboanga del Sur than via ARMM's regional capital located in Cotabato City.

Other provinces with lower likelihood of school attendance relative to the NCR at the elementary level include Bukidnon (-3.9%), Capiz (-3.5%), Ifugao (-2.8%), Negros Oriental (-3.2%), Palawan (-3.2%), Sarangani (-2.7%), Sultan Kudarat (-4.1%) and Zamboanga del Norte (-4.4%). Some of these provinces like Capiz, Northern Samar, and Sarangani are relatively poor, which means that such a province has more limited job or earning opportunities than other areas. Others like Ifugao, Palawan, and Negros Occidental have rugged terrain with remote *barangays* in the mountains. However, neither relative poverty nor unfavorable terrain have deterred children in Benguet, Mountain Province, Romblon, and Zambales, where the likelihood of their education participation in either the elementary or secondary level appear to be even higher than those in the NCR. In sum, the results indicate possible area-level factors that households do not control but which influence their schooling decisions.

Following the methodology outlined above, the estimated coefficients of the provincial dummies in the logit regression of school attendance (Table 9.14) are regressed using the ordinary least-squares method against province-level average school-level inputs, local government expenditures, and poverty incidence or severity (to account for the general socioeconomic conditions of the population in the provinces). Table 9.15 shows the statistically significant factors: presence of a principal (0.0006), pupils per seat (-0.0324), and poverty severity (-0.0053). The signs of the coefficients are as expected, in that, arguably, children are more

Table 9.15 Effects of area-level characteristics on school attendance

Explanatory variables	Model 1		Model 2	
	Coefficient	Robust standard error	Coefficient	Robust standard error
Principal	0.0005*	0.0003	0.0006*	0.0003
Pupils per room	−0.0025	0.002	−0.0016	0.0017
Pupils per chair	−0.00009	0.0001	−0.0001	0.0001
Pupils per seat	−0.0295	0.0215	−0.0324*	0.0193
Pupils per desk	0.0015	0.0028	0.0012	0.0028
Pupils per teacher	0.0014	0.0019	0.0003	0.0015
LGU expenditure per capita	0.00000121	0.00000184	0.00000103	0.00000240
LGU education expenditure per pupil	0.00000951	0.00000962	0.00001	0.00000943
Poverty incidence	−0.0003	0.0003	0.0006	0.0004
Poverty severity	n.a.	n.a.	−0.0053*	0.0032
Constant	0.055**	0.0229	0.0516*	0.026
Number of observations	71		1	
F-statistic	5.09		4.71	
Prob > *F*	0.000		0.000	
R-squared	0.4881		0.5234	

LGU = local government unit; n.a. = not applicable.
** Significant at the 5% level; * Significant at the 10% level.

Sources: Authors' calculations based on Annual Poverty Indicator Survey 2007.

enticed to go to class if each is assured of a seat (fewer pupils per seat ratio), and the general community is well off (which implies that other children are also in school). Note that, ostensibly, it is the severity of poverty (how poor a household is) rather than its mere incidence (whether the household is poor) that matters. This implies that it is the extremely poor households that are unable to access public education services. Finally, the province-level fixed effects are also positively influenced by the proportion of principal-led schools, which could mean that principals are better at managing schools, inspiring the teaching staff, and engaging the local community for the benefit of the school.

Equity of policy options for education

While Metro Manila is the richest "province," the fact that its school attendance rate is not much different from most other provinces or cities indicates the presence in these areas of both facilitating and hindering environmental factors that influence household decisions. Of these, the government directly controls the proximity or quality of public schools, peace and order, local government support to schools (principally, the Special Education Fund), or directly to children (like scholarships). The government also regulates tuition fees in private schools and corporate sponsorships of education activities. By tweaking these community-level or environmental factors, the government can then influence the circumstance variables that have direct bearing on a household's schooling decisions.

Three policy options for improving access to education are simulated in this study: (i) the average proportion of principal-led public elementary schools in each province is placed at no less than 20%; (ii) the average number of pupils per seat in all provinces is set to no more than one; and (iii) a combination of the first and second policy options. In 2007, in 58 provinces there was more than one pupil per seat, and in 46 provinces fewer than 20% of schools were run by principals. Targeting at least 20% of the schools to have principals (rather than teachers) as school heads seems conservative given the dearth of qualified principals.

Table 9.16 shows the OIs and EIOs corresponding to the three policy scenarios. Without the assumed policy changes, the baseline EIO is 0.9845. The first policy scenario—adjusting the number of pupils per seat—leads to an EIO of 0.9847, a slight improvement over the baseline EIO. On the other hand, raising the proportion of principal-led schools results in an EIO of 0.9840, while a combination of the two policy scenarios yields an EIO of 0.9842. These results indicate that while the three policy scenarios each can improve the rate of attendance in public schools in each province, only the first (pupils per seat not more than one) can improve overall equity. In contrast, increasing the proportion of principal-led schools seems to worsen equity, which means it could induce higher enrollment among all children, but perhaps slightly more of them from high-income families. This can be inferred from Figure 9.3, in which the opportunity curves corresponding to each of the policy scenarios are higher than the baseline, although somewhat parallel to it.

In sum, the policy simulation exercises here show how selected policy variables can improve the overall rate of school attendance, but not necessarily overall equity. Put differently, school-based or supply-based interventions benefit all and do not discriminate in favor of poor households. Alternatively, the government thus has to resort to demand-side interventions to get children from poor households to attend school.

Conclusion and policy recommendations

In summary, we find both choice and circumstance factors to be relevant in explaining household decisions to seek care for family members or to send their

Table 9.16 Equity impacts of policies on school attendance

Policy scenarios	OI	EIO
Baseline	0.9366	0.9845
Pupil per seat (≤ 1)	0.9382	0.9847
Proportion of principal-led schools ($\geq 20\%$)	0.9447	0.9840
All policy options	0.9464	0.9842

Source: Authors' calculations based on Annual Poverty Indicator Survey 2007.

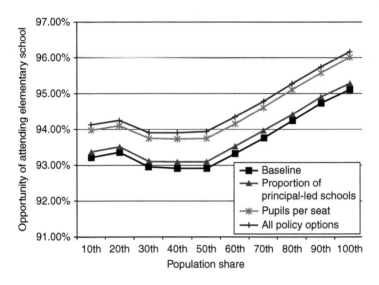

Figure 9.3 Opportunity curves for school attendance.
Source: Authors' calculations based on Annual Poverty Indicator Survey 2007.

children to school. Particularly at the household level, lack of income and capacity to pay, family composition, mother's age and education status, and the child's age and gender are found to be critical. These results are broadly consistent with those found in other studies (e.g., Mesa 2008; Orbeta 2009; Son 2009; Son and San Andres 2009), which also reported significant geographical variations in household access to health or education services.

In this chapter, we further investigated the differential effects of several area-level characteristics that are captured together with others as part of location-fixed effects in the usual regression analyses of household decisions. Applying a two-step procedure, we were able to tease out the impact of province-level health and education service variables on the probability of skilled-birth attendance, seeking care for children with fever, and elementary schooling. The presence of accredited facilities, the number of health personnel, the type of school resources available, and local government support to public schools in the community help to define the circumstances that condition household decisions. We also considered PhilHealth coverage as another circumstance variable, which the government automatically extends to poor households. Our simulation results reveal that PhilHealth coverage has a bigger impact than facility-based circumstance factors on improving overall equity of access to health services. In addition, we find that while school-level factors may improve overall enrollment, the impact is felt less among the poor.

The results have two major policy implications. First, demand-side interventions, especially when targeted to the poor, such as PhilHealth coverage, will improve overall health access and its equity, and may even induce greater school participation. Second, while location-specific barriers may be capturing the inadequate levels, distribution, or quality of public health facilities or schools, it is still important to tease out the relative effectiveness of the components of possible supply-side interventions. For example, doctors may be more important than just the health facility to improve access to healthcare among pregnant mothers. In education, principals may be more critical than facilities such as chairs or desks in improving scholastic achievements. Thus, the impact of demand-side interventions can be maximized if supply-side constraints are likewise addressed.

Notes

1 This chapter was prepared by Joseph J. Capuno and Aleli D. Kraft who are associate professors at the University of the Philippines. This paper is based on their country report submitted to the Asian Development Bank (ADB) under a regional technical assistance on Equity in the Delivery of Public Services in Selected Developing Member Countries. The authors acknowledge the overall research guidance of Hyun H. Son, the comments and suggestions from Jacques Silber and the participants in the ADB workshop on 19 April 2010, and the excellent research assistance of Emmanuel San Andres, Paul Mariano, Hannah Morillo and Vigile Marie Fabella. The authors remain responsible for all remaining errors.
2 Infant mortality is deaths of children less than 1 year old per 1,000 live births and child mortality of children less than 5 years old.
3 To save on space, the tables containing the descriptive statistics of the variables in the regression analysis of household health-seeking and schooling decisions are not included here. The relevant tables are reported in Capuno and Kraft (2010).
4 As of December 2007, there were officially 79 provinces, excluding the National Capital Region (NCR) in the Philippines. For the purposes of this study, the NCR is considered a province.
5 The underlying reduced-form model links school attendance with the characteristics of the child, household-level characteristics, and province-level fixed effects. The province-level dummy variables are introduced to account for area-specific factors like geography, peace and order, transportation facilities, and cultural values that condition the household's decision to enroll their school-age members.

10 Equity in education and health services in Nepal[1]

Bal Gopal Baidya and Nephil Matangi Maskay

Introduction

Nepal recently emerged from a traumatic 10-year armed conflict that killed 13,000 persons, displaced more than 50,000 internally, and significantly reduced economic growth. A high poverty rate and increasing inequality, unequal access to basic services and economic opportunity, and centuries-old discriminatory laws and social practices (i.e., the caste system) are generally believed to have significantly contributed to the conflict (Central Bureau of Statistics [CBS] 2005). In recent years, this has led to a greater emphasis on the inclusive development of the country as reflected in the periodic development plans, such as the Three Year Interim Plan 2007–10 and Three Year Plan for 2010–13, which were formulated after the cessation of armed hostilities in April 2006.

As equitable access to quality basic services is necessary for inclusive growth, there is an emphasis on improving equity in access to and use of basic services, especially health and education. This is crucial to enhancing human capabilities and among the basic rights of Nepalis, as guaranteed by the Interim Constitution of Nepal (2007).

This chapter assesses equity in health and education services in Nepal to better understand the barriers and constraints to their equitable provision. It uses Ali and Son's (2007) equity index of opportunity and opportunity curve methods, which take into account not only the average level of opportunity, but also its distribution among various population segments. Because this method gives greater weight to the access of the poor to these services, it can be considered "pro-poor." Furthermore, logistic regressions on health service utilization and participation in education and performance indicators were done to identify the factors explaining the inequalities. The next two sections of this chapter discuss findings on equity in health and education services, with each sector analysis starting with an overview of service delivery followed by empirical analysis of access and outcome indicators. The concluding section looks into major policy implications for improving the delivery of these social services.

The health sector

At a policy level, the Government of Nepal acknowledges the necessity of quality public health services and provides a supportive policy environment to encourage the equitable delivery and financing of public health services. In 2007, aiming to lower financial barriers to health service access, the government announced its Free Health Care Policy, which provides free health services at sub-health posts, health posts, primary healthcare centers, and district hospitals. Although adequate financing to implement the policy could be a challenge, early indications are very encouraging, with the increased use of health services by marginalized groups in several districts.

Both public and private sectors provide health services in Nepal. Public health services are very extensive: they are delivered by a network of 3,126 sub-health posts and 677 health posts at the village level, 209 primary healthcare centers at the electoral constituency level, 65 district hospitals, eight zonal hospitals, and four regional and/or sub-regional hospitals. In addition, there are eight central level hospitals and 291 *Ayurvedic* (traditional medicine) health institutions. Private services are mostly confined to urban areas or market centers in the rural areas.

The public health sector used to be a highly centralized structure managed by the Ministry of Health and Population (MOHP). However, in 2002/03, in coordination with the Ministry of Local Development, MOHP began handing over financial and administrative management of the public health institutions to village development committees. It has handed over slightly more than one-third of existing public health institutions with promising preliminary indications. The Decentralization Policy has seen an increase in user satisfaction, increased patient flow, a greater sense of local ownership, better monitoring, increased transparency, improved drug supply and resource mobilization, and more timely decision-making (MOHP 2008). This has occurred despite the significant constraints imposed by an absence of elected bodies at the local level and limited management capacity.

Nepal's public health expenditure is about 5% of the national budget or about 1% of gross domestic product (GDP). While low, when out-of-pocket health expenditures are considered—at nearly two-thirds of the total—total health expenditure as a proportion of GDP is one of the highest in South Asia.

Per-capita public expenditure on health was a meagre US$4 in 2007/08, and public financing has not increased significantly despite the supportive policy environment. In part this is because the MOHP, with little absorptive capacity, has never been able to spend more than 80% of its allocated budget. This is due partly to the way funds are released by the Ministry of Finance: funds are released over the three trimesters of a fiscal year but very much loaded into the last trimester, forcing ministries to spend most of their budget in the final four months and thus undermining their effectiveness.

There is also a problem of inequitable distribution of health personnel across the country, with a high concentration in the Central Development Region (CDR).

This reflects the large number of health facilities in the region and that more people prefer to be in the CDR's Kathmandu Valley. Rural health institutions, especially those in remote regions, are short of health workers as a result.

With regard to financing health services, private health insurance is limited (Pande, Maskay, and Chataut 2004), although the government has started a community health insurance scheme to help bridge the health financing gap. Community health insurance was piloted in the districts of Morang and Nawalparasi in 2003/04, and extended to Udayapur, Rautahat, Dang, and Kailali in 2006/07.[2] It aims to increase community access to healthcare services, introduce an alternative healthcare financing mechanism, pool health risks, and develop community solidarity. The schemes are managed by the community and provide a subsidized premium for poor households. Premiums per household (up to maximum of six members) ranged from NRs500 to NRs1,000 per year in 2007/08. Benefits are provided through the local primary healthcare centers, with referral provision in two districts[3] up to a maximum ceiling amount. Coverage is very low, however, and usually less than 10% of the households are covered by community health insurance, even in those areas where it is in operation.

Equity in access to health services

This study uses Ali and Son's (2007) opportunity index and opportunity curve method to assess equity in health services. It analyses data from the Nepal Demographic and Health Surveys of 2001 and 2006; these surveys are conducted every five years with rigorous mechanisms for checking quality. Progress on most of Nepal's health and demographic indicators is assessed using these surveys. Indicators on prenatal checkup by health personnel and postnatal checkup by health institutions were used for this analysis. The results are discussed below.

The equity index of opportunity for prenatal checkup by health assistants or workers was 1.0 in 2001 and 2006, indicating equal access among poor and rich. By contrast, prenatal checkup services by doctors and nurses/midwives were inequitable, with not much change in equity between 2001 and 2006, although average access improved slightly (Table 10.1 and Figure 10.1).

Inequitable access to prenatal checkups by doctors, nurses, and midwives may be explained by the uneven distribution of these health personnel. In the CDR, where the Kathmandu Valley is located, there was one doctor for every 12,000 people, compared with one for every 19,000 or higher in other regions. The distribution of nurses shows the same pattern of concentration in CDR. By contrast, health assistants and health workers are much more equitably distributed and are thus more accessible.

The opportunity index and opportunity curves clearly show that access to postnatal checkups in government health posts or sub-health posts is the most pro-poor (generally downward sloping), and private hospitals or clinics are very pro-rich (upward sloping). Even government hospitals are not pro-poor

Table 10.1 Opportunity index of health personnel consultation for prenatal checkups by wealth quintile

Population share	Doctor		Nurse/midwife		Health assistant/worker	
	2001	2006	2001	2006	2001	2006
10%	3.7	4.4	10.2	15.6	10.1	11.4
20%	5.2	6.7	13.3	18.1	11.9	12.9
30%	6.7	7.1	16.4	20.9	13.3	13.8
40%	8.7	9.1	20.6	25.6	14.6	15.7
50%	9.4	10.4	22.8	27.2	14.8	16.0
60%	11.4	12.3	24.1	29.7	15.3	16.6
70%	12.1	13.9	25.1	31.8	14.6	16.4
80%	14.7	16.6	28.3	36.4	14.1	16.9
90%	18.9	21.8	29.3	37.8	14.0	15.8
100%	23.5	25.1	34.7	40.1	13.2	14.6
Opportunity index	11.4	12.7	22.5	28.3	13.6	15.0
Equity index of opportunity	0.5	0.5	0.6	0.7	1.0	1.0

Source: Authors' calculations using Nepal Demographic and Health Survey 2001 and 2006.

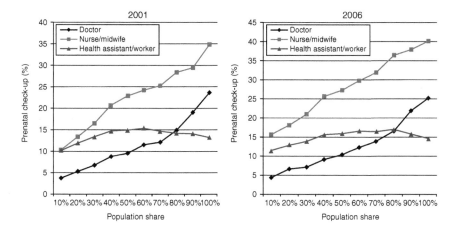

Figure 10.1 Opportunity curve of prenatal checkup by health personnel.
Source: Authors' calculations using Nepal Demographic and Health Survey 2001 and 2006.

(Table 10.2 and Figure 10.2) as this curve is generally upward sloping, that is, they are utilized more by the rich than the poor.

The wide distribution of government health posts and sub-health posts in rural areas and the easy access of rural dwellers to these facilities—95% of the poor live in rural areas (CBS 2005)—may explain their pro-poor characteristics. In 2008 there were 3,126 sub-health posts and 677 health posts; there is one health post or sub-health post in each of the village development committees, the lowest

Table 10.2 Opportunity index of health institution utilization for postnatal checkups by cumulative wealth quintile

Population share	Government hospital		Government health and sub-health post		Private hospital/clinic	
	2001	*2006*	*2001*	*2006*	*2001*	*2006*
10%	18.1	19.9	29.8	31.9	4.3	6.2
20%	18.8	17.9	29.0	27.7	5.0	7.0
30%	19.1	21.1	29.5	29.7	5.5	7.2
40%	19.7	23.3	29.2	27.5	6.4	7.7
50%	21.1	24.9	28.7	28.1	6.8	8.1
60%	22.6	25.5	27.4	27.3	7.8	8.6
70%	24.5	27.8	25.6	25.8	8.9	9.6
80%	25.5	28.9	24.1	24.3	10.1	11.4
90%	27.2	31.6	21.2	22.9	12.0	13.7
100%	30.4	34.3	19.2	21.4	14.8	15.8
Opportunity index	22.7	25.5	26.4	26.6	8.2	9.5
Equity index of opportunity	0.7	0.7	1.4	1.2	0.6	0.6

Source: Authors' calculations using Nepal Demographic and Health Survey 2001 and 2006.

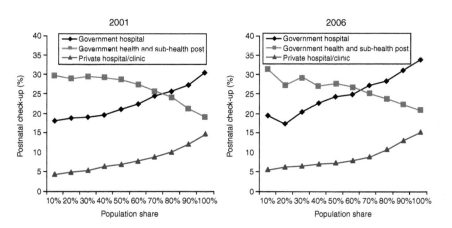

Figure 10.2 Opportunity curve of postnatal checkup by type of health institution.
Source: Authors' calculations using Nepal Demographic and Health Survey 2001 and 2006.

administrative tier in the country. In contrast, government hospitals and private facilities are mostly located in district headquarters or market towns. As a result, the rural poor must travel much farther to access hospitals than they do for health posts and sub-health posts.

Determinants of health service utilization

Logistic regression on the utilization of the services of skilled birth attendants (SBAs) during child delivery[4] was carried out using plausible demographic variables (e.g., women's age and marital status), socioeconomic variables (e.g., caste/ethnicity, mother's education, working status of mother, wealth status of the family, and others), and geographical variables (e.g., development region, ecological region, urban or rural residence) as controls. Unfortunately, no supply-side variables could be used because they were not included in the data sets.

The results of the logistical regressions indicated that a rural woman is much less likely than an urban woman to get SBA assistance during delivery (Table 10.3). Similarly, the mother's education level affects the likelihood of SBA use, rising with education level, while family wealth status is another important determinant. Caste is also an important determinant of access to an SBA, with women of lower-ranked castes such as Dalits much less likely to have an SBA during delivery. Women who did not have prenatal checkups—which are widely available in health posts and sub-health posts—were also less likely to have SBA assistance.

The equity analysis of health services clearly shows that rural-based health personnel and health institutions are most accessible to the general population and, accordingly, equitably provide services. By contrast, doctors and nurses are not equitably distributed, although the distribution improved slightly from 2001 to 2006, while government hospital services are also not easily accessible. Moreover, these results reiterate the importance of women's education in the utilization of health services. Similarly, having prenatal service increases the chances of a woman getting SBA assistance during delivery, a critical factor in attaining Millennium Development Goals 4 (maternal health) and 5 (child mortality). Prenatal services are easily available from health posts and sub-health posts.

The education sector

Nepal recognizes education as one of the fundamental rights of its citizens. The Interim Constitution of Nepal (2007) says that (i) each community shall have the right to receive basic education in its mother language and (ii) each citizen shall have the right to free education up to the secondary level. Nonetheless, specific laws to operationalize these provisions have yet to be formulated. The existing Education Act of 2002 deals mainly with the management and regulation of schools. It does not mention anything about compulsory education for children, nor does it refer to the operationalization of the education rights of Nepalese citizens. Thus, Nepal has tried to ensure the education rights of its citizens through its education policies and programs rather than by enacting laws.

The reality is that about one-tenth of primary-age children (6–10 years) have yet to realize these constitutional rights, while the situation for secondary-age children (11–15 years) is even worse: nearly one in eight secondary-age children is out

Table 10.3 Determinants of having a skilled birth attendant during delivery, 2001 and 2006

Independent variable	2001		2006	
	Coefficient	*Standard error*	*Coefficient*	*Standard error*
Constant	1.1782**	0.512	1.509*	0.44
Residence (Ref. urban)				
Rural	−0.410**	0.52	−0.513***	0.577
Ecological belt (Ref. hill)				
Mountain	−0.122*	0.203	−0.192**	0.243
Terai	−0.280**	0.177	−0.121**	0.189
Development region (Ref. Central)				
Eastern	−0.108*	0.128	−0.108*	0.223
Western	−0.117*	0.121	−0.191	0.202
Mid-western	−0.204**	0.109	−0.213**	0.243
Far-western	−0.229**	0.256	−0.225**	0.175
Mother's education (Ref. school leaving certificate and above)				
No education	−0.554*	0.541	−0.512*	0.409
Primary	−0.248*	0.174	−0.241*	0.223
Some secondary	−0.109**	0.275	−0.138**	0.134
Prenatal checkup (Ref. yes prenatal)				
No prenatal	−0.490*	0.257	−0.216*	0.307
Wealth quintile (Ref. tenth)				
First	−0.631*	0.34	−0.604*	0.52
Second	−0.638	0.411	−0.611	0.351
Third	−0.571	0.56	−0.581	0.57
Fourth	−0.559*	0.595	−0.542	0.501
Fifth	−0.472*	0.422	−0.465	0.373
Sixth	−0.45	0.431	−0.437	0.331
Seventh	−0.222*	0.213	−0.185*	0.197
Eighth	−0.117	0.204	−0.107*	0.162
Ninth	−0.063*	0.244	−0.071	0.075
Family's caste (Ref. Brahmin and Chettri)				
Other Madeshi caste	−0.174	0.121	−0.144*	0.162
Dalits	−0.139**	0.097	−0.149**	0.102
Newar	0.128	0.075	0.144*	0.181
Janajati	−0.036*	0.052	−0.029*	0.019
Muslim	−0.251	0.222	−0.237	0.176
Others	−0.027	0.047	−0.074	0.06
Working status of women (Ref. professional work and labor)				
No work	−0.250*	0.115	−0.215	0.341
Agro employed	−0.034*	0.155	−0.073**	0.143
Other	0.023	0.001	0.078	0.09
Marital status (Ref. married)				
Widowed	−0.007	0.076	−0.011	0.067
Divorced/separated	0.003	0.074	−0.017	0.07
Age of women (Ref. less than 20)				
20–34	0.021	0.072	0.014	0.041
35–49	−0.051	0.018	−0.083	0.05

*** Significant at 1% level, ** Significant at 5% level, and * Significant 10% level.

Source: Authors' calculations using Nepal Demographic and Health Survey 2001 and 2006.

of school. Education is an important human asset that helps to reduce poverty, and lack of it helps perpetuate poverty from one generation to the next. As such, educational opportunity should be available to all without discrimination.

Public spending on education is almost entirely focused on public schools. Public schools are largely managed by the district level officers of the Ministry of Education, although the ministry is handing over management of schools to local communities, with nearly one-third of schools in community hands as of August 2009. The government also allows the operation of private schools, which finance themselves usually by charging tuition fees. Private schools may be run on either a profit or non-profit basis. The existing policy allows parents options on where to send their children.

To encourage school participation, primary education (i.e., Grades I–V) in public schools is completely free while secondary education is fee-free, although students have to buy textbooks. However, parents still incur significant direct and indirect costs, even when a child attends public primary school. Direct education costs are also higher at the secondary level, while opportunity costs rise as children get older.

Incentive programs targeted to deprived groups have been implemented to offset the direct and indirect costs of education; however, the incentive amount—NRs350 yearly per student—is far too low to offset direct and indirect costs. Moreover, incentive schemes are not implemented as envisaged: although they are targeted to deprived castes and ethnic groups, they are distributed to all members of that group regardless of income status and are often paid late. As a result of these implementation weaknesses, the incentive scheme has not been as effective as expected.

Blanket implementation of the incentive scheme presents an equity problem. The scheme defines a caste or ethnic group as being deprived and all children from this group, rich or poor, are eligible to receive benefits. This has led to situations where a poor Hill Chhetri child is still considered advantaged and deprived of benefits, whereas a Hill Dalit child from a rich family is considered disadvantaged and gets the benefit. Lack of proper targeting also enlarges the beneficiary base of the scheme, reducing the average benefit per child.

Nonetheless, given its national commitments, Nepal has significantly increased its public investment in education—from 8.8% of the national budget or 1.8% of GDP in 1990/91 to 16.8% of the budget or 4.1% of GDP in 2008/09. The growth rate in education expenditures has exceeded enrollment rates, pushing expenditure per student at the primary level up a remarkable four times in real terms.[5] As a result, it has made significant progress toward achieving the Millennium Development Goal on universal primary education.

Equity in access to education

The equity analysis presented in this section is also based on the opportunity index and opportunity curve method of Son and Ali (2007). The data used for the analysis are from the Nepal Family Health Survey 1996 and Nepal Demographic Health

Surveys of 2001 and 2006. These national surveys focus on demographic and health issues, but also include information on education such as school enrollment, educational attainment, and the literacy status of household members. The analysis also uses the most recent Nepal Labor Force Survey 2008 conducted by the Central Bureau of Statistics (CBS 2008) and data from a Department of Education survey (DOE 2008), which reports achievement test scores of students in Grades I, III, and V.

School participation rates among primary-age children 6–10 years old clearly show Nepal's significant progress from 1996 to 2008. There was improvement in both overall participation rates and equity (Figures 10.3 and 10.4), with the same pattern of improvement observed between girls and boys, urban and rural children, and among children in different ecological regions.

Despite this, disparities still exist between rich and poor children, boys and girls, urban and rural children, and children living in mountains and plains. More significant disparities are seen when children are compared by caste or ethnicity. School participation among Terai Dalits and Muslim children is much lower than in other groups (Table 10.4). Moreover, female participation is generally low for almost all groups, especially for secondary school-age girls. This implies that targeted incentive programs for girls have to be expanded and strengthened to make them more effective. In addition, school participation rates among Terai Dalits slipped between 2006 and 2008: this may be due to the weak implementation of incentive programs as well as the unfriendly school environment for Dalits. Discrimination against Dalits is much more prevalent in the Terai—an alarming trend needing further examination.

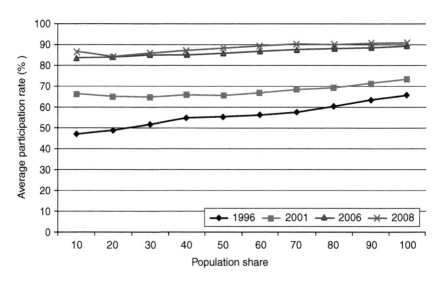

Figure 10.3 Opportunity curves for school participation of primary age children (6–10 years).

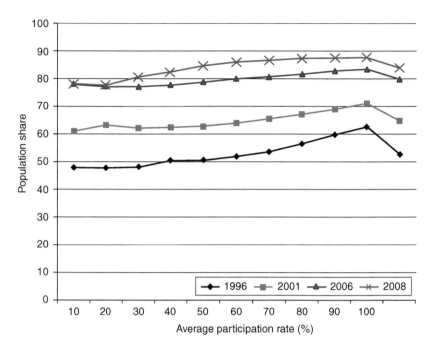

Figure 10.4 Opportunity curves for school participation of secondary age children (11–15 years).

Table 10.4 School participation rates of primary and secondary age children by gender, caste, and ethnicity, 2008

Caste and/or ethnicity	Primary (6–10 years)		Secondary (11–15 years)	
	Boys	Girls	Boys	Girls
Hill Brahmin	98.4	98.8	98.7	98.9
Hill Chhetri	97.3	94.1	96.1	91.6
Terai Brahmin/Chhetri	98.4	100.0	99.0	84.3
Other Terai/Madhesi	90.6	83.7	83.9	62.9
Hill Dalits	96.9	91.9	91.0	86.0
Terai Dalits	65.7	64.4	66.6	39.7
Newar	98.0	97.9	65.7	97.8
Hill Janjati	94.1	93.1	92.2	91.1
Terai Janjati	95.3	93.2	91.1	88.0
Muslim	72.5	74.1	74.8	49.4
Other	87.5	84.7	91.5	76.4
All	92.4	89.7	91.0	84.7

Source: Authors' calculations using Nepal Labor Force Survey 2008.

Although data sets of the Nepal Demographic and Health Surveys do not have information on types of schools attended, this information is available in the DOE 2008 data. Analysis of this data indicates that public schools are very pro-poor both for primary and secondary age children (Tables 10.5 and 10.6 and Figures 10.5 and 10.6) while private schools are very pro-rich, as would be expected.

Given the implications for greater equity of public schools, focusing public investment on public schools is justified. At the same time, policy measures should be explored to make private schools more equitable. For instance, private

Table 10.5 Opportunity index for type of school attended by children of primary age (6–10 years), 2008

Population share	Public school	Private school
10	96.9	3.1
20	97.1	2.9
30	96.6	3.4
40	95.5	4.5
50	93.8	6.2
60	92.2	7.8
70	90.2	9.8
80	86.7	13.3
90	82.5	17.5
100	76.6	23.4
Opportunity index	90.8	9.2
Equity index of opportunity	1.2	0.4
Comments	Equitable	Not equitable

Source: Authors' calculations based on Department of Education 2008.

Table 10.6 Opportunity index for type of school attended by children of secondary age (11–15 years), 2008

Population share	Public school	Private school
10	97.30	2.70
20	97.00	3.00
30	96.60	3.40
40	95.90	4.10
50	94.70	5.30
60	93.40	6.60
70	91.50	8.50
80	87.70	12.30
90	83.70	16.30
100	78.60	21.40
Opportunity index	91.64	8.36
Equity index of opportunity	1.17	0.39
Comments	Equitable	Not equitable

Source: Authors' calculations based on Department of Education 2008.

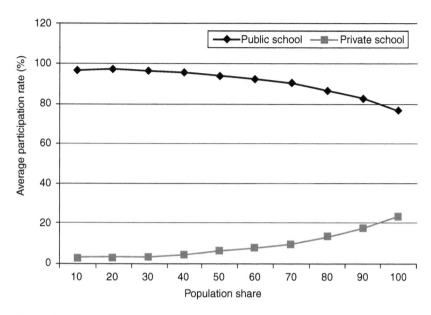

Figure 10.5 Opportunity curves for type of school attended by children 6–10 years old.
Source: Authors' calculations based on Department of Education 2008.

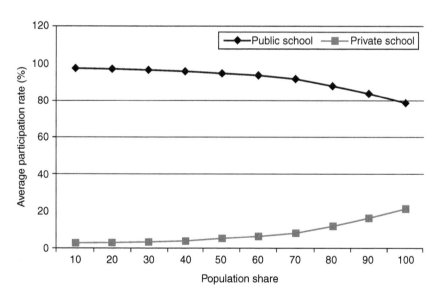

Figure 10.6 Opportunity curves for type of school attended by children 11–15 years old.
Source: Authors' calculations based on Department of Education 2008.

schools could be required to provide a certain proportion of seats free of cost or at discounted rates to poorer children.

Logistic regression was applied to the data to identify the determinants of school participation of primary and secondary age children. The results indicate that children start relatively late in primary school (Table 10.7). Wealth status has a significant effect on the odds of school participation of primary age children: lower wealth status of a child's family reduces the odds of the child attending school, although the wealth influence has gradually weakened over the years.

Caste or ethnicity also matters in primary enrollment: the Terai and/or Madhesi castes, Janajatis (Terai and Hill), and Muslim children had much lower odds of attending school compared with Hill Brahmins. The case of Terai Dalits and Muslims is particularly poignant: they need to be specifically targeted to increase their school participation. Distance to schools also played a role: in 2008, the residence in the Terai, where distance to schools is generally much less, increased the odds of school attendance when other factors were controlled. As for education of the head of household, if the head is not educated the chances of his or her children attending school is much reduced.

Table 10.8 shows that children above 12 years old have lower and progressively decreasing odds of being in school. This could point to the increasing likelihood that children will drop out of school as the opportunity costs of education rise as they grow older (i.e., entering the labor force becomes more attractive). This implies the need for greater effort to encourage secondary age children to attend school.

As is the case among primary age children, wealth is an important determinant of school participation of secondary age children, with the odds of participation declining as wealth declines. There are also large caste and ethnic disparities, with Terai Dalits being the most deprived group. Educated household heads also increase the odds of secondary age children attending school. Surprisingly, once other factors are controlled, rural residence does not reduce the odds of school participation of secondary age children. This may be because, for older students, school proximity or ease of access to school is a less important factor than for the younger pupils.

Equity in student performance

Two data sets are used to assess equity in student achievement: the first is a six-district World Bank-funded study of 80 schools carried out in 2005. It includes test scores for Nepali, English, mathematics, and social studies for Grades III and V. The second is a DOE 2008 survey, which reports achievement test scores of students in Grades I, III, and V in three subjects: Nepali, English, and mathematics. Because Grade I students are generally very young, achievement test scores for students at this level are not appropriate indicators of student performance, so only achievement test scores of Grades III and V pupils are considered. Similarly, mathematics test scores from the DOE 2008 survey are implausibly[6] higher than test scores of Grades III and V students in 2005, meaning they are unreliable and

Table 10.7 Determinants of school participation of children 6–10 years old (odds ratio from logistic regression)

Independent variables	2001		2006		2008	
	Odds ratio	p-value	Odds ratio	p-value	Odds ratio	p-value
Sex (Ref. males)						
Female	0.401	0.000	0.484	0.000	0.713	0.000
Age (Ref. 6 years)						
7 years	2.063	0.000	1.765	0.000	1.278	0.031
8 years	2.287	0.000	2.208	0.000	2.126	0.000
9 years	2.823	0.000	2.379	0.000	2.045	0.000
10 years	2.900	0.000	2.494	0.000	1.791	0.000
Wealth (Ref. richest quintile)						
Poorest quintile	0.122	0.000	0.142	0.000	0.157	0.001
Second quintile	0.164	0.000	0.383	0.001	0.202	0.005
Third quintile	0.266	0.000	0.608	0.089	0.641	0.449
Fourth quintile	0.313	0.000	0.692	0.211	0.740	0.638
Caste and/or ethnicity (Ref. Hill Brahmin)						
Hill Chhetri	2.517	0.081	0.563	0.165	0.610	0.098
Terai Brahmin/Chhetri	8.848	0.000	0.421	0.998	1.760	0.697
Other Madeshi Caste	0.631	0.376	0.109	0.000	0.167	0.000
Hill Dalit	1.759	0.288	0.397	0.030	0.680	0.218
Terai Dalit	0.309	0.028	0.086	0.000	0.064	0.000
Newar	2.543	0.096	0.649	0.469	0.739	0.522
Hill Janjati	2.385	0.099	0.237	0.000	0.428	0.003
Terai Janjati	1.509	0.433	0.293	0.003	0.456	0.020
Muslim	0.180	0.001	0.034	0.000	0.074	0.000
Others	3.501	0.207	0.095	0.000	0.134	0.000
Ecological region (Ref. hill)						
Mountain	0.594	0.000	0.362	0.000	0.856	0.368
Terai	0.727	0.004	0.383	0.000	1.728	0.001
Residence (Ref. urban)						
Rural	1.056	0.769	1.344	0.126	0.802	0.239
Household head's education (Ref. secondary+)						
No education	0.237	0.000	0.262	0.033	0.174	0.000
Primary	0.390	0.008	0.397	0.142	0.514	0.053
Secondary	0.740	0.401	0.705	0.584	0.519	0.066
Constant	25.800	0.000	421.188	0.000	457.282	0.000

Source: Authors' calculations based on Nepal Demographic and Health Survey 2001 and 2006 and Nepal Labor Force Survey 2008.

Table 10.8 Determinants of school participation of children 11–15 years old (odds ratio from logistic regression)

Independent variables	2001		2006		2008	
	Odds ratio	p-value	Odds ratio	p-value	Odds ratio	p-value
Sex (Ref. males)						
Female	0.280	0.000	0.428	0.000	0.455	0.000
Age (Ref. 11 years)						
12 years	0.856	0.148	0.665	0.008	0.651	0.002
13 years	0.699	0.001	0.410	0.000	0.532	0.000
14 years	0.452	0.000	0.266	0.000	0.292	0.000
15 years	0.321	0.000	0.160	0.000	0.191	0.000
Wealth (Ref. richest quintile)						
Poorest quintile	0.237	0.000	0.270	0.000	0.343	0.001
Second quintile	0.271	0.000	0.487	0.000	0.531	0.040
Third quintile	0.444	0.000	0.715	0.097	1.274	0.443
Fourth quintile	0.627	0.001	0.997	0.988	0.938	0.844
Caste and/or ethnicity (Ref. Hill Brahmin)						
Hill Chhetri	2.830	0.064	0.498	0.003	0.262	0.000
Terai Brahmin/Chhetri	5.911	0.002	0.396	0.149	0.146	0.002
Other Madeshi Caste	0.503	0.215	0.123	0.000	0.046	0.000
Hill Dalit	1.503	0.469	0.363	0.000	0.145	0.000
Terai Dalit	0.360	0.076	0.068	0.000	0.024	0.000
Newar	2.805	0.076	0.639	0.216	0.316	0.004
Hill Janjati	2.449	0.109	0.440	0.000	0.183	0.000
Terai Janjati	1.403	0.545	0.529	0.011	0.162	0.000
Muslim	0.151	0.001	0.054	0.000	0.026	0.000
Others	0.932	0.927	0.242	0.000	0.078	0.000
Ecological region (Ref. hill)						
Mountain	0.576	0.000	0.528	0.000	0.456	0.000
Terai	0.799	0.032	0.557	0.000	1.075	0.556
Residence (Ref. urban)						
Rural	1.136	0.418	1.411	0.032	0.991	0.950
Household head's education (Ref. secondary+)						
No education	0.388	0.001	0.528	0.053	0.314	0.000
Primary	0.525	0.021	0.657	0.206	0.468	0.000
Secondary	1.057	0.847	1.189	0.609	0.836	0.416
Constant	26.558	0.000	212.620	0.000	1048.646	0.000

Source: Authors' calculations based on Nepal Demographic and Health Survey 2001 and 2006 and Nepal Labor Force Survey 2008.

are therefore not analyzed. Moreover, unlike test scores in Nepali and English, inequity in mathematics scores was very low in 2005 and practically equitable in 2008. Again, this is a quite implausible, and for this reason, the opportunity index analysis for mathematics is not discussed.

Student performance in Grade III generally improved from 2005 to 2008 (Figure 10.7), but inequity increased in student performance in Nepali (Figure 10.7). Grade III English was not tested in 2005 and the trend cannot be assessed; however, the relatively low equity index of opportunity (0.78) and the shape of the opportunity curve clearly indicates an inequitable performance of students in English, with students from richer families performing better than poorer children (Figure 10.8). This is probably attributable to the household environment of richer children, which may be considered more conducive to learning English owing to the presence of English reading materials, television, radio, or better English knowledge of the parents and other family members.

It may be noted that although Grade III performance in Nepali has improved, disparities between the rich and poor have widened: the equity index of opportunity declined from 0.94 in 2005 to 0.89 in 2008. One reason for this may be the higher enrollment of poorer children, for many of whom Nepali is not a mother tongue.

Achievement among Grade V students indicates that there was not much change in performance in Nepali between 2005 and 2008 (Figure 10.9). However, performance has become more inequitable in that poorer children performed much worse in Nepali in 2008 than richer children. This is probably because more non-Nepali speaking and poorer children are now in schools, and inequity in achievement in Nepali may be a negative side-effect of improving access to education. The deprived home environment of poorer children may have hurt

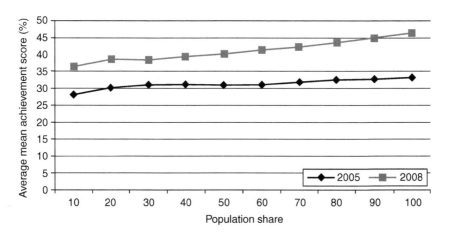

Figure 10.7 Opportunity curves for mean achievement test score of Grade III Nepali, 2005 and 2008.

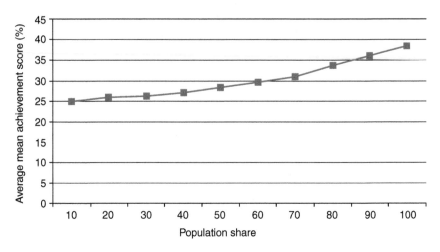

Figure 10.8 Opportunity curves for mean achievement test score of Grade III English, 2005.

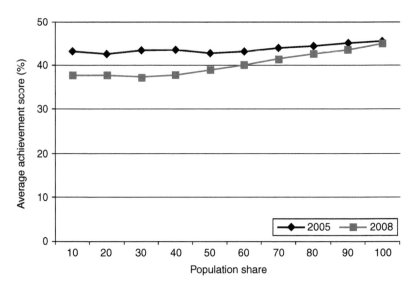

Figure 10.9 Opportunity curve for mean achievement test score of Grade V Nepali, 2005 and 2008.

their performance, and generally, children whose mother tongue is not Nepali have difficulty with the language.

In English, the performance of Grade V students changed little from 2005 to 2008 (Figure 10.10), but disparities between poor and rich children increased in 2008. Greater access to private schools among children from richer families

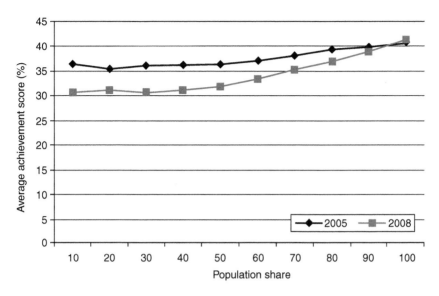

Figure 10.10 Opportunity curves for mean achievement test score of Grade V English, 2005 and 2008.

probably explains this increased inequity. Given its international importance and despite its higher cost, many parents opt to send their children to private schools because they think the quality of education is better than in public schools.

This study attempted to identify the determinants of achievement in Nepali and English for Grades III and V. A linear regression was performed with scores as the dependent variable and various households and student characteristics as independent variables. The results are given in Table 10.9 (Grade III) and Table 10.10 (Grade V). Given the limitations of the data set, results here should be considered indicative. The results indicate that household wealth status and the educational attainment of the household head are very important determinants of student performance in Nepali and English at Grades III and V. The wealthier the family background or the higher the education level of the household head, the higher are the scores in Nepali and English. The results also indicate that non-Nepali speakers do poorly in Nepali, which is to be expected. Other Madheshi castes (one of the relatively disadvantaged non-Nepali-speaking Terai groups) do poorly in both Nepali and English, which, again, may be expected given their disadvantaged background.

Another implication of the results is the poorer performance of children in public schools compared to private schools. Even after controlling for other background characteristics of students, simply attending a public school substantially lowers the score of students in all subjects in both grades. Reasons for the better performance of private schools could include greater teacher accountability, more

Table 10.9 Determinants of student performance in Grade III, 2008

Independent variable	Nepali		English	
	B	Significance	B	Significance
Constant	74.676	0.000	64.057	0.000
Age of child	−0.218	0.285	0.287	0.218
Sex (Ref. female)				
Male	−2.449	0.000	0.207	0.788
Caste ethnicity (Ref. Hill Brahmin)				
Hill Chhetri	1.642	0.162	1.232	0.333
Terai Brahmin/Chhetri	−10.509	0.271	0.375	0.972
Other Madeshi Caste	−5.059	0.002	−4.058	0.032
Hill Dalit	−1.153	0.418	−1.935	0.217
Terai Dalit	−0.476	0.860	−2.675	0.355
Newar	−4.820	0.007	3.539	0.073
Hill Janjati	0.780	0.519	0.617	0.639
Terai Janjati	1.821	0.307	−1.646	0.405
Muslim	−8.137	0.125	2.000	0.668
Others	12.651	0.089	11.189	0.147
Ecological region (Ref. mountain)				
Hill	−10.945	0.000	−6.528	0.000
Terai	−10.026	0.000	−1.720	0.227
Wealth (Ref. poorest quintile)				
Second quintile	−0.595	0.572	0.228	0.848
Third quintile	3.039	0.005	4.169	0.001
Fourth quintile	4.086	0.000	7.744	0.000
Richest quintile	5.099	0.000	10.466	0.000
Education of household head (Ref. illiterate)				
Primary	2.081	0.018	0.617	0.531
Secondary	4.680	0.000	2.343	0.028
SLC and above	4.698	0.001	3.866	0.008
School type (Ref. private)				
Public	−26.082	0.000	−38.515	0.000

SLC = school leaving certificate.

Source: Authors' calculations based on Department of Education 2008.

resources per student, better physical facilities, and overall better educational quality.

With policies and programs backed by increased public investment on education, Nepal has made significant progress toward achieving the Millennium Development Goal of universal primary education. But gaps remain—there is significant inequity in school participation of children aged 6–15 years from different economic backgrounds, and inequity in student performance.

Multivariate analysis identifies household wealth, education status, and caste or ethnicity as important determinants of school participation. Greater wealth and a more educated household head improve school participation, while the children of

Table 10.10 Determinants of student performance in Grade V, 2008

Independent variable	Nepali		English	
	B	Significance	B	Significance
Constant	56.265	0.000	58.103	0.000
Age of child	−0.108	0.626	0.011	0.957
Sex (Ref. female)				
Male	−2.357	0.001	0.517	0.437
Caste ethnicity (Ref. Hill Brahmin)				
Hill Chhetri	−0.252	0.827	1.322	0.223
Terai Brahmin/Chhetri	−21.716	0.022	−13.739	0.212
Other Madeshi Caste	−10.587	0.000	−8.720	0.000
Hill Dalit	0.692	0.641	−0.444	0.753
Terai Dalit	−11.144	0.000	−9.707	0.001
Newar	0.708	0.674	1.279	0.420
Hill Janjati	−1.247	0.281	−1.048	0.339
Terai Janjati	−3.349	0.058	−2.527	0.132
Muslim	−8.575	0.088	−14.091	0.028
Others	−3.105	0.744	−19.687	0.206
Ecological region (Ref. mountain)				
Hill	−4.616	0.000	−2.140	0.035
Terai	−2.151	0.092	9.673	0.000
Wealth (Ref. poorest quintile)				
Second quintile	−0.801	0.469	−2.376	0.023
Third quintile	5.248	0.000	2.183	0.043
Fourth quintile	7.220	0.000	5.775	0.000
Richest quintile	5.842	0.000	7.049	0.000
Education of household head (Ref. illiterate)				
Primary	2.678	0.003	2.209	0.009
Secondary	4.850	0.000	3.486	0.000
SLC and above	7.594	0.000	5.956	0.000
School type (Ref. private)				
Public	−13.200	0.000	−29.453	0.000

SLC = school leaving certificate.

Source: Authors' calculations based on Department of Education 2008.

deprived castes and ethnic groups (such as Hill Dalit, Terai Dalit, other Medhesi Caste, and Muslim) are less likely to attend school. These findings should be kept in mind when designing incentive policies. Similarly, student performance in primary school improves as household economic status and the education of the household head rise.

Due to data limitations, the contribution of different education inputs to achievement level could not be assessed. However, regression results clearly indicate the better performance of students in private schools. This may be attributable to a higher level of inputs—such as higher expenditure per student in private school—and more effective use of available resources—such as making teachers more accountable.

There is preliminary evidence of improvement in community-managed schools and that communities in the Hill districts are more willing to take over the management of schools than communities in Terai areas. But the implementation of school decentralization policy is taking place at a very difficult time: there are no elected local bodies and the general security situation remains challenging.

Conclusion and policy implications

The results of the health sector analysis clearly indicate that policy should focus on rural health institutions and personnel. Strengthening these and improving the quality of rural-based health personnel will significantly improve equity in access to health services and its outcomes. The early success of decentralization in the health sector suggests further expansion and deepening of this process for better health services and results.

There is also need for greater public investment in the health sector: current per-capita public investment is very low and needs to be significantly increased. Improving the educational status of Nepalese women will also help to increase the use of health services and improve outcomes. In this regard, improving school participation among deprived groups, such as girls and the poor, will not only positively impact educational outcomes, but health outcomes as well.

There has been significant improvement in school participation and equity, but important gaps remain. School participation of children from certain deprived groups and regions, especially among girls, is still low; thus, the main focus of education policy should be on these out-of-school children. Appropriate measures—such as increasing the incentive amount and improving its targeting— should be implemented to increase the school participation of deprived groups. Quality of education in public schools also needs to be improved: results suggest that school decentralization is working to improve the teaching and learning environment in schools and thus should be continued.

Notes

1 This chapter was prepared by Bal Gopal Baidya and Nephil Matangi Maskay who are Senior Research Fellows at New Era in Kathmandu. It is based on their country report submitted to the Asian Development Bank under a regional technical assistance on Equity in the Delivery of Public Services in Selected Developing Member Countries. The authors acknowledge the overall research guidance of Hyun H. Son and the comments and suggestions from Dr. Lava Deo Awasthi and Emmanuel San Andres and the participants in the regional workshop in Manila on 19 April 2010. The authors remain responsible for all remaining errors.
2 Apart from community health insurance schemes, the government does not have plans for social health insurance, although discussions on this are ongoing.
3 The premium was higher for those who wished to cover referral services as well.
4 This indicator was used for analysis in view of its direct implication in reducing maternal and infant mortality.

5 Public investment has gone mostly to finance teacher salaries, with little left to meet the non-salary expenses at the school level.
6 Mathematics is generally considered a difficult subject and many students fail it. Average scores are usually low, as evident from the 2005 average score. The sudden increase in average mathematics scores in 2008 is difficult to explain. A New ERA survey reports an average mathematics score of 34.2, which is more in line with the 2005 average score (New ERA 2008).

11 Equity in education and health services in Sri Lanka[1]

Nisha Arunatilake and Priyanka Jayawardena

Introduction

Sri Lanka has long been recognized for its achievements in human development. In large part, this achievement is credited to the policies of successive governments that provided widespread access to health and education services free of charge for over 50 years. However, the country's social sectors are now faced with new challenges. Recent policy debates have highlighted the need to improve the quality of services, especially in rural areas, and to modernize and make them more relevant to current market demands. Despite a long-standing separatist conflict and recurrent exposure to external shocks, Sri Lanka's economy has maintained growth above 5% since 1990.

This study seeks to better understand whether access to social services and social sector outcomes has improved. Are opportunities for health and education services equitable in Sri Lanka, and how has equity changed over time? What factors affect the opportunities for health and education services? Are household expenditures on health and education progressive in Sri Lanka? The first section below discusses the country's socioeconomic background, while the next section provides an overview of the health and education sectors. This is followed by a section which describes the data and methodology used and, afterwards, two sections detailing the empirical findings on education and health, respectively. We conclude with a summary of the study's major findings.

Background

Sri Lanka is a small island nation with an area of 65,610 square kilometers in the Indian Ocean. In 2008, gross domestic product (GDP) was US$40 billion or US$2,014 per capita (Central Bank of Sri Lanka 2008). Its population of nearly 20 million is 74% Sinhalese, 12.7% Sri Lankan Tamil, 5.6% Indian Tamil, 7% Muslim, and the rest are Burghers and other groups.[2] According to the 2001 census,[3] 80% of the population was rural, while the rest were urban (15%) and estate (5%).[4] Despite an ethnic conflict that lasted over 25 years as well as recurrent natural disasters and external price shocks, the country has managed to maintain average economic growth rate above 5% since 1990, while growth from 2004 to 2008 averaged 6.4%. But this rate of growth has not been sufficient to alleviate poverty in the more disadvantaged areas of the country, reduce economic disparities, and improve employment conditions. Further, provincial GDPs and their growth rates vary widely across the country: Western Province, the location of the capital, Colombo, is the most affluent and accounts for nearly half of GDP.

According to the Department of Census and Statistics (2008), poverty as measured by the head-count ratio declined from 26% in 1990/91 to 15% in 2006/07, albeit with variance at the sub-national level. Despite marked improvements in this ratio in the urban and rural sectors, poverty in the estate sector worsened during the same period, from 20.5% to 32.0%. Around a quarter of the population lives in poverty in the poorest provinces, while in others poverty levels are significantly lower. Interprovincial disparities in poverty have widened over time, with poverty levels in the more affluent provinces, such as Western and Southern Provinces, declining more sharply than in the poorer provinces of Uva, Sabaragamuwa, and Central Provinces. There is no time series data for Eastern Province and Northern Province, but because they were affected by the recently concluded armed conflict they are likely to have performed poorly.

Overview of the education and health sectors

The education sector

General education, for children aged 5–18 years, is organized into four cycles: primary (grades I–V), junior secondary (grades VI–IX), senior secondary (grades X–XI) and collegiate (grades XII–XIII). Students face national exams in grade V (the grade V scholarship exam), at the end of grade XI (the Ordinary level exam or O-levels), and at the end of grade XIII (the Advanced level exam or A-levels).

Under the 13th amendment to the constitution in 1987, education was devolved and more authority was given to provinces in school management and supervision. The education administration consists of five levels: the Ministry of Education (MOE) at the center, Provincial Ministries/Departments of Education (PME), Zonal Education Offices, Divisional Education Offices, and schools. About 3% of schools (324 in 2006) are classified as national schools, while the rest are provincial schools. National schools are governed directly by the Ministry of Education, while provincial schools are governed by respective PMEs. Terminal grade schools are categorized into four types: 1AB, 1C, Type 2 and Type 3. The 1AB and 1C schools have classes up to A-level. The main difference between these two types of schools is that at A-level, 1AB schools offer all subject streams, while 1C schools only offer subjects in the arts and commerce streams. Type 2 schools offer classes up to O-level, and Type 3 schools offer classes up to grade V. In the majority of schools the medium of instruction is either Sinhala or Tamil, the country's two main languages.

Government expenditure on education[5] in 2008 was Rs100,083 million or 2.3% of GDP, fluctuating around this level in the past decade. Investment in education is low compared to the averages for South Asia, and for low- and middle-income countries in general (World Bank 2005). It is also low compared with Sri Lanka in the 1960s, when this share was around 4.7% of GDP (National Education Commission [NEC] 2003). Low investment in education has limited essential investment in improving facilities and developing human and other resources in schools (World Bank 2005). However, studies show that recurrent expenditure on primary and secondary schools is distributed fairly across provinces (World Bank 2005). Another source of disparity in the sector could be the reliance on households to finance a large proportion of education. The share of private investment in education is substantial, with 21% financed through out-of pocket expenditure by households in 2002, according to the World Bank (2005).

Table 11.1 provides time trends in national enrollment rates for different education cycles.[6] Given that data is not comparable it is difficult to comment on these statistics for all years. In general, however, enrollment rates seem to have stagnated at the primary level and improved initially at the junior secondary levels, while they have declined at the senior secondary and collegiate levels. These results are of concern given that the country is striving to achieve universal education at the compulsory primary and junior secondary school cycles (Arunatilake 2006).

Despite good access to education, especially at the primary level, improving equity in access to good quality and relevant education opportunities has been a challenge for the sector for several decades (NEC 2003). Several recent policy documents on education highlight the need to upgrade quality of education. Despite high access rates, educational outcomes of students at all levels have room for improvement (NEC 2003; World Bank 2005).

Table 11.2 shows completion rates for major education cycles.[7] Almost a fifth of children do not complete primary education at the appropriate age. Furthermore, there are wide disparities in school completion rates across class, gender, sector, and provinces, with poor males in the estate sector performing worst. Completion rates are lower for higher school cycles, and their disparities are also wider. The data suggest that particular attention should be given to improving school

Table 11.1 Time trends for net enrollment rates in major education cycles

Variables	1996/97	2003/04	2006/07
Net primary enrollment rate	97.0	96.7	96.5
Net junior secondary enrollment rate	84.2	91.5	88.2
Net senior secondary enrollment rate	62.6	73.6	54.5
Net collegiate level enrollment rate	13.8	28.3	19.8

Note: The calculations used the following definition as used by UNESCO: Enrollment of the official age group for a given level of education expressed as a percentage of the corresponding population. Calculations using Consumer Finance and Socio Economic Survey 1996/97 and Consumer Finance and Socio Economic Survey 2003/04 are approximate values calculated using age at time of survey. Household Income and Expenditure Survey 2006/07 data are more accurate as in this survey information on survey dates and birth dates of children are available.

Source: Authors' calculations using Consumer Finance and Socio Economic Survey 1996/97 and 2003/04 and Household Income and Expenditure Survey 2006/07.

Table 11.2 Completion rates[a] in major education cycles (2006/07)

	Grade 5	Grade 9	Grade 11
By quintile[b]			
Poorest quintile	73.4	61.2	22.6
2nd quintile	81.3	69.2	35.4
3rd quintile	85.0	71.7	32.8
4th quintile	82.2	76.6	47.3
Richest quintile	87.4	75.4	60.6
By gender			
Male	81.9	67.7	35.3
Female	80.8	73.3	42.9
By sector			
Estate	64.2	46.1	7.9
Rural	83.3	74.5	42.7
Urban	84.9	72.0	42.3
By province			
Western	80.7	69.2	41.8
Central	79.4	75.3	33.1
Southern	86.3	74.8	45.5
Northern	n.a.	n.a.	n.a.
Eastern	n.a.	n.a.	n.a.
North-Western	82.8	69.9	28.8
North-Central	89.9	78.4	37.4
Uva	71.0	55.8	28.4
Sabaragamuwa	79.3	67.2	45.1
Sri Lanka	**81.4**	**70.5**	**39.1**

[a] Completion rate is defined as follows: percentage of children in the official age group completing the education cycle.
[b] Quintiles are based on a welfare index based on consumption.
n.a. = data not available.
Source: Authors' calculations using Household Income and Expenditure Survey 2006/07.

cycle completion among poorer groups, males, and those in the estate sector. These disparities in school cycle completion rates, especially at higher education cycles, are reflected in the O-level and A-level success rates. While more than two-thirds of children in the richest quintile pass O-levels, a similar proportion in the poorest quintile either never takes the exam or does not pass. Similar disparities are seen in A-level success rates.

The health sector

The public health sector is managed at two levels: the Ministry of Health (MOH) at the center and Provincial Ministries of Health (PMOHs) in the provinces. Initially, all teaching hospitals and hospitals established for special purposes (e.g., a cancer hospital) were under the MOH and the rest, including provincial hospitals, were under PMOHs. In the past 10 years, however, the MOH took over management of several provincial hospitals and district general hospitals, thereby re-centralizing management. In 1992, divisional secretariats and divisional directors of health services were introduced as an organizational framework for implementing provincial functions. The PMOHs establish and maintain hospitals and dispensaries other than those under the MOH. However, some vital functions such as manpower management are still largely in the hands of the MOH. In general, lack of capacity for planning and management is a central issue in the provincial system.

Total national expenditure on health in 2008 was Rs176,982 million, or 4% of GDP, and has increased steadily over the past decade. The government's contribution in that time has fluctuated around 45%, while the rest came from private sources. In 2008, 7.6% of government expenditure was on health.[8] Nearly 90% of private contributions are out-of-pocket, with the remainder coming from insurance schemes and non-government organizations (Arunatilake, Attanayake, and Jayawardena 2009).

Based on traditional indicators for measuring health, the country's health status has improved. The infant mortality rate dropped substantially from 17.7% in 1991 to 11.3% in 2003 (Department of Census and Statistics 2008), and life expectancy at birth improved to 71.7 for males and to 76.4 for females (Central Bank of Sri Lanka 2008). The prevalence of some communicable diseases has also declined, although other communicable diseases such as dengue hemorrhagic fever and HIV/AIDS continue to trouble the system (Arunatilake et al. 2009). Health status at present is gradually moving toward an era in which non-communicable diseases are dominant. For example, the prevalence of diabetes, hypertensive disease, ischemic heart disease, and asthma has steadily increased since 2000 (Arunatilake et al. 2009). Another area of concern for policymakers is malnutrition. Jayawardena (2010) finds that malnutrition affects one out of five under-five year olds and one out of six reproductive age females. However, systematically collected information on non-communicable diseases is not available, and hence we concentrate on child and maternal health outcomes in this analysis.

For the country as a whole, outcomes related to child nutrition (i.e., height-for-age, weight-for-age, and weight-for-height) have increased only marginally over the two years (2000 and 2006) for which data are available (Table 11.3). The number of newborns with minimum birthweight has also declined marginally over the years. These health outcomes are in general better in urban areas, but relative to the other two sectors have deteriorated more in urban areas over the two years. In contrast to trends in child health outcomes, maternal health outcome indicators have improved over time. Both child and maternal health outcomes are worst in the estate sector, although they have improved by most indicators.

Data and methodology

Data

The methodology we adopt, which will be described in the succeeding section, requires information on income and expenditure of households as well as their

Table 11.3 Health outcomes (means)

	2000				2006			
	Sri Lanka	Urban	Rural	Estate	Sri Lanka	Urban	Rural	Estate
Child health								
Under-five children with at least minimum height-for-age	81.5	89.8	81.8	56.3	82.6	85.4	83.7	59.0
Under-five children with at least minimum weight-for-age	77.0	84.2	76.1	65.4	78.6	82.7	78.5	69.9
Under-five children with at least minimum weight-for-height	84.5	88.5	83.0	86.0	84.9	85.3	84.8	85.7
Newborns with at least minimum birth-weight	83.9	86.0	83.7	77.2	83.4	87.1	83.5	69.3
Maternal health								
Maternal body mass index > 18.5	76.4	87.5	75.4	52.3	83.8	90.3	83.9	68.5
Access to healthcare								
Delivery assisted by health personnel	96.6	98.7	97.2	85.8	99.3	99.7	99.4	97.3
Delivery in hospital (public or private)	97.9	99.6	98.9	83.8	98.6	99.0	98.7	95.3
Tetanus injection received during pregnancy	95.8	93.6	97.2	89.9	95.4	95.3	95.6	92.7

Note: Child anthropometric indices are expressed as percentage above − 2 standard deviations from the median of the World Health Organization 2005 Child Growth Standards.

Source: Authors' calculations.

access to education and health services and outcomes across time. Since such data are not available from one source, we had to use several.

The data for the education sector analysis come mainly from two household surveys: (i) the Consumer Finance and Socio Economic Survey carried out by the Central Bank of Sri Lanka during 1996/97 (CFS 1996/97) and 2003/04 (CFS 2003/04), and (ii) the Household Income and Expenditure Survey (HIES 2006/07) carried out by the Department of Census and Statistics (DCS). Since the CFS was discontinued after 2003/04 and since the earlier versions of HIES 2006/07 did not include detailed information on health and education, we are compelled to rely on two sources of information. As such, it must be noted that results are not strictly comparable between the two surveys. Both surveys for the specified years collect detailed information on health and education and information on household expenditures.

The information for the health sector analysis comes from the Demographic and Health Survey (DHS 2000 and 2006/07) conducted by the DCS. This survey gathers nationally representative information on maternal and child health issues. One shortcoming of this survey for our purposes is its lack of income and expenditure data. Thus, for the health sector analysis we have used an asset index using principal component analysis to rank households. Details on how this was constructed are given in Jayawardena (2010). Expenditure on healthcare is obtained from HIES data.

Methodology

The concept of equity assumes that households have access to the same opportunities, whatever their socioeconomic status. This is a broad definition as the level of opportunity can be measured by a variety of indicators and the socioeconomic status can be measured along several dimensions. This study specifically considers the equity of opportunity in resources, access, and outcomes as described below.

Indicators used for education include (i) access to education (school enrollments at different cycles of schooling), (ii) education outcomes (school cycle completion), and (iii) the progressivity of out-of-pocket expenditure on education. Access to school is measured by net enrollment for different education cycles. The net enrollment rate is defined as the percentage of children in the official age group in school for a given educational level (UNESCO 2009). The official age groups for primary and junior secondary school are 5–10 years and 11–14 years, respectively. Quality of education is measured using completion of different school cycles by the official age group. Following the Ministry of Education (MOE) (2008), school completion is the proportion of children in the corresponding age group completing the relevant school cycle by official age. For example, officially, children who are 10 years old by end of January in a particular year should have completed their primary education by the end of the previous year.

Indicators used for the health sector analysis include (i) access to healthcare (delivery in a medical institution, delivery assisted by health personnel, and receiving a tetanus injection during pregnancy); (ii) health outcomes of mothers (body mass index of mothers); (iii) health outcomes of children (anthropometric measures of children under five, including height-for-age, weight-for-age and weight-for-height, and birth weight); and (iv) the progressivity of out-of-pocket expenditure on health.

Although there are a variety of important health indicators, we have focused our analysis on child and maternal health indicators due to data availability. Access to health institutions is measured by the ability to access a health institution for delivering a child. A health institute is defined as any government or private hospital or maternity home. Access to a qualified "health professional" is measured by the receipt of assistance by health personnel during delivery. Doctors, nurses, midwives and assistant midwives are considered qualified health professionals (Gwatkin et al. 2000). Receiving a tetanus injection during pregnancy is considered an important aspect of prenatal care as it prevents infections during delivery; thus, the proportion of women receiving tetanus shots during the most recent birth (as a percentage of all women who have given birth in the last five years) is used as an indicator of access to prenatal care. In addition to these access indicators, we use several indicators to measure the nutritional levels of mothers and children. The nutritional level of mothers is measured by their body mass index[9] and that of children by the anthropometric measures of children under five: height-for-age, weight-for-age and weight-for-height (International Food Policy Research Institution 2003; Jayawardena 2010). The birthweight of new-born babies is also used as a measure of prenatal care received.[10]

Following Ali and Son (2007), this study constructs opportunity curves for the population for the years where data are available to assess the equity impacts of access to education and health opportunities. In order to quantify the precise magnitude of the change, we also calculate the opportunity index (OI) and the equity index of opportunity (EIO).

Four probit regressions are done to assess the factors affecting opportunity for education services. Two of these are on school participation and the other two on school completion. The regressions on school participation assess participation at the primary and the junior secondary levels, while the regressions on school completion assess completion of primary (grade V) and junior secondary (grade IX) school cycles. The independent variables used include individual-, household- and community-level information. To avoid problems with endogeneity, direct and indirect costs faced by the household are "proxied" by the average costs incurred by all households in the community.

Two sets of regressions are assessed to examine the factors affecting child nutrition status and access to medical services. In the first set, regressions are run for four different types of indicators measuring different aspects of nutritional outcomes such as stunting, being underweight, wasting, and low birthweight. In the second set, access to medical services are assessed using three indicators to proxy access to facilities (place of delivery), access to medical personnel (delivery assisted by a medical professional), and access to medicine (getting a tetanus injection). The independent variables in these regressions include the mother's characteristics, the child's characteristics, household wealth status, and the hygiene practices of the household. Details of the dependent and independent variables used are given in Tables 11.9 and 11.10.

Households incur out-of-pocket costs when using a service. The benefits from public education can be greater for those households that are able to complement these services with out-of-pocket spending. Examining out-of-pocket spending per student in different income groups can reveal whether there are other types of inequalities in the system that affect health and education outcomes. We thus examine the progressivity of out-of-pocket payments using information provided in the HIES 2006/07 data. The government and other charitable sources also provide education-related welfare items to households (such as textbooks and uniforms); however, the values of these items are excluded from the calculations.

Empirical findings on education

Figure 11.1a shows the opportunity curve for access to primary schooling. Data suggest that although average opportunity has declined over time the equity in access to primary education may have increased (the 2003/04 curve is above the 1996/97 curve for poorer households). The average opportunity for access to education has also improved for all other education cycles considered over the 1996/97 to 2003/04 period (Figure 11.1b–d). Further, as seen by the opportunity curves, these improvements were felt at all levels of income. The upward slope of the opportunity curve indicates that children from lower income groups have lower access to education at all levels of education.

Overall, the EIO for school access is below one for all school cycles in 2006/07, indicating that equity can be further improved at all levels. However, on the positive side, the EIO improved over the 1996/97 to 2003/04 period, indicating that growth has been equitable during this period. The improvements in equity are largest for the senior secondary level followed by the junior secondary level (Table 11.4). School completion rates are also not equitable for all school cycles, and the equitability of school completion decreases for higher school cycles. It is particularly low for the senior secondary level.

Table 11.5 shows the equity indices for different provinces. Uva and Sabaraga-muwa provinces are the worst performing in terms of equity in school participation. The opportunity for school participation is equitable only in the North Central province, and is true for both primary and junior secondary levels. Equity in opportunity for school participation is worst in the Sabaragamuwa province at both the primary and junior secondary levels. An interesting finding is that even in the wealthiest Western province, equity in opportunity is lower than the national average at the junior secondary level (the EIO is 0.943 for the Western province compared with 0.963 for the country).

For 2006/07, the EIO for school completion is below 1 for all school cycles, and equity in school completion decreases with higher school cycles. The OI for school completion is also far below 100, and this decreases sharply with higher school cycles. The OI of school completion is 70.49 at the primary cycle, while it drops to 21.63 at the senior secondary cycles. These statistics show that although growth in access to education has been equitable, the opportunity for school completion is low, especially at higher school cycles.[11]

Probit analyses were conducted to better understand the reasons for school non-participation and the disparities in education completion. Results in Table 11.6 show that school participation is significantly explained by health status, education of the head of the household, and community non-participation rates (i.e., the children not in school divided by the total number of children in a community in a given age group) for both school cycles considered. In addition, ethnicity explains school participation at the primary and junior secondary levels.

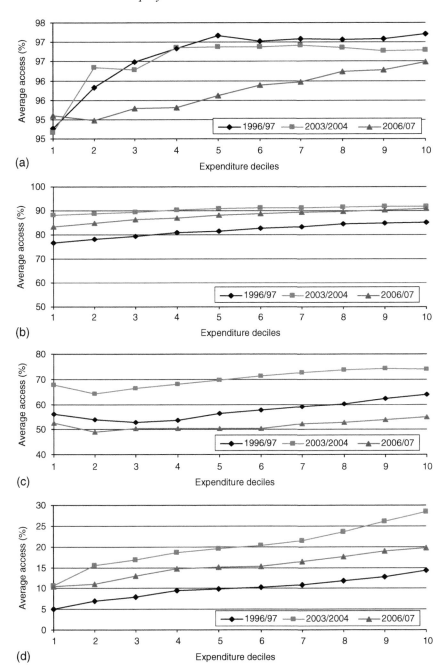

Figure 11.1 Opportunity curves for access to (a) primary education, (b) junior secondary education, (c) senior secondary education, and (d) collegiate level education.

Source: Authors' calculations using CFS 1996/97, CFS 2003/04, and HIES 2006/07

Table 11.4 Equity indices of opportunity in education by cycle

		Access to school		
		1996/97	*2003/04*	*2006/07*
Primary education	CI	0.004	0.001	0.008
	OI	96.7	96.500	95.9
	EIO	0.994	0.997	0.994
Junior secondary	CI	0.030	0.010	0.028
	OI	81.7	90.500	85.3
	EIO	0.959	0.986	0.963
Senior secondary	CI	0.079	0.043	0.058
	OI	57.6	70.200	51.7
	EIO	0.902	0.949	0.942
Collegiate level	CI	0.223	0.209	0.182
	OI	9.9	20.1	15.2
	EIO	0.694	0.707	0.773
		School completion rates		
Primary (Grade V)	CI	n.a.	n.a.	0.028
	OI	n.a.	n.a.	78.46
	EIO	n.a.	n.a.	0.959
Junior secondary (Grade IX)	CI	n.a.	n.a.	0.058
	OI	n.a.	n.a.	66.16
	EIO	n.a.	n.a.	0.933
Senior secondary (Grade XI)	CI	n.a.	n.a.	0.211
	OI	n.a.	n.a.	29.47
	EIO	n.a.	n.a.	0.741

CI = concentration index; OI = opportunity index; EIO = equity index of opportunity; n.a. = data not available.

Note: Calculations exclude Northern and Eastern Provinces as data are not available for these provinces for all the years considered. 2006/07 data are not strictly comparable to earlier years as this data is from a different source. School completion cannot be accurately calculated using CFS 1996/97 and CFS 2003/04.

Source: Authors' calculations using CFS 1996/97, CFS 2003/04, and HIES 2006/07.

At the primary level, school participation increases with age, but at a decreasing rate. This could be due to the delayed start of schooling. As expected, disability and chronic illnesses are significant reasons for school non-participation in both school cycles. The marginal effects[12] for this variable were relatively large for both age groups considered. School participation was lower for children 11–14 years old of all other ethnic groups relative to that of Sinhalese. School participation did not vary across different income levels, but the education level of parents had a significant effect on school participation, especially at higher school cycles. This indicates that more than income, the lower know-how and interest of parents may be affecting school participation. Lastly, children from communities with high dropout rates were significantly more likely not to participate in schooling.[13] As shown by marginal effects, this effect is relatively large, indicating that special attention should be given to improving school participation in communities with low participation rates.

Table 11.5 Measures of equity in school enrolment by province, 2006/07

	Concentration index	Opportunity index (%)	Equity index of opportunity
Primary			
Sri Lanka	0.008	95.928	0.994
Western	0.004	96.178	0.999
Central	0.007	96.037	0.992
Southern	0.009	95.787	0.986
North Western	0.006	97.083	0.994
North Central	0.000	97.779	1.005
Uva	0.015	95.431	0.989
Sabaragamuwa	0.015	93.510	0.986
Junior secondary			
Sri Lanka	0.028	85.276	0.963
Western	0.032	82.487	0.943
Central	0.017	87.938	0.982
Southern	0.001	86.054	0.972
North Western	0.030	83.445	0.946
North Central	−0.003	94.511	1.002
Uva	0.041	83.999	0.973
Sabaragamuwa	0.052	81.758	0.940

Source: Authors' calculations.

The results for school completion show that ethnicity and living in a community with a low school participation rate affects school completion at both the primary and junior secondary levels. In addition, poor health and poverty negatively affect school completion at the primary level, while being male and not living in a household headed by a public servant negatively affect school completion at the junior secondary level. These results indicate that community-level factors that affect both the demand (e.g., remoteness, alcoholism, violence, and poverty) and the quality of supply (e.g., availability of teachers, school facilities, and so forth) of education and the opportunity cost of schooling affect the likelihood of school completion.

As with opportunity costs, direct costs of education are also important factors in school attendance and completion. As can be seen in Table 11.7, households allocate about 3.2% of their total expenditure to education. This proportion gradually increases with income, but comes down again for the highest income decile. These results show that there is some progressivity in out-of-pocket expenditure on education. The major portion of education expenditure (42%) is spent on tuition and boarding fees, followed by stationery (22%), and transport (20%) (Figure 11.2). Household expenditure on uniforms and textbooks is only a small portion of total household expenditure on education, largely because the government provides these items free of charge.

Figure 11.3 compares household expenditure on education for different expenditure items. The data indicate that, as expected, the rich spend much

Table 11.6 Factors affecting school participation and school completion for different age groups (probit regressions)[c]

Factors	School participation		School completion	
	Age 5–10	*Age 11–14*	*Grade 5*	*Grade 9*
Male	0.03	−0.02	0.10	−0.24**
Age	2.60***	0.83		
Age squared	−0.16***	−0.05		
Disabled / chronic illness	−1.11***	−1.08***	−0.57**	−0.27
Ethnicity (Ref. Sinhales)[a]				
Tamil	−0.26	−0.76***	−0.80***	−0.72***
Moor and other	−0.10	−0.67***	−0.42**	−0.29*
Expenditure quintile (Ref. richest quintile)				
Poorest quintile	−0.06	−0.22	−0.50**	0.21
2nd quintile	−0.06	−0.02	−0.19	0.26*
3rd quintile	−0.06	−0.06	−0.02	0.17
4th quintile	−0.16	0.09	−0.18	0.13
Employment of household head (Ref. public)				
Private	−0.03	−0.07	0.14	−0.39**
Self employed	0.07	0.02	−0.04	−0.36**
Not working	−0.09	−0.07	0.09	−0.33*
Education of household head (Ref. secondary+)				
Less than primary	−0.31*	−1.00***	−0.10	−0.22
Less than secondary	−0.10	−0.60**	0.20	0.01
Community characteristics				
Direct cost (monthly 100s of rupees)	0.00	0.00	−0.01	0.01
Indirect cost (monthly 100s rupees)	−0.02	0.02	0.03	−0.01
Time to primary school[b]	−0.07		−0.05	
Time to secondary school[b]		−0.03		−0.04
Not in school rate	−2.88***	−2.10***	−1.53**	−2.32***
Sample size	7,996	5,552	1,355	1,457
Pseudo R^2	0.27	0.29	0.08	0.09

[a] Reference category given in parentheses.
[b] Expressed in minutes.
[c] Controls for residence at province level and sector level were included in the regression.

Note: Statistical significance at 1%, 5%, and 10% confidence levels are indicated by ***, **, and *, respectively.

Source: Authors' calculations using HIES 2006/07.

more on education for all categories of out-of-pocket expenditure compared with their poor counterparts. Moreover, the results reveal that education spending on private school fees is much more concentrated among the rich than the poor. According to Figure 11.3, the rich spend proportionally much more than their total household expenditure, as indicated by the fact that the concentration curve for the expenditure on private school fees lies below the Lorenz curve.

Table 11.7 Average monthly household expenditure on education and health

Expenditure decile	Total consumption expenditure (Rs.)	Expenditure on education (Rs.)	Expenditure on health (Rs.)	Expenditure on education as % of total expenditure	Expenditure on health as % of total expenditure
Poorest decile	9,797	280	270	2.9	2.8
2	11,867	354	364	3.0	3.1
3	13,503	398	451	2.9	3.3
4	15,889	489	548	3.1	3.4
5	17,590	574	537	3.3	3.1
6	20,559	673	728	3.3	3.5
7	24,192	820	708	3.4	2.9
8	29,016	950	913	3.3	3.1
9	36,626	1,337	1,155	3.7	3.2
Richest decile	66,039	2,050	1,692	3.1	2.6
All	24,019.59	775.59	723.91	3.2	3.0

Source: Authors' calculations using HIES 2006/07.

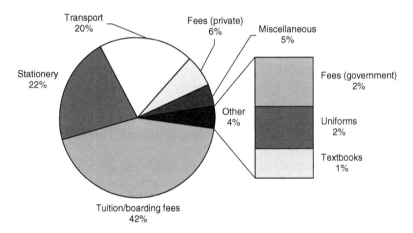

Figure 11.2 Distribution of out-of-pocket expenditure on education.
Source: Authors' calculations using HIES 2006/07.

Empirical findings on health

As with education services, opportunity to access medical institutions and medical personnel during delivery is quite high and has improved over time, although it is still inequitable, as most EIOs are below 1. On the other hand, the opportunity to receive a tetanus injection during pregnancy is also high, although less than for the other two indicators considered. Moreover, opportunity and equity in access to tetanus shots has declined marginally over time, mainly due to a decline in the access to this service in rural areas and in the estate sector.

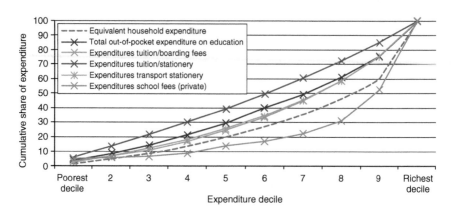

Figure 11.3 Distributional incidence of out-of-pocket payments on education, 2006.
Source: Authors' calculations using HIES 2006/07.

The opportunity indices show that nutritional levels among under-five children, new born babies, and mothers have a lot of room for improvement. At the national level, EIOs for child nutrition have mainly improved, except for a marginal deterioration in the indicator for birth weight of newborns, mainly due to a large decline in the estate sector (Table 11.8).

The relatively bad performance of the estate sector can partly be explained by the results in Table 11.9. The results show that children from very poor and poor households are less likely to have adequate nutrition, while children with low birthweight are more likely to have nutritional deficiencies. The mother's nutritional status also has a negative effect on child nourishment, while similar factors affect birthweight.

Children whose mothers read newspapers regularly tend to have better nutrition, indicating better awareness. Results also indicate that the education level of the mother and her income status are significant factors affecting access to health services (Table 11.10). In particular, poorer families have less access to qualified health personnel during delivery of a child.

On average, households allocate about 3% of their monthly expenditures on health. This proportion fluctuates around that level across different income levels (Table 11.7). The results in Figure 11.4 show that although the concentration curves for total expenditure on health as well as on out-patient departments and consultations lie below the 45 degree line but above the Lorenz curve, indicating that, as expected, out-of-pocket health spending is proportionally greater for rich people than for poor.

Conclusion and policy recommendations

This chapter examined opportunities to access education and health services and equity in access to these services and their changes over time. The results show that

Table 11.8 Equity indices of opportunity in health by sector

		2000		2006	
		Opportunity index (%)	*Equity index of opportunity*	*Opportunity index (%)*	*Equity index of opportunity*
Child health[a]					
Under-five children with	Sri Lanka	72.7	0.899	76.3	0.926
at least minimum	Urban	76.5	0.910	73.0	0.905
height-for-age	Rural	76.0	0.928	78.7	0.940
	Estate	57.0	0.933	63.1	0.917
Under-five children with	Sri Lanka	69.1	0.903	73.3	0.934
at least minimum	Urban	65.1	0.846	67.9	0.883
weight-for-age	Rural	69.2	0.907	73.9	0.940
	Estate	66.6	0.968	70.4	1.017
Under-five children with	Sri Lanka	80.9	0.962	83.2	0.980
at least minimum	Urban	85.8	0.986	79.7	0.968
weight-for-height	Rural	79.1	0.955	83.1	0.977
	Estate	86.0	1.018	83.8	1.050
Newborns with at least	Sri Lanka	80.4	0.965	80.1	0.962
minimum birthweight	Urban	85.8	1.020	83.4	0.978
	Rural	80.7	0.963	80.9	0.968
	Estate	74.4	1.012	72.5	0.940
Maternal health					
Maternal body mass	Sri Lanka	69.5	0.917	78.1	0.931
index > 18.5	Urban	85.9	0.997	80.3	0.930
	Rural	70.6	0.931	78.9	0.938
	Estate	52.7	0.913	71.4	0.929
Access to healthcare					
Delivery assisted by health personnel[b]	Sri Lanka	94.6	0.980	98.8	0.995
Delivery in public or private hospital[b]	Sri Lanka	95.6	0.978	97.9	0.993
Received tetanus	Sri Lanka	94.8	0.991	94.0	0.987
injection during	Urban	86.0	0.949	93.8	0.989
pregnancy	Rural	97.1	0.999	94.3	0.988
	Estate	90.9	0.966	92.9	0.963

[a] Child anthropometric indices are expressed as percentage above − 2 standard deviations from the median of the World Health Organization 2005 Child Growth Standards.
[b] Sample size is too small to disaggregate by sector.
Source: Authors' calculations based on DHS 2000 and 2006/07.

the opportunity to access education services is high in Sri Lanka, particularly at the primary level. However, access to education is still inequitable even though it has improved over time, particularly at the senior and junior secondary education cycles. On the other hand, data show that the opportunity to complete school is inequitable at present. These results indicate a need to continue existing efforts

Table 11.9 Factors affecting child nutrition status

Variables	Not stunted[b]	Not under-weight[b]	Not wasted[b]	Adequate birthweight
Child's characteristics				
Child age (in months)	−0.01	−0.10***	−0.05***	
Male child	−0.09**	−0.06	−0.13**	0.16***
Birth order of child	−0.08***	−0.06**	−0.02	
Low birthweight child	−0.57***	−0.71***	−0.49***	
Child sick recently[a]	−0.01	−0.08*	−0.06	
Twin birth				−1.96***
Mother's characteristics				
Mother's education (Ref. secondary completed)				
Primary schooling	−0.17*	−0.12	−0.11	−0.12
Secondary schooling	−0.08	−0.05	−0.01	0.03
Mother reads newspaper regularly	0.11*	0.19***	0.09	0.14**
Mother engages in an economic activity	−0.08	−0.06	0.08	0.08
Mother's age at first child's birth (Ref. 24–34 years)				
15–24 years	−0.07	0.00	0.05	−0.18***
35–49 years	0.07	−0.04	−0.27**	−0.02
Mothers height (in centimeters)	0.05***	0.04***	0.00	0.03***
Mother underweight	−0.09	−0.24***	−0.30***	−0.35***
Household characteristics				
Number of people in the household	−0.01	0.01	0.01	0.01
Number of children between 0 and 5	−0.01	0.04	0.02	0.13***
Sector of residence (Ref. urban)				
Rural	0.10	0.01	0.06	−0.09
Estate	−0.28**	0.06	0.19*	−0.48***
Safe drinking water	0.00	0.00	0.10	0.06
Water sealed separate toilet	−0.04	−0.07	0.00	−0.01
Wealth quintiles (Ref. wealthiest quintile)				
Poorest quintile	−0.46***	−0.34***	−0.17*	−0.13
Second poorest quintile	−0.39***	−0.38***	−0.10	−0.09
Middle quintile	−0.27**	−0.25**	−0.18**	0.00
Second wealthiest quintile	−0.25**	−0.23**	−0.25***	−0.11
Sample size	5,678	5,678	5,678	6,079
Pseudo R^2	0.12	0.11	0.04	0.09

[a] Child had diarrhea, fever, or cough in the past two weeks.

[b] Not stunted = adequate height-for-age, not underweight = adequate weight-for-age, and not wasted = adequate weight-for-height.

Note: Statistical significance at 1%, 5%, and 10% confidence levels are indicated by ***, **, and *, respectively.

Source: Authors' calculations based on DHS 2006/07.

Table 11.10 Access to health services

Variables	Getting tetanus injection	Delivery assistance	Place of delivery
Mother's characteristics			
Mother's age (Ref. 25–34 years)			
15–24	0.30**	0.11	0.10
35–49	−0.31***	0.08	−0.18*
Lives with partner	0.08	−0.07	−0.28
Mother's education (Ref. secondary completed)			
Primary schooling	−0.74***	−0.98***	−0.81***
Secondary schooling	−0.27**	−0.41**	−0.32**
Reads newspaper regularly	−0.01	−0.10	0.01
Mother's economic activity	0.14*	−0.07	0.06
Household characteristics			
Household size	−0.04**	0.01	−0.01
Number of children between 0 and 5	−0.29***	−0.26***	−0.21***
Sector of residence (Ref. urban)			
Rural	−0.01	−0.13	−0.08
Estate	0.04	−0.22	−0.33**
Safe drinking water	0.00	0.25*	0.11
Water sealed separate toilet	0.19**	0.16	0.15
Wealth quintiles (Ref. wealthiest quintile)			
Poorest quintile	0.11	−3.39***	0.11
Second poorest quintile	0.11	−3.27***	0.12
Middle quintile	0.31**	−3.27***	0.39**
Second wealthiest quintile	0.22*	−3.29***	0.10
Sample size	5,874	6,850	6,864
Pseudo *R*-squared	0.0891	0.1466	0.0932

Statistical significance at 1%, 5%, and 10% confidence levels are indicated by ***, ** and *, respectively.
Source: Authors' calculations based on DHS 2006/07.

at improving school attendance at higher school cycles and the need to focus on programs to keep children in school.

On the health front, access to qualified medical personnel and health facilities for child delivery is high. There is also fairly high opportunity for receiving tetanus injections; however, it remains inequitable. On the positive side, the opportunity for utilizing qualified medical professionals and health facilities has improved; however, equity in access to medicines, as measured by having a tetanus injection during pregnancy, has declined, mainly due to a decline in opportunity in the rural and estate sectors. Results also indicate that although there has been a marginal improvement in the nutrition levels of children and mothers, around one-fifth of children and mothers still do not have adequate nutrition. Overall, the equity in opportunity for adequate nutrition has improved and for some sectors nutritional outcomes are equitable across households.

The study also estimated probit regressions to assess factors influencing disparities in access to education and health. The education sector analysis reveals

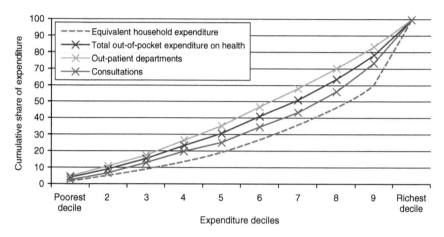

Figure 11.4 Distributional incidence of out-of-pocket payments on health, 2006.
Source: Authors'calculations using HIES 2006/07.

that the system needs to put more effort into including children with special needs, such as those with health issues. The results also indicate that community-level factors play a major role in explaining disparities, suggesting that community-level policies could improve access to education facilities. Further studies are needed to assess lower school participation of children from minority ethnic groups. More effort is also needed to ensure that children enrol in school at the correct age. On the other hand, the results on health indicators show that poverty is the main factor affecting low levels of nutrition, but increasing awareness and educating mothers could also improve the nutritional status of children. Poverty and low education are the main factors affecting access to medical personnel and institutions.

The data show that high out-of-pocket expenditures for education may contribute to observed inequities, although government provision of tuition and textbooks free of charge seems to have lessened the out-of-pocket expenditure on those items. Improving geographical access to quality schools and subsidizing transport may lessen household expenditure on transport and boarding fees, which may in turn improve the progressivity of household expenditure on education. In addition, the need for private tuition could be minimized by improving the quality of education at the collegiate level. Also, reducing the competitiveness of the A-level exam would reduce the need for extensive private tuition.

In general, 3% of household spending goes to healthcare, and the poor allocate a relatively higher proportion of expenditure on health. This is true for total out-of-pocket expenditure, expenditure on consultations, and out-patient visits. These results are somewhat unexpected, given that healthcare is provided free of charge at government hospitals. These results may reflect the poor quality of services, the longer waiting times to receive treatment, or the unavailability of different types of services at government hospitals. This suggests a need to improve the availability and quality of care in government hospitals.

Notes

1 This chapter was prepared by Nisha Arunatilake and Priyanka Jayawardena, who are Research Fellows at the Institute of Policy Studies in Colombo. It is based on their country report submitted to the Asian Development Bank (ADB) under a regional technical assistance on Equity in the Delivery of Public Services in Selected Developing Member Countries. The authors acknowledge the overall research guidance of Hyun H. Son and the comments and suggestions from Jacques Silber and Emmanuel San Andres and the participants in the regional workshop in Manila on 19 April 2010. The authors remain responsible for all remaining errors.
2 Percentages are based on 1981 Department of Census and Statistics information. Although a census was conducted in 2001 it did not cover the districts of Jaffna, Mannar, Vavunia, Mullativu, Killinochchi, Batticaloa, and Trincomalee.
3 These statistics should be treated with caution for several reasons. First, the 2001 Census was complete only in 18 districts. Due to the prevailing conflict, the census could only be partly completed in the Northern and Eastern Provinces. Second, due to changes in the administrative make-up, town councils (considered urban) were abolished and their administration given to Pradesheeya Sabhas (considered rural). As a result, the urban sector was underestimated in the 2001 census (DCS 2006).
4 Any tea, rubber, or coconut cultivation with ten or more resident workers is referred to as the estate sector.
5 Refers to government expenditure on general and higher education.
6 Note that these trends are not exactly comparable because 2006/07 data comes from HIES 2006/07, while data for the other two years come from CFS 1996/07 and CFS 2003/04. HIES is conducted by the Department of Census and Statistics, while the CFS is conducted by the Central Bank of Sri Lanka.
7 It is not possible to examine time trends in these indicators as earlier household survey data do not contain the necessary information for accurate calculations.
8 Based on data from www.who.int/nha/en/ accessed 27 September 2010.
9 Body mass index (BMI), an indicator commonly used in health, is the weight in kilograms divided by the square of the height in meters (km/m^2). An adult with BMI below 18.5 is considered acutely undernourished (Jayawardena 2009).
10 A child who has adequate height-for-age is considered to be not stunted, a child who has adequate weight-for-age is considered to be not under-weight, and a child who has adequate weight-for-height is considered to be not wasted. A new-born weighing at least 2,500 grams is considered to have an adequate birthweight.
11 Although an attempt was made to calculate various equity indices at the provincial level for school completion, the results are not reliable as the sample sizes at the provincial level are very small.
12 Not reported, available upon request.
13 In calculating community drop-out rates, leave-out means were used (following a method adopted by Lanjouw and Ravallion 1999) to avoid biases caused by implicitly including the dependent variable to calculate an independent variable.

References

Alderman, H., Hoddinott, J., and Kinsey, B. (2006) "Long-term Consequence of Early Childhood Malnutrition," *Oxford Economic Papers* 58(3): 450–474.

Ali, I. and Son, H.H. (2007) "Measuring Inclusive Growth," *Asian Development Review* 24(1): 11–31.

Annual Poverty Indicators Survey (2007) National Statistical Office, Philippines.

Arrow, K., Cline, W.R., Maler, K.G., Munasinghe, M., Squitieri, R., and Stiglitz, J.E. (1995) "Intertemporal Equity, Discounting, and Economic Efficiency," in J. Bruce, H. Lee, and E. Haites (eds) *Climate Change 1995: Economic and Social Dimensions of Climate Change*, Cambridge, England: Cambridge University Press.

Arunatilake, N., Attanayake, N., and Jayawardena, P. (2009) "Equitability in Education and Health Services in Sri Lanka," report submitted to the Asian Development Bank under RETA 6461.

Arunatilake, N. (2006) "Education Participation in Sri Lanka—Why all are not in school," *International Journal of Education Research* 45: 137–152.

Asian Development Bank (2007) *South Asia Economic Report: Social Sectors in Transition*, Mandaluyong City: Asian Development Bank.

Asian Development Bank (2008) *Key Indicators for Asia and the Pacific 2008*, Mandaluyong City: Asian Development Bank.

Atkinson, A.B. (1970) "On the Measurement of Inequality," *Journal of Economic Theory* 2: 244–263.

Atkinson, A.B. and Stiglitz, J. (1980) *Lectures on Public Economics*, New York: McGraw-Hill.

Bentham, J. (1781) *The Principles of Morals and Legislation*, online version at http://www.utilitarianism.com/jeremy-bentham/index.html.

Bhalla, S. and Glewwe, P. (1986) "Growth and Equity in Developing Countries: A Reinterpretation of the Sri Lankan Experiences," *World Bank Economic Review* 1(1): 35–63.

Bourguignon, F., Ferreira, F., and Menendez, M. (2007) "Inequality of Opportunity in Brazil," *Review of Income and Wealth* 53(4): 585–618.

Bourguignon, F., Ferreira, F., and Leite, P. (2002) "Ex-ante Evaluation of Conditional Cash Transfer Programs: The Case of Bolsa Escola," Policy Research Working Paper Series 2916, World Bank, Washington, DC.

Bruns, S., Mingat, A., and Rakomalala, R. (2003) *Achieving Universal Primary Education by 2015: A Chance for Every Child*, World Bank, Washington, DC.

Capuno, J.J. and Kraft, A. (2010) "Equity in the Delivery of Public Services in Selected Developing Member Countries: Philippines Country Report," report submitted to the Asian Development Bank under RETA 6461.

Central Bank of Sri Lanka (2008) *Annual Report in 2008*, Colombo: Central Bank of Sri Lanka.

Central Bureau of Statistics (2005) *Poverty Tends in Nepal (1995–96 and 2003–04)*, Kathmandu: CBS.

Central Bureau of Statistics (2008) *Report of the Nepal Labour Force Survey 2008*, Kathmandu: CBS.

Checchi, D. and Peragine, V. (2005) "Regional Disparities and Inequality of Opportunity: The Case of Italy," IZA DP No. 1874, Institute for the Study of Labor, Bonn, Germany.

Coady, D., Grosh, M., and Hoddinot, J. (2004) *Targeting of Transfers in Developing Countries: Review of Lessons and Experience*, Washington, DC: World Bank.

Coase, R.H. (1960) "The Problem of Social Cost," *Journal of Law and Economics* 3(1): 1–44.

Cogneau, D. and Mesple-Somps, S. (2008) "Inequality of Opportunity for Income in Five Countries of Africa," Document de Travail 2008–04, Development Institutions and Analyses de Long Terme (DIAL), Paris, France.

Consumer Finance and Socio-Economic Survey data (1996/97) Department of Census and Statistics, Sri Lanka.

Consumer Finance and Socio-Economic Survey data (2003/04) Department of Census and Statistics, Sri Lanka.

Cooter, R. and Ulen, T. (2000) *Law and Economics*, Reading, MA: Addison-Wesley Longman, Inc.

Dasgupta, P. (1990) "Well-being and the Extent of its Realization in Poor Countries," *Economic Journal* 100(Supplement): 1–32.

Dasgupta, P. (1993) *An Inquiry into Well-Being and Destitution*, Oxford: Clarendon Press.

Dasgupta, P., Sen, K., and Starrett, D. (1973) "Notes on the Measurement of Inequality," *Journal of Economic Theory* 6: 180–187.

Deaton, A. (2000) "Price Indexes, Inequality, and the Measurement of World Poverty," *American Economic Review* 100(1): 5–34.

Department of Census and Statistics (2006) *A brief analysis of population and housing characteristics*, online version at http://www.statistics.gov.lk/PopHouSat/PDF/p7%20population%20and%20Housing%20Text-11-12-06.pdf (accessed 13 July 2009).

Department of Census and Statistics (2008) *Poverty Indicators: Household Income and Expenditure Survey – 2006/07*, Colombo: DCS.

Department of Education (2006) *Basic Education Sector Reform Agenda Program Implementation Plan*. Department of Education Central Office: Pasig City.

Department of Health (2007) *Annual Report: Making F1 Work through Better Health Governance*, Manila: DOH.

Department of Health (2008a) *National Objectives for Health, 2005–2010*, Manila: DOH.

Department of Health (2008b) "Accelerate a unified strategy to save mothers, newborns, and children," *Health Policy Notes* 1(2).

Drewnowski, J. (1974) *On Measuring and Planning Quality of Life*, The Hague: Institute for Social Studies.

Dreze, J. and Sen, A. (1989) *Hunger and Public Action*, Oxford: Oxford University Press.

Dworkin, R. (1981) "What is Equality? Part 1: Equality of Resources," *Philosophy and Public Affairs* 10: 185–246.

Easterly, W. (2001) *The Political Economy of Growth without Development: A Case Study of Pakistan*, Washington, DC: World Bank.

Family Income and Expenditure Survey [FIES] (2006) National Statistical Office, Philippines.

Fehr, E. and Schmidt, K. (1999) "A Theory of Fairness, Competition and Cooperation," *The Quarterly Journal of Economics* 114(3): 817–868.

Filmer, D. (2003) *The Incidence of Public Expenditures on Health and Education. Background Note for World Development Report 2004: Making Services Work for Poor People*, Washington, DC: World Bank.

Foster, J., Greer, J., and Thorbecke, E. (1984) "A Class of Decomposable Poverty Measures," *Econometrica* 52(3): 761–766.

Gemmel, N. (2001) "Fiscal Policy in a Growth Framework," UNU-WIDER Research Paper No. 84, World Institute for Development Economic Research.

Goldstein, J. (1985) "Basic Human Needs: The Plateau Curve," *World Development* 13: 595–609.

Graham, W., Bell, J., and Bullough, C. (2001) "Can Skilled Attendance at Delivery Reduce Maternal Mortality in Developing Countries?," in V. Brouwere and W. Van Lerberghe (eds) *Safe Motherhood Strategies: A Review of the Evidence*, Antwerp: ITG Press.

Greene, W. (2003) *Econometric Analysis, 6th edition*, New Jersey: Prentice Hall.

Grosse, R. and Perry, B. (1983) "Correlates of Life Expectancy in Less Developed Countries," *Research in Human Capital and Development* 3: 217–253.

Gwatkin, D.R., Rustein, S., Johnson, K., Pande, R., and Wagstaff, A. (2000) *Socio-Economic Differences in Health Nutrition and Population in Nepal*, Washington, DC: World Bank.

Haddad, L. and Kanbur, R. (1991) "Intrahousehold Inequality and the Theory of Targeting," Development Economics Working Paper No. 789, World Bank, Washington, DC.

Harsanyi, J. (1976) *Essays on Ethics, Social Behaviour, and Scientific Explanation*, Dordrecht, Netherlands: D. Reidel.

Heinrich, J., Boyd, R., Bowles, S., Camerer, C., Fehr, E., and Gintis, H. (2004) *Foundations of Human Sociality: Economic Experiments and Ethnographic Evidence from Fifteen Small-Scale Societies*, Oxford, England: Oxford University Press.

Heller, P. (1981) "The Incidence of Taxation in Korea," International Monetary Fund DM Series No. 14, Washington, DC.

Hicks, N. (1979) "Growth vs. Basic Needs: Is there a Trade-off?," *World Development* 7: 985–994.

Hicks, N. and Streeten, P. (1979) "Indicators of Development: The Search for a Basic Needs Yardstick," *World Development* 7: 567–580.

Household Income and Expenditure Survey (2006/07) Department of Census and Statistics, Sri Lanka.

Hussain, I. (1999) *Pakistan: The Economy of an Elitist State*, Karachi: Oxford University Press.

Ico, R. (2008) "Catastrophic health care, poverty and impoverishments in the Philippines," *Philippine Review of Economics* 45(1): 109–126.

International Food Policy Research Institution (2003) "The Importance of Women's Status for Child Nutrition in Developing Countries," Research Report 131, International Food Policy Research Institution, Washington, DC.

Isenman, P. (1980) "Basic Needs: The Case of Sri Lanka," *World Development* 8(3): 237–258.

Jaywardena, P. (2009) "Measuring and Decomposing Socioeconomic Inequalities: Methods and Examples," unpublished mimeo, Institute of Policy Studies of Sri Lanka, Colombo.

Jayawardena, P. (2010) "Socio-economic determinants and inequalities in maternal and childhood malnutrition," unpublished Masters thesis, University of Colombo.

Kakwani, N. (1977a) "Applications of Lorenz Curves in Economic Analysis," *Econometrica* 45: 719–727.

Kakwani, N. (1977b) "Measurement of Tax Progressivity: An International Comparison," *Economic Journal* 87: 71–80.

Kakwani, N. (1980) *Income Inequality and Poverty: Methods of Estimation and Policy Applications*, New York: Oxford University Press.

Kakwani, N. (1984) "On the Measurement of Tax Progressivity and Redistributive Effect of Taxes with applications to Horizontal and Vertical Equity," *Advances in Econometrics* 3: 149–168.

Kakwani, N. (1986) *Analyzing Redistribution Policies: A Study Using Australian Data*, New York: Cambridge University Press.

Kakwani, N. (1993a) "Performance in Living Standards," *Journal of Development Economics* 41: 307–336.

Kakwani, N. (1993b) "Poverty and Economic Growth with Application to Côte d'Ivoire," *Review of Income and Wealth* 39(2): 121–139.

Kakwani, N. (1997) "Growth Rates of Per-Capita Income and Aggregate Welfare: An International Comparison," *Review of Economics and Statistics* 79(2): 201–211.

Kakwani, N. and Pernia, E. (2000) "What is Pro-Poor Growth," *Asian Development Review* 16(1): 1–22.

Kakwani, N. and Son, H.H. (2008) "Poverty Equivalent Growth Rate," *Review of Income and Wealth* 54(4): 643–655.

Kaplow, L. and Shavell, S. (2002) *Fairness versus Welfare*, Cambridge, MA: Harvard University Press.

Killick, T. (2002) "Responding to Inequality," ERC Inequality Briefing Paper No. 3, DFID.

Klasen, S. (2003) "In Search of the Holy Grail: How to Achieve Pro-Poor Growth?" Discussion Paper No. 96, Ibero-America Institute for Economic Research, Georg-August-University, Göttingen.

Kolm, S. (1976) "Unequal Inequalities," *Journal of Economic Theory* 12: 82–111.

Kraft, A.D., Quimbo, S.A., et al. (2009) "The Health and Cost Impact of Care Delay and the Experimental Impact of Insurance on Reducing Delays," *Journal of Pediatrics* 155(2): 281–285.

Lanjouw, P. and Ravallion, M. (1999) "Benefit Incidence, Public Spending Reforms, and the Timing of Program Capture," *World Bank Economic Review* 13(2): 257–274.

Le Grand, J. (1984) "Equity as an economic objective," *Journal of Applied Philosophy* 1(1): 39–51.

Le Grand, J. (1991) *Equity and Choice: An Essay in Economics and Applied Philosophy*, London: Harper Collins.

Lorenz, M. (1905) "Methods of Measuring the Concentration of Wealth," *Journal of the American Statistical Association* 9: 209–219.

Mahalanobis, P.C. (1960) "The Method of Fractile Graphical Analysis," *Econometrica* 28: 325–351.

Maligalig, D.S. and Albert, J.R.C. (2008) "Ensuring More Evidence-Based Policy for Basic Education," *PIDS Policy Notes* 2008–03, Makati City: Philippine Institute for Development Studies.

Manasan, R.G. (2000) "Basic Education: Improving Quality and Quantity," *PIDS Policy Notes* 2000–20, Makati City: Philippine Institute for Development Studies.

Marx, K. (1867) *Capital, Volume I*, B. Fowkes (trans.), London: Penguin Books, 1990.

McCulloch, N. and Baulch, B. (1999) "Tracking Pro-Poor Growth," ID21 Insights No. 31, Institute of Development Studies, Sussex, UK.

McKay, A. (2002) "Assessing the Impact of Fiscal Policy on Poverty," UNU-WIDER Research Paper No. 43, World Institute for Development Economic Research.

Mesa, E.P. (2008) "Measuring education inequality in the Philippines," *Philippine Review of Economics* 44(2): 33–70.

Mill, J.S. (1848) *Principles of Political Economy*, W. Ashley (ed.), New York: Kelly, 1965.

Ministry of Education (2008) *School Census 2008*, Battaramulla, Sri Lanka: MOE.

Ministry of Health and Population (2002) *Nepal Demographic and Health Survey 2001*, Kathmandu: MOHP, New ERA, and Macro International Inc.

Ministry of Health and Population (2007) *Nepal Demographic and Health Survey 2006*, Kathmandu: MOHP, New ERA, and Macro International Inc.

Ministry of Health and Population (2008) *A Report on Assessment of Management by Local Health Facility Management Committees in Decentralized Health Facilities FY 2064/65*, Kathmandu: MOHP.

Morris, D. (1979) *Measuring the Conditions of the World Poor: The Physical Quality of Life Index*," New York: Pergamon Press.

National Economic and Development Authority (2005) *Second Philippines Progress Report on the Millennium Development Goals*. Pasig City: National Economic and Development Authority.

National Education Commission (2003) *Proposals for a National Policy Framework on General Education in Sri Lanka*, Colombo, Sri Lanka: NEC.

National Statistical Coordination Board (2010) *Philippine National Health Accounts 2006*, Makati City: NSCB.

Nozick, R. (1974) *Anarchy, State and Utopia*, New York: Basic Books.

O'Donnell, O., Van Doorslaer, E., Wagstaff, A., and Lindelow, M. (2008) *Analyzing Health Equity Using Household Survey Data*, Washington, DC: World Bank.

Oh, Y.C. (1982) "An Evaluation of the Tax Reform for a Value-Added Tax in Korea, with Special Reference to the Distribution of the Tax Burden, Administrative Efficiency and Export," unpublished Ph.D. Dissertation, New York University.

Oosterbeek, H., Sloof, R., and van de Kuilen, G. (2004) "Differences in Ultimatum Game Experiments: Evidence from a Meta-Analysis," *Experimental Economics* 7: 171–188.

Orbeta, A.C. Jr. (2009) "Number of children and their education in Philippine households," *Philippine Review of Economics* 46(2): 123–154.

Paes de Barros, R., Ferreira, F., Molinas Vega, J.R., and Chanduvi, J.S. (2009) *Measuring Inequality of Opportunities in Latin America and the Caribbean*, Washington, DC: World Bank.

Pande, B.R., Maskay, N.M., and Chataut, B.D. (2004) "Health Insurance Models in Nepal: Some Discussion on the Status of Health Insurance," in T. Sein (ed.) *Social Health Insurance in South-East Asian Region*, Geneva: WHO.

Posner, R. (2003) "Norms and Values in the Economic Approach to Law," in A. Hatzis (ed.) *Norms and Values in Law and Economics*, London: Routledge.

Pyatt, G. (1987) "A Comment on Growth and Equity in Developing Countries: A Reinterpretation of the Sri Lankan Experience by Bhalla and Glewwe," *World Bank Economic Review* 1(3): 515–520.

Ravallion, M. (2009) "A Comparative Perspective on Poverty Reduction in Brazil, China and India," Policy Research Working Paper Series 5080, World Bank, Washington DC.

Ravallion, M. and Chen, S. (2003) "Measuring Pro-Poor Growth," *Economics Letters* 78: 93–99.

Rawls, J. (1971) *A Theory of Justice*, Cambridge, MA: Harvard University Press.

Rawls, J. (1993) *Political Liberalism*, New York: Columbia University Press.

Reyes, C. and Due, E. (2009) *Fighting Poverty with Facts*, Ottawa: International Development Research Centre.

Roemer, J. (1998) *Equality of Opportunity*, Cambridge, MA: Harvard University Press.

Ross, D. (1998) *Aristotle: The Nicomachean Ethics*, Oxford, England: Oxford University Press.

Rothschild, M. and Stiglitz, J. (1973) "Some Further Results on the Measurement of Inequality," *Journal of Economic Theory* 6: 188–204.

Rowntree, B.S. (1901) *Poverty: A Study of Town Life, Sixth and Seventh Annual Reports of the Commissioner of Labor, 1891 and 1892*, Washington, DC: Government Printing Office.

Sen, A. (1973) "On the Development of Basic Economic Indicators to Supplement GNP Measures," *United Nations Economic Bulletin for Asia and the Far East* 24.

Sen, A. (1981) "Public Action and the Quality of Life in Developing Countries," *Oxford Bulletin of Economics and Statistics* 43: 287–319.

Sen, A. (1985a) *Commodities and Capabilities*, Amsterdam: North Holland.

Sen, A. (1985b) "Standard of Living Lecture 1: Concepts and Critiques," in G. Howthorne (ed.) *The Standard of Living (The Tanner Lecture in Human Values)*, Cambridge, England: Cambridge University Press.

Sen, A. (1985c) "Standard of Living Lecture 2: Lives and Capabilities," in G. Howthorne (ed) *The Standard of Living (The Tanner Lecture in Human Values)*, Cambridge, England: Cambridge University Press.

Sen, A. (1987) *Standard of Living*, New York: Cambridge University Press.

Sen, A. (1989) "Development as Capabilities Expansion," *Journal of Development Planning* 19: 41–58.

Sen, A. (1993) "Capability and Well-Being," in M. Nussbaum and A. Sen (eds) *The Quality of Life*, New York: Oxford Clarendon Press.

Sen, A. (1999) *Development as a Freedom*, Oxford, England: Oxford University Press.

Sheehan, G. and Hopkins, M. (1979) *Basic Needs Performance: An Analysis of Some International Data*, Geneva: International Labor Organization.

Shorrocks, A. (1983) "Ranking Income Distributions," *Economica* 50: 3–17.

Silber, J. and Son, H.H. (2010) "On the Link between the Bonferroni Index and the Measurement of Inclusive Growth," *Economics Bulletin* 30(1): 421–428.

Skoufias, E., Davis, B., and Vega, S. (2001) "Targeting the Poor in Mexico: An Evaluation of the Selection of Households into PROGRESA," *World Development* 29(10): 1769–1784.

Slesnick, D. (1994) "Consumption, Needs, and Inequality," *International Economic Review* 35(3): 677–703.

Smith, A. (1759) *Theory of Moral Sentiments*, London: A. Millar.

Smith, A. (1776) *An Inquiry into the Nature and Causes of the Wealth of Nations*, London: W. Strahan and T. Cadell.

Son, H.H. (2004) "A Note on Pro-Poor Growth," *Economics Letters* 82: 307–314.

Son, H.H. (2008) "Explaining Growth and Inequality in Factor Income: The Philippines Case," ADB Economics Working Paper No. 120. Asian Development Bank, Manila.

Son, H.H. (2009) "Equity in Health and Health Care in the Philippines," ADB Economics Working Paper Series 171, Asian Development Bank, Manila.

Son, H.H. and Kakwani, N. (2008) "Global Estimates of Pro-Poor Growth," *World Development* 36(3): 1048–1066.

Son, H.H. and San Andres, E, (2009) "Equity in the Delivery of Health and Education Services in the Philippines: Key Findings and Recommendations," unpublished report, Asian Development Bank, Manila.

Steiner, H. (1994) *An Essay on Rights*, Oxford, England: Blackwell.

Streeten, P. (1979) "Basic Needs: Premises and Promises," *Journal of Policy Modelling* 1: 136–146.

Svensson, L. (1980) "Equity Among Generations," *Econometrica* 48(5): 1251–1256.

Theil, H. (1967) *Economics and Information Theory*, Amsterdam: North-Holland.

UNDP (1990) *Human Development Report 1990*, New York: Oxford University Press.

UNDP (2007) *Human Development Report 2006: Beyond Scarcity: Power, Poverty and the Global Water Crisis*, New York: Oxford University Press.

UNDP (2010) *Human Development Report 2010: The Real Wealth of Nations: Pathways to Human Development*, New York: Oxford University Press.

UNESCO (2009) UNESCO Institute for Statistics, http://glossary.uis.unesco.org/glossary/en/home.

UNRISD (1972) *Contents and Measurement of Socio-Economic Development: A Staff Survey*, New York: Praeger.

Van Parijs, P. (1995) *Real Freedom for All: What (If Anything) Can Justify Capitalism?*, Oxford, England: Oxford University Press.

Watts, H.W. (1968) "An Economic Definition of Poverty," in D. Moynihan (ed.) *Understanding Poverty*, New York: Basic Books.

Williams, A. and Cookson, R. (2000) "Equity in health," in A.J. Culyer and J.P. Newhouse (eds) *Handbook of Health Economics, Vol. 1*, Amsterdam: Elsevier Science.

World Bank (2001) *World Development Report 2001: Attacking Poverty*, New York: Oxford University Press.

World Bank (2004) *World Development Report 2004: Making Services Work for Poor People*, Washington, DC: World Bank.

World Bank (2005) *Treasures of the Education system in Sri Lanka: Resorting Performance, Expanding Opportunities and Enhancing Prospects*, Colombo, Sri Lanka: World Bank.

World Bank (2006) *World Development Report 2006: Equity and Development*, New York: Oxford University Press.

World Bank (2008) *World Development Indicators 2008*, Washington, DC: World Bank.

World Health Organization (2008) *Maternal Mortality in 2005: Estimates Developed by WHO, UNICEF, UNFPA, and the World Bank*, Geneva: WHO.

Zajac, E. (2001) *Political Economy of Fairness*, Cambridge, MA: MIT Press.

Index